RELIGIOUS FUNDAMENTALISM IN ASIA

RELIGIOUS FUNDAMENTALISM IN ASIA

BY
V. D. CHOPRA

Foreword By
MAHARAJA KRISHNA RASGOTRA

GYAN

ISBN : 978-81-212-0841-1

Published, 2018

Published by

Gyan Publishing House
5, Ansari Road
Daryaganj, New Delhi-110002
Phone: 011-47034999, 9811692060
www.gyanbooks.com
E-mail: books@gyanbooks.com

Printed at: G. Print Process, Delhi.

CONTENTS

FOREWORD

This book is the outcome of a seminar organised by the International Institute of Asia-Pacific Studies in October 1993 to examine the recent phenomenon of Hindu religious revival in Indian politics and its consequences on India's future. The destruction, on 6 December 1992, of a mosque of the early Mughal period at Ayodhya, one of the most Hindu holy cities, had sent shock waves not only across India and her neighbouring muslim countries of Bangladesh and Pakistan, but even to the far away countries of Europe and America. In the latter countries the sense of shock arose from a perceived realisation that India had abandoned or was about to abandon secularism, one of the most progressive features of the modern Indian state.

In the Muslim countries of West Asia and Africa, the assault by Hindu fanatics on a mosque, whatever its disputed history, followed by communal violence in several parts of the country had given rise to dismay and anguish over India's fall from its high ideals of tolerance, and to some worry about the well-being of India's large muslim population. There was also concern over the consequences of recent events to the stability of India, a country to which many had looked as a source of strength and support in times of difficulty.

Perhaps in Pakistan's ruling elite alone there was a sense of gratification over the Ayodhya episode and the wave of violence that followed. There—and in Bangladesh—the destruction of the mosque was exploited as a pretext for the unleashing of an anti-India campaign and an orgy of violence and destruction directed at the few remaining places of Hindu worship. In Pakistan in particular, nothing gladdens the rulers more than the evidence, howsoever incredible or tragic, of India acquiring the attributes of a theological state rather like their own. The rise of a "Hindu Rashtra" in India would be prejudicial to the interests of Indian Muslims, but it would help define and justify Pakistan's fundamentalist Islamic identity and lend some credibility to its pretense of being the protectors of Indian muslims.

The tragedy at Ayodhya came as the climax of a long campaign on the part of a major political formation to incite Hindu religious sentiment to gain political ascendency. It was an act of Hindu chauvinism and there was little evidence of remorse in the circles that had planned and perpetrated it. In the rest of the country, the sense of sorrow was pretty widespread. On the country's intellectual elite in particular, the effect was traumatic, and there was a deeply felt apprehension that something had gone terribly wrong with Indian politics. Where would the tendency to exploit religious sentiment and religious symbols for political ends lead India? It is not comforting to contemplate the menace to India's internal harmony and her external security and the threat to her very character and integrity posed by the explosive mixture of religious bigotry and political opportunism.

Though tolerance and synthesis have generally characterised the progress and consolidation of the Indian society through the millenia, religious fanaticism and exploitation of religion for political purposes are not unknown in India's long and chequered history. It is an important lesson of history that periods marked by religious bigotry or the state patronage of a particular religion in preference to others have also been the periods of the decline and disruption of India's polity. Whereas Emperor Akbar's tolerant rule and his encouragement of the efforts of the saint-poets and philosophers of the time to create a new Indian synthesis resulted in the broad acceptance of the Mughals by their Hindu subjects, Aurangzeb's attempt to impose theocratic rule on India marked the beginning of the Mughal empire's ruin.

In recent times, polarisation of Indian politics and society on religious lines was consciously encouraged by our British rulers to weaken the freedom movement and delay India's independence. The introduction of separate electorates for different religious communities early this century had nourished muslim separatism which eventually resulted in the country's partition at independence. With British instigation and support, the Muslim League successfully exploited religion to gain political power in a new country carved out of the old India, but at great cost to Indian muslims. The partition divided the Muslim community and weakened Indian Islam. But, perhaps, its greater disservice to Islam lay in the setback it administered to the evolution of a tolerant and forward-looking, Indianised Islam as a powerful civilisational influence in the modern world.

The Islamic state of Pakistan has not displayed any capability to generate such an influence: It only uses Islam to mark its own identity and to settle political scores with India. It has contributed little, unlike Egypt, Indonesia, Iran or Turkey, to the Muslim world's cultural panorama or to Islam's wealth of thought. The reason for this is that in adopting Islam, Egypt, Indonesia, Iran and Turkey did not, unlike Pakistan, sever their historical and cultural moorings or disown their past. The socio-political outlook of Pakistan, especially in its approach to India of which it was once a part, is, therefore, marked by an unusually embittered fanaticism born of separatism and a certain lack of self-assurance. Pakistan's aggresive Islamic orientation received encouragement from the West in the cold war environment of the world in which it was born. Britain and the United States of America were, then, engaged in forging an Islamic front against Soviet Russia's 'godless communism'. That policy, designed essentially to protect the West's vital economic and political interests in the Middle East, fitted well with Pakistan's own ambition of a larger-than-life military and political role in that region and in South Asia. Other than Saudi Arabia and Sudan, of all the preponderantly muslim countries of the world, Pakistan is the only truly fundamentalist Islamic state in the commonly understood meaning of that phrase.

This legacy of India's partition and the block politics of the cold war era is not going to go away easily, and its effects are bound to be felt in India-Pakistan relations for quite some time. We in India have to be careful how we react to the periodic outbursts of Islamic zealotry in Pakistan's internal and external policies. Manifestations of Hindu reaction in Indian politics would inhibit and undermine India's global role. In no sense whatever is Pakistan a fit role-model for India; and I can think of nothing more fatal to India's foreign policy, and indeed to her internal cohesion, than Hindu fundamentalism.

Religious fundamentalism or religious revivalism, are perhaps, not the most appropriate descriptions of the recent Indian Phenomenon of an aggressive inclination to inject issues of caste and religion into politics to gain votes. Revival of the true spirit of religion, or return to the basics of any faith in a society, are not to be feared or looked down upon. The fundamental tenets of all religions are the same: belief in God or an Higher Power, man's innate divinity and the sanctity of life, the importance of prayer and contemplation and service in daily life, the emphasis on tolerance and peace for the soul's progress in life's pilgrimage etc. etc. In their basic teachings all religions are paths to the same goal of a more elevated human existence. Since all religions aim at universality, a true religious revival should lead humanity to a life of harmony and a fellowship of the spirit. The cultivation of a truly religious outlook and behaviour on the part of all communities in a multi-religious country like India would make it the role model for an evolving global society.

On the other hand, religions have their local particularities, such as rites and customs, laws, languages of their scriptures, the modes of dress and worship etc., which distinguish their followers from one another. These particularities do tend to distinguish one community from another, and in backward societies in particular, these distinctions lend themselves to easy exploitation by unscrupulous politicians in search of votes and power. Politics by nature is mundane, competitive, and divisive, and religion, which is a means for the elevation of the spirit, ought not to be allowed to become the politician's tool. Mixing of the two breeds intolerance, pits different religious groups and communities against one another, and demeans religion by reducing Allah, Ram and Waheguru to the status of political partisans.

As a practising Hindu, I find it galling that anyone should try to highjack my faith to promote a purely political aim in the name of cultural nationalism. Hinduism is a perennial search for life's higher truths and, as such, it is not merely tolerant but comprehensive of all other efforts in that direction. In its social dimensions, it represents a ceaseless endeavour to evolve human society into a true fellowship of the spirit. Attitudes of exclusionism, intolerance and fanaticism are alien to Hindusim.

A world society which is a synthesis of all human civilisations and communities is no longer a dream. The on-going revolution in modern communications has brought that goal within man's reach. In a world which grows smaller and more intimate by the day, local particularities and divisions are bound to get increasingly blurred. India, where every major religions has a large following, is the crucible of tomorrow's global human civilisation. Therefore, the pursuit of divisive, religion-based politics in our country is tantamount to denying our own future. Here, religion and politics must remain separate and the State must be secular in the sense that it is free from all bias and is equally the protector of all faiths. In adopting the secular model for the modern Indian state, our founding-fathers were seeking a synthesis of the best in India's age-old tradition and the compulsions of her present reality. The disharmony and destruction caused in the last five years by the pursuit of religion, caste or class-based politics by some of the country's major political formations are sufficient proof of the dangers inherent in any departure from that model.

There are strong practical reasons for maintaining and strengthening India's secular character. Islam's advent in India goes back a thousand years, and muslims ruled most of India for half that period. Two centuries of European dominance added further to India's cultural and religious diversity. These and other foreign impacts of the last thousand years, indigenised and assimilated in some measure already, have greatly influenced India's life-styles, her thought-processes and her ethos. It is not possible to reverse history and take India back to the golden age of pure Hinduism. Even though 85 per cent of India's population is Hindu, her 120 million Muslims constitute the world's second largest concentration of Islam's followers. Besides, there are large numbers of Christians, Buddhists, Jains and Sikhs—some with concentrations in majority areas of their own, others mostly scattered in the length and breadth of this vast land. The pursuit of chauvinist Hindu politics even by sections of the dominant majority community can tear holes in the multi-coloured fabric of our society and encourage unfriendly outside forces to intervene in India's domestic problems with infiltration of arms, explosives, money and agents.

The pursuit of religion-based politics by India's Muslim population is even more irrelevant: indeed it can prove ruinous to the community by leaving it out of the mainstream of India's socio-economic advance, which to some extent has already happened. Muslim politicians of India need to understand and appreciate the fact that India is secular precisely because the majority of her population is Hindu, that Indian secularism best suits their interest and they owe it to themselves to reinforce it in every possible way. Pakistan can cause some mischief or irritation for India, but it can do very little that is good for the Indian Muslims. India's answer to Pakistan's Islamist jingoism must be synthesis and secularism.

In recent years, a great deal has been said in the Western media about the threat, so-called, of Islamic fundamentalism. Much of it is purely propaganda intended to serve a particular Western interest at a given time. While American propaganda condemned the Islamic fervour of revolutionary Iran, America unscrupulously exploited Islam for its proxy war against the Soviet Union in Afghanistan. It rewarded Pakistan with an abundance of munitions and money for stimulating the 'jehad', of which the most tragic victim today is Afghanistan. American encouragement and support of the current phase of Pakistan's 'jehad' against India in Kashmir are no longer a secret. Could it be that there is a design to keep the "forces of Islam" engaged in some conflict somewhere, to weaken the countries directly involved and to reinforce influence and presence in their region ? That certainly was the case in the Gulf region where Western influence and presence are stronger today than in the 'hey-day' of the British empire.

Narrow-minded and jingoistic Hindu reaction in India is not the right answer to manifestations of Islamist assertion in the policies of Pakistan or any other country. We should deal with Pakistan's Indian obsessions in the knowledge that the Muslim world is not a political monolith inimical to India, that our large Muslim population is a valuable link between the two and Muslim countries are cognisant of India's great potential as a source of friendly support and cooperation with them.

It is my belief that the trend of our times, stimulated by the vital influences of modern education and ongoing developments in science and technology, is opposed to fanatical or fundamentalist approaches. Even in Pakistan, the influence and popularity of the 'mullah' is on decline. In a world of ever-widening inter-action between civilisations, an outlook of liberatism in politics and international relations even in deeply religious societies is increasingly bound to come to the fore. This trend is evident in post-revolutionary Iran. It is in India's interest to reinforce this trend by cultivating, in ever growing measure, the spirit of tolerance, rationality and secularism in its own political behaviour.

India's commercial, cultural, political and strategic interests in Muslim countries are very large indeed. The needs of our interaction with these countries and the requirements of India's role in the world beyond call for an India that is strong and self-assured in its diversity, an India that is forward-looking and open-minded, aware of its great past and confident of own vision of the future. Our politics and our policies must reflect the true reality of India which is not merely a nation but also a civilisational force in the world. An India that presents itself as a self-besieged fortress of obscurantism and reaction is a self-diminishing vision.

Maharaja Krishna Rasgotra

PREFACE

This book represents an effort to discuss the impact of Religious Revivalism on Nation-State building from the Asian perspective though with emphasis on India. Thus, it presents the problems in intellectual history from a different perspective than most European and American experts, who view them through European thought as the norm or criterion. This is the unique thrust of this study. It has to be underlined that all contributors have taken into account the humanistic aspect of all the religions. What is of deep concern today is that religious philosophies are being distorted to rouse passions for political ambitions and objectives. At the same time, however, it appears that many of the problems of what is called "modern thought" of Nation-State did not manifest themselves in Asia before the period of "Westernization", except in scattered instances. Therefore, Nation-State building in ancient societies has been more complex.

The reader will find this work as a source book in at least two important aspects. In the first place, most of the contributors are outstanding scholars who have made rich contribution in their respective disciplines. Secondly, the problem of religious revivalism in all the major countries of Asia has been critically examined.

The contributors specialize in diverse academic disciplines. If there is a strong consistency in their analyses and conclusions, it is neither by design nor chance. Instead, it indicates an important confluence of critical perspective. Though most of the papers included in this book were presented in a seminar organised by the international institute of Asia Pacific Studies, they were up-dated and revised on the basis of further discussions.

Through this book, I have aimed to present an objective picture of two parallel developments now taking place in this region: the modern nation-state building in the specific conditions of this area, where the religious systems—Hinduism, Buddhism, Islam, Sikhism and the teachings of countless different sects have something in common. These religions have not witnessed any major movements or reformations, and yet have managed to sustain themselves as a major link in the entire superstructural sphere, including the state and polity. That being the position, a new ideological structure is being carefully constructed by certain political forces to obfuscate the social reality. This wilful distortion of reality and deliberate relegation of the social problems indeed create divisions and fissures among the people, which in turn, retard the nation-state building process.

Over four decades of independent economic development has consolidated the nation-state concept. The nationwide territorial economic integration, the mass media (both print and electronic) etc. are factors which have created a new national awareness. All things considered, Asian countries, above all India, are at the crossroads. One obvious danger is that the psyche of emotional injury to the religious sentiments of the various communities is being exploited by conservative forces and certain external powers.

Two articles published in this book were originally published in periodicals. We gratefully acknowledge the fact that excerpts from the Iranian Journal of International Affairs (Vol. III, Number 4, 1990-1991) on the 'Power of Religious Rituals and Revolution' by Dr. Cyrus Vakili-Zad been included in the book. We are also grateful to Dr. Inayatullah Baloch: we have published an article based on his doctoral dissertion entitled "The Problem of Greater Baluchistan". I am extremely grateful to all the contributors to this book. But for their active cooperation, my endeavour would not have succeeded.

Finally, I must thank Mr. M. Rasgotra, an outstanding expert on international affairs, for writing the introduction to this book, notwithstanding his preoccupations. In fact, without his intellectual and moral support, it would not have been possible for the International Institute for Asia-Pacific Studies, a non-governmental and non-official organisation, to make its modest contribution.

I must also express my thanks to Mr. Ashok K. Chatterjee for scrutinising and reading the manuscript of the book. I must also compliment the senior members of the staff of the Gyan Publishing House for their cooperation.

V.D. Chopra

L/3, Kailash Colony,
New Delhi - 110 048

CONTRIBUTORS

1.	Mr. Maharaja Krishna Rasgotra	:	Former Foreign Secretary, Former High Commissioner of India to U.K. and Chairman International Institute for Asia-Pacific Studies.
2.	Mr. V.D. Chopra	:	Former Head of Economics Department Rawalpindi (Pakistan) Author and Columnist, Vice Chairman International Institute for Asia-Pacific Studies.
3.	Mr. D. R. Goyal	:	Chief Editor, Secular Democracy and well known Columnist.
4.	Dr. Girish Mishra	:	Teachers Economics in Delhi, well known Economic Analyst.
5.	Dr. Asghar Ali Engineer	:	Chairman, Centre for Study of Society & Secularism and a well known Author.
6.	Dr. Nirmal Singh	:	Former Associate Professor of Jawaharlal Nehru University & Researcher on Current Political trends.
7.	Dr. Prem Singh	:	Expert on Contemporary History of Punjab.
8.	Prof. Kalim Bahadur	:	Professor of South Asian Studies & Chairperson Centre for South, Central Southeast Asian & South West Pacific Studies, Jawaharlal Nehru University.

9.	Dr. Inayatullah Baloch	:	Well known Scholar of Pakistan, an expert on problem of Nationalities in developing countries. Teaches Political Science in one of the University in Germany.
10.	Dr. S.R. Chakravarty	:	Associate Professor, South Asian Studies Division, Jawaharlal Nehru University.
11.	Dr. Cyrus Vakili-Zad	:	Assistant Professor at the Centre for Middle Eastern Studies, Harvard University.
12.	Prof. M.S. Agwani	:	Former Vice Chancellor of Jawaharlal Nehru University, Member National Commission for Minorities Government of India.
13.	Dr. Jagdish P. Sharma	:	Teaches Political Science in Delhi His Doctoral Dissertation was on West Asia.
14.	Major General D. Banerjee AVSM	:	Deputy Director, The Institute for Defence Studies and Analyses, New Delhi.
15.	Prof. Devendra Kaushik	:	Chairperson Centre for Soviet Area & East European Studies, Jawaharlal Nehru University, New Delhi.
16.	Prof. R. R. Sharma	:	Director for Soviet Area Studies Programme, Jawaharlal Nehru University, New Delhi.
17.	Dr. Ajay Kumar Patnaik	:	Associate Professor, Centre for Soviet Area Studies, Jawaharlal Nehru University, New Delhi.
18.	Mr. P. Stobdan	:	Research Officer, At Institute for Defence Studies & Analyses, New Delhi.
19.	Mr. Darbara Singh	:	Former Chief Minister of Punjab and A Member of the Congress working. This Piece is an excerp from an article before his death.

Religion and Human Consciousness

V.D. CHOPRA

Religion has played, and perhaps will continue to play a major role in moulding human consciousness. According to one theory, the essence and structure of such consciousness is a reflection of the social being, of the material basis of the society. The other theory is that human conciousness is moulded by different philosophies, and some of these, particularly religious philosophies, have been revealed to man though philosophy in its totality differs from religion in its cognition of the objective laws of development of nature, society and human thought theoretical assimilation of the world is the mainline of all human cognition. It is a fact that in the pre-independence period, Indian political leaders and social reformers had utilised the appeal of India's ancient past for progressive social and political aims. But after independence, social and political reactionaries have been utilising our ancient heritage for purposes extremely harmful to India's all-round progress. Our glorious heritage has been turned into a handmaid of chauvinism, communalism, superstition, antiscientific outlook, and all kinds of narrow and obscurantist purposes.

Liberal leaders and patriots have been repeating again and again that our culture and civilisation is imbued with a spirit of humanism and tolerance, and that India's unique unity in diversity must be preserved. But, in today's world of growing offensive reaction, such arguments do not cut much ice with the new generation. Young Indians need to be told in clear language, what was really noble and progressive in our ancient past, and what is reactionary, oppressive and unjust. They must know what they have to be proud of, what can inspire them for the solution of modern problems. They must also know what has to be renounced and rejected.[1]

Many of our distortions in the nation-state building process, such as rise of communalism, casteism, chauvinism, etc., can be explained by the fact that in the post independence period, ground was not prepared in terms of culture. Gandhiji and Jawaharlal Nehru saw the Indian revolution as a historically necessary condition for raising the cultural standard among the broad masses, but very few steps were taken in this direction during their lifetime, while subsequently, emphasis to cultural policy was made on the platform of populist politics with an eye on election. Nehru's thesis that modern nation-state should be built only by making use of the entire wealth of mankind's historical and cultural development, was sent into oblivion, and "cultural construction" was mostly led by incompetent, ignorant and unprofessional people, who were at times led by political cynics.

The people were befogged by myths and slogans. They were stupefied by propaganda. Moral values and notions of decency, duty, honour, conscience, noble behaviour and charity, which were for ages inherent part of our people, thought and action, were contemptuously cast aside in "abstract humanistic" categories. The recent developments in India have focussed on the interaction of religion on politics, and vice versa. This unholy alliance, of course, relates directly to the centuries-old colonial heritage in all facets of Indian life, particularly in the realm of ideology. This is also closely related to the complicated social reality.

Like any other religion, the Hindu religion continues to supply some deeply felt needs of human nature. It had given a set of values to human life, some of which may not be of relevance today. Yet, it did furnish the foundation of our morality. Religion often merges into mysticism and metaphysics; and metaphysical philosophy of life does appeal to mind, particularly to the irrational mind. In countries still in their transitional stage and yet to emerge as full-fledged modern nation-states, emphasis is laid on the "inward life". Such a philosophy of life embedded in religion becomes an article of faith for a vast mass of the people.

It is necessary to destroy the cobwebs of the myth of the alleged inadequacy of Indian philosophical and sociological thoughts, of its "one hundred per cent" idealism, mysticism, stagnation and pessimism. In the past 200 years our colonisers had distorted and belittled the great culture of the Indian people in every possible way, endeavouring to exterminate the progressive cultural traditions from the consciousness of the Indian masses. That is why the most absurd and distorted information of Indian sociological thought had spread in Europe.

It had become almost a habit with some British and American scholars to clothe Indian philosophical thought in mysticism, and identify it mostly with religious thoughts. It was Hegel who wrote: "What we refer to as Eastern philosophy is, generally speaking, to a much greater extent a religious mode of perception and a religious worldview of the Oriental people which can easily be mistaken for philosophy..."[2] American philosopher William T. Harris (1833-1909) in his numerous works characterises Indian philosophy as negative absolutism, abstractionism and nihilism. This view has proved to be extremely tenacious and still has some adherents. In 1957, a bulky collection of texts of Vedic literature translated from Sanskrit was published in Princeton (USA). Characteristically, the book contains texts mostly of religious content and ignores the philosophical significance of the ancient Indian thought structures evolved over the centuries.

Finally, a widely current notion of the colonialists is that the peoples of developing countries are, in general, incapable of "genuine" and independent philosophical thinking. In short, "the West tried its best to persuade India that its philosophy is absurd, its art puerile, its poetry uninspired, its religion grotesque and its ethics barbarous..."[3] This was the situation before India became independent; yet such theories are still being spun even today. One cannot ignore another aspect of Indian philosophy, its history of political orientation. Treating history idealistically, some scholars ignore the material basis of the society. In their opnion, the development of philosophical views, theories and ideology in general is independent of the social basis. This methodological defect is characteristic of the so-called traditional historical-philosophical thought in our country. It is this thought structure which provides ideological basis for obscurantism and the so-called religious revivalism.

The Main Precepts

Some experts on Indian philosophy identify the main trends of Indian thought deserving special attention as:

(1) The attempt to base philosophy on all aspects of experience and not only on some experience;
(2) The practical insistence that philosophy is for life and must be lived in all its spheres—private, social, and international;
(3) The emphasis on the necessity to control the body and mind, the necessity of moral purity and meditation, to make philosophical truths effective in life;

(4) The recognition of the fundamental unity of all beings, particularly mankind, and the consequent consciousness that our moral or religious duties are toward all, and not simply to the members of our own group, country, or race;

(5) The conviction that the Ultimate Reality (*Brahma*) manifests itself or can be conceived in different ways, and consequently the conviction that there are divergent paths to perfection any one of which can be adopted in accordance with one's inner inclination;

(6) The belief that political freedom and material progress are necessary, but only as means to ultimate spiritual peace and perfection, so that they should be attained in ways not detrimental to the latter; and

(7) The contention that the ultimate aim of every individual is to perfect himself with a view to raising the world to perfection.[4]

These perhaps represent the basic propositions of the Vedanta, although within Vedantism itself there have been various trends. However, what is relevant to the current Indian situation is that Hindu religious philosophy is being imparted different interpretations with a view to erasing from the consciousness of the followers of this religion, its humanistic content. The Indian nation-state today is at an early stage of its formation, and the process will be prolonged and contradictory and often painful one. Two parallel processes of nation-state building, are currently on—the secular-democratic one and the communal-theocratic.

In the area of theory and ideology, the exponents of secular-democratic nation-state have to interpret the entire Indian philosophy, including the religious philosophy, objectively drawing lessons particularly from the period when India was engaged in the freedom struggle. The *Bhagvat Geeta,* basing itself on the thesis that *Brahma* and *Atma*, although being totally unattached, were, at the same time, the supreme driving power of the universe, emphatically concludes that unattached, selfless action was the essence of life, the truest and the highest path leading to *Moksha.*

Lokamanya Tilak, wanting to rouse our people from the slumber of despair and demoralisation during the British rule, plumped for the *Geeta* interpretation of Vedanta. "The materialist body is transient and perishable, but the *Atma* is eternal and imperishable. So, go forward dauntlessly to face British prisons and even the gallows", was his message to the people.

For a long time, Indian aggressive revolutionaries also drew inspiration from the *Geeta* or the cult of *Durga* and *Kali*. *Shree Krishna*, in the *Geeta* claims to be the destroyer of tyrants. That was also the legendary role of *Durga*, the consort of *Shiva*. This admirably suited the revolutionaries who wanted to destroy the British tyrants.

But the humanist saints of the medieval *Bhakti* movement were different. The bigoted Brahmin priesthood of the time insisted that '*Chaturvarnya*' had been ordained by the Vedas, and revealed by *Brahma*, and that the *smritis*, swearing in the name of the Vedas had laid down that "vaishyas" and "shudras", the untouchables, must be treated with the utmost rigour and hate.

The *Bhakti* saints, imbued with the spirit of humanism, naturally differed with this interpretation. They accepted the theory of the four *Varnas* emanating from four different limbs of *Brahma*—the mouth, the arms, the thighs and the feet. But that did not negate the fact that all of them had emanated from *Brahma* himself, and as such, had the same *Atma* and were the children of the same supreme creator. Thus, within the framework of *Chaturvarnya*, they had to be given compassionate and humane treatment.

These illustrations from the Hindu religious philosophy are evidences that idealist and religious motivations, idealist and religious forms, serve the cause of human progress under certain conditions. The modern social thought not only recognises them, but also gives scientific explanation to them. Yet, one should not ignore the limitations of such religious consciousness. For instance, the *Bhakti* movement did not go beyond preaching and practising humanism in socio-religious matters, did not raise the question of economic exploitation or political oppression of the masses.

Traditions of Sikh Religion

The founding Gurus of the Sikh religion had themselves perceived a different religious identity for their followers. The Sikh faith came to flourish in the 15th and the 16th centuries. A new ferment was sweeping the land then, and the common people were compelled to re-examine their values and refurbish their faith. India was face to face with a new situation, trying to absorb the then established presence of the foreign Muslim element. Out of this ferment rose a new set of religious reformers who consciously preached a synthesis and unsparingly condemned the ills which had beset the Hindu religion and society. There was the Hindu saint Ramanand in the south in the 15th century, with his more well-known disciple Kabir, a Muslim weaver of Varanasi. Kabir's poems and songs of wisdom became, and still are, very popular. In the north, Guru Nanak, the founder of the Sikh religion, held sway. The influence of these reformers went far beyond the limits of the particular sects that grew around them. Hinduism came under an inescapable impact of new ideas and new ethical principles. Hindus, Muslims and Sikhs were not only becoming integrated within themselves, but they were also giving birth to a new class structure within the confines of the Indian society as a whole.

The word Sikh is derived from Sanskrit *"shishya"*, meaning a disciple or learner.[5] Guru Nanak was a revolutionary and a religious and social reformer, according to whom the political and cultural domination of the people by the ruling classes was chiefly responsible for their degeneration. Their emancipation, he thought, could only be brought about by a new consciousness which would instill into them the unity and fatherhood of God and the equality and fraternity of man. He refused to recognise the distinction between man and man, and between the sexes, created by the old caste system and other outmoded social conventions and proclaimed that all human beings were born equal. He felt that the real cause of the misery of the people was their disunity, caused by the diversity of their faiths and beliefs. Thus, in his own way, Guru Nanak was arousing the people to the changing realities. The fifth Guru Arjan Dev, a worthy heir to Nanak's teachings, unpraised the low castes debarred for centuries from receiving religious teachings and ministration. "To the knowledge of the basic creed religion all are entitled. Among all the four castes all are free to give utterance to God's holy name", declared Guru Arjan Dev.

In the holy scripture of the Sikhs, the *Granth Sahib*, are included hymns by saints from different castes and religions. Among these are Kabir, Ravi Das, a cobbler, and Namdev, a tailor. These saints have freely given expression to the doctrine of caste equality.[6]

The intolerance unleashed by the Mughal emperors, especially after

Akbar, was mainly responsible for turning the peaceful and peace-loving followers of Guru Nanak into a militant sect. Jehangir, suspicious of the spreading influence of the teachings of the Sikh Gurus, tortured Guru Arjan Dev to death in 1606 on a false charge of treason. His son, Guru Hargobind, though in the employment of Jehangir, had to undergo 12 years' imprisonment in Gwalior. He rebelled against Shah Jehan and defeated the Moghul imperial army at Sangrama near Amritsar in 1628. Guru Teg Bahadur, who succeeded Guru Har Kishan, was seized by Aurangzeb and beheaded on flimsy charges.

It was in these historical conditions that the character of Sikhism underwent drastic transformation at the hands of the tenth Guru, Gobind Singh. It was he who created the Khalsa. He initiated five persons into the Khalsa who, in turn, initiated him. By this one act, he terminated the Guruship, transferring its sanctity to the Sikh community and their holy book, *Guru Granth Sahib*. Staunch Sikhs were commanded to observe the five symbols that clearly demarcated them from other religious communities. The five symbols prescribed were: keeping long hair and unshorn beards (*kesh*), carrying a sword (*kirpan*), wearing a knee-length underwear (*kachha*), a bracelet (*kara*) and having a comb in the hair (*kangha*). Under his leadership the first serious blow to undermine the Mughal empire in the north was made.

It is significant to mention that Guru Gobind Singh considered Hindustan as mentioned in the *Adi Granth* as his homeland. The Guru has nowhere used the word "Punjab". He has called Bengal as his "spiritual homeland" as stated in one of his letters addressed to his followers in Dhaka. The Guru in fact was aware of the distress of the whole country, and not merely of the Punjab. Aurangzeb's successor, Bahadur Shah, was on friendly terms with Guru Gobind Singh and wanted the latter's help for the subjugation of the Marathas and the Rajputs. The Guru refused any such help point blank, because this was against his deep devotion for his country.

Four of the Guru's "Panj Piaras" were non-Punjabis by caste and origin.[7] Sikhs, inspired by their religion, have played a glorious role in India's struggle for independence. Here one important historical fact may be recalled to illustrate this.

In May 1857, the Indian army at Meerut revolted against the British.

It was much more than a simple military revolt, and it spread rapidly and assumed the character of a mass rebellion and a war of independence, but mainly confined to Delhi, United Provinces and parts of central India and Bihar. This revolt strained British resources to the full, though it was ultimately suppressed with the help of "loyal" Indian soldiers. The 1857 rebellion exposed all the inherent weaknesses of the feudal chieftains and princes, who had the sympathy of the masses over large areas, but were divided and unorganised, without any constructive ideal or community of interests guiding their efforts.

In meeting this armed challenge, the British had leaned heavily on the support of the Gurkhas. But more shocking was the fact that Sikh chieftains played an important role in suppressing this war of independence. In return for this "service" to the British rulers, they were given big "Jagirs", both in Punjab and UP.

Punjab's history is replete with some of the shiniest examples of opposition to tyranny. The strategic geography of the state, the many foreign invasions over the centuries and the inherent disposition of its strong, sturdy and brave people have all combined to give birth to sagas of valour during different periods of its chequered history. Some of the finest and noblest specimens of human endurance, grandeur and glory have come from Punjab. It has been the cradle of many a religion at whose altar the faithfuls have sacrificed themselves smilingly. Its soil has been hallowed by the memories of youthful patriots rushing headlong to the gallows, and old stalwarts braving cheerfully the blows of naked British imperialism for the liberation of their motherland.

The long, relentless struggle of the Sikh gurus against tyranny and bigotry and the martyrdoms of Guru Arjun Dev, Guru Tegh Bahadur, Bhai Mani Singh, Bhai Mati Dass, the four Sahibzadas of Guru Gobind Singh and of Banda Bairagi constitute an awe-inspiring saga of sacrifice. The stirring deeds of the brave sons of Rewari and Gurgaon during India's first war of Independence in 1857 and the cannon-blasting of the brave Namdharis in 1872 have all built up the heroic traditions of the Punjabi people.

Punjab, especially the area of the central districts of the erstwhile united Punjab, is the hallowed ground for the Sikh community because every inch of this land is associated with some important event in the lives of the gurus or other great martyrs of the community. The Sikh movement turns round what may be called the 'Gurdwara-cum-Sacred Book' axle. To the devotees of the Sikh religion, the 'gurdwara' is more than a mere place of worship and the '*Granth Sahib*' much more than a book of spiritual guidance. Both are interwoven with the social and spiritual life of the people, and the growth of the Sikh religion over the centuries. To the Sikhs, *Guru Granth Sahib* represents the body and soul of their lives and teachings of the gurus, while the gurdwaras are not only the embodiments of the struggles of the Sikhs but are also integrated with the day-to-day social life and religion of the community.

In such a background, the Sikh religious fundamentalists of today and the activities of the terrorists violate the noble traditions of the Sikh religion. Punjab currently is at the crossroads. One obvious danger is that the "hurt" psyche of the Sikhs, the so-called emotional injury to their religious sentiments because of the tragic developments of the eighties, is being exploited to create conditions of instability. A new collusion between internal reaction on the one hand and Pakistan on the other has surfaced in Punjab. An added disturbing factor has been the fact that in the post-cold war era, Washington has again begun to raise the bogey of the "threat to the Sikhs" under the cover of human rights. United States President Bill Clinton's observation about "solution that protects Sikh rights" conceals more than what it reveals.[8] Though the U.S. officially has tried to clarify that President Clinton did not mean "Khalistan" when he talked about the "Sikh Rights" in Punjab, and that what he had in mind was the "protection of human rights of all the minorities", the fact that the US Administration is openly talking about human rights in Punjab and Kashmir is ominous.[9] The crux of the problem is that religious fundamentalist forces are being given overt and covert support from outside India. President Clinton's comments were made in a letter to Democratic Congressmen Gary Condit in the last week of January, 1994. That the American President should have openly declared that he shares the "desire for a peaceful solution that protects Sikh rights" was indeed an extraordinary statement by the head of a foreign state. This has to be seen in the context of certain other statements by the American policy makers. (i) A senior US State Department official John Mallot openly advised India, from a public platform, how to conduct not only its relations with other countries but also its domestic affairs.[10] (ii) Not so senior an American official Robin Raphel has questioned the accession of Kashmir to India; (iii) Another official of the State Department told an

Indian newsman that the US "disapproves" of India's human right record in Kashmir and that this country's right to put down insurgency in any state did not entitle it to violate human rights. President Clinton himself has bracketed India with Bosnia in his UN speech.[11]

All these facts pieced together, make it clear that the old policy of Washington of backing religious fundamentalist forces in countries which follow an independent path has not undergone any basic change in the post-cold war period. To substantiate this, one more fact may be mentioned.

Harry Barnes, a former US ambassador in India, has equated the 'Khalistan' demand with the freedom struggle of the people of Puerto Rico in an interview in mid-June 1983. This was widely reported in the Indian press. It may be mentioned that Barnes has been listed in authoritative 'Who's Who in CIA', compiled by Dr Julius Mader (pages 46-47), though the US ambassador has covered more areas since then. This controversial book is taken seriously by American researchers into, and campaigners against, the CIA.[12] This is how foreign forces are disorienting the consciousness of our people.

Islam and Christianity

Let us now briefly examine the humanistic aspect of Islam and Christianity and their role in human consciousness. The origin of Christianity was in the misery of the slaves in Rome and their yearning for emancipation. Islam arose as a movement for uniting the warring tribes, by assuring equality to all who recognised one Allah and Mohammed as the only Prophet. These religions appeared in the Middle Ages when they replaced the local pagan cults.

Islam can be interpreted either as a sum total of the fundamental Islamic social and revolutionary principles and doctrines aimed at ameliorating the social conditions of the masses, as a brotherhood of believers, their equality and collectivization of means of production and distribution; or as a complex of Muslim institutions belonging to certain historical epochs and modes. Islamic ideology, therefore, is amenable to different interpretations depending on those who invoke it. The traditional literature of Islam relates to various historical periods: the pristine period of the

Prophet (peace be upon Him) and the Rightly-guided Caliphs. The Muslim community of those times was a cohesive fraternity of believers, and their Islam was a revolutionary social principle. Later, under the Umayyads and Abbasids, Islam developed as a part of the general social formation in the context of a feudal mode of production. All institutions, ideas and theories elaborated during these later periods bear a deep imprint of the feudalist approach. The later social and legalistic Islamic literature deals with the problems faced by the medieval society. Islamic ideology in its theory and history is thus, strictly speaking, a historical category in the social or institutional sense.[13]

In the industrial society, separation of the social order and sciences from the restrictions of religion is a modern phenomenon. The religious, ideological structure of Islam in the new historical conditions, is being distorted to change the consciousness of the people; the main thrust being on building a religious dogma and superstition among the common people.

This distortion of reality and deliberate confusion of the social problem by the ruling elites through political use of religion is characteristic of the developing societies of Africa, Asia and Latin America which were annexed by world capitalism as its periphery. The loot of the natural and human resources of the underdeveloped societies under ideological camouflage has been made possible with the help of the indigenous upper classes. As self-appointed custodians of ideology, these elites, as part of the international capitalist system, formulate and develop religio-political ideas, concepts and theories which conserve the existing neo-colonial economic structures of these societies.

Islam: Feudalism and Commonwealth

Under the Umayyads, Abbasids and latter regimes, feudal mode of production, in general, prevailed in the Muslim world throughout the medieval times. This socio-economic formation mainly rested on the division of the society into a minority of landlords, tax-farmers and slave-owners, and a vast majority of slaves and serfs. This feudal system, and its religio-political ideology, is reflected in the medieval legal literature, which essentially deals with the contemporary feudal economic and social relationships. Religion was exploited by the absolute autocrats for their own purpose. This post-Quranic feudal ideology is the main source of inspiration even for some of the modern States, such as Pakistan.

The traditional institutions and ideas are deliberately taken up by the ruling elites to "fit" in their grand scheme, in full knowledge that such superficial nods in the direction of tradition would not affect the existing economic structures and relationships between landlords and their tenants, capitalists and the labourers. Similar intent is there in the official religious policy of the State. The "call to prayer" is broadcast by the official media, and the masses are asked to pray regularly, to fast in the month of Ramadan and to pay *Zakat* from their savings. These rituals have no effect on the existing economic structures; on the contrary, they render them sacrosanct, as the poor people are reminded again and again that poverty and riches are divinely decreed and their distribution is not a function of the economic system. In the early Islamic period, the universal ethical principles enunciated in the *Quran* and the *Hadith* of the Prophet and his illustrious companions—like brotherhood, egalitarianism and social solidarity among the believers—were realized by abolishing the systems of *riba* and *muzara'a* (share-cropping/ground rent) and making all capital, land and natural resources the collective property of the entire community, to be used for the benefit of all. The community is a *Jama'a* a collectivity, not in the religious or theological sense only, but the social and economic resources were to be used for the equal development of all. This principle negates all self-aggrandizements, the profit motive, self-interest and private ownership of the social means of production. But this original Islamic ideology, with its collectivist theory of social organization, is not convenient to the ruling classes.

Early Islam was a social movement and a code of action rather than a collection of religious rituals. It was a community, a fraternity of believers, with its principles verbalized in a religious framework and religious terminology, without which the people of the time could not understand the spirit and message of Islam, nor translate their theories into action. In essence, the *Quran* is a "book of action", a declaration of war against all exploiters of weaker human beings, and against all vested interests.[14]

What is being today labelled as the resurgence of Islamic fundamentalism has little to do with any real renaissance of Islamic values or civilization. The renewed trend towards revivalism is not an autonomous collective phenomenon involving the entire *ummah*, the community of believers. The niceties being exchanged at diplomatic levels between the Western powers, particularly the United States, and the ruling elite of some Islamic countires, do not amount to recognition of the political strength or cultural integrity of Islamic countries, individually or collectively. As in the past, the imperial interest of the Western powers is best served by maintaining hold on the material and human resources of the Islamic world and using some of the Islamic states for geopolitical interests in the fast changing international co-relation of forces in the post-cold war period.

Christianity

The religious systems of the East—Hinduism, Sikhism, Islam—and the teachings of countless different religious sects are diverse, yet they do have something in common: not one of these religions, which to this day constitute a major unit linking the entire superstructural sphere, has ever experienced any profound reformation like European Christianity has. Nor one of them could provide such a powerful spiritual justification for the political and socio-economic activities of the society and the individual as European Christanity did at one time, especially, Protestantism, under the protection of which capitalism developed faster and put the European peasantry and urban population in the foreground of the struggle for a modern nation-state. The religions of the East, like of the West in the past, do not include just adoration of a deity, but prescribe "consecrated" way of life and thinking of both the society and the individual. Students of religious philosophies may be competent to draw a line of demarcation between Christianity and other religions, yet social scientists cannot ignore the fact that Christianity had undergone a basic transformation unlike Hinduism, Islam, Sikhism etc. the social structure of the East could have been very different today if the envelop of ideas surrounding its material existence had undergone some changes on a scale on which Europe did. The religious systems of the Western world, especially from the 14th and 15th centuries onwards, did much more to promote social and economic development than the corresponding systems did in the East. It is therefore not by chance that the Christian countries of the West, and not the Islamic, Buddhist or the Hindu ones, became the cradle of capitalism.

The lag in the East's economic development meant that modern capitalist states began to take shape there later than in the West. It were national states that, in their turn, acted as powerful accelerators of capitalist development. The delay in the emergence of national states in the East is largely explained, of course, by foreign invasions and domination, but hardly by these alone. A considerable role here was played by the extremely narrow and shallow entrepreneurial and economic base; above all, the social division of labour and the development of commodity-money relations. The economic base did not suffice for the formation of a national state owing to the stagnant nature of the superstructure, too.[15]

National consciousness surfaced earlier in the countries of Asia and Africa, primarily as a response to foreign aggressions, foreign oppression and exploitation and everything that the imperialist countires brought with them. The significance of this factor needs to be investigated by the intellectuals of the East, though some social reformers and religious leaders have made some valuable contributions in this area of social thought-structure.

The nation-state concept and the delinking of religion from politics emerged in Europe in the 16th century, and we have had four centuries of the evolution of the nation-states in Europe and the last one and half century in western hemisphere as well. This period of history was marked by extraordinary violence, such as the 30-year war, Napolionic wars, the Balkan wars, the first and second world wars, the American civil war, the decimation of the Red Indian population, the French revolution, the Bolshevik revolution, etc. Countries which are today known for their commitment to peace, such as Sweden and Switzerland have had their full share of violence. Religious intolerance, genocide, ethnic conflicts and oppression have marked this period. The development of science and technology, industrialisation, spread of education and a spirit of secularism over a period of a century, and finally two horrible wars within a span of two successive generations, have seemingly stabilised the industrialised world.

The role of the Church in modern-state building has taken different directions, though in Europe by and large, a clear line of demarcation has been evolved between the nation-state and the church.

Here it must be recalled that in Tsarist Russia Christianity was at its worst. The Tsar was the supreme autocrat of the Orthodox Church, and he had, during the last few years of his reign, Rasputin as his spiritual adviser. This adventurer had, by his unsavoury combination of drinking bouts, sexual orgies, religious fanaticism and habitual venality, completely disgusted not only the ordinary capitalist but also the corrupt inner circles of the Russian society—a disgust so great that it eventually led to his violent removal from the scene by a relative of the Tsar himself. The village priesthood taken as a whole was illiterate and grasping. The monasteries enjoying large revenues, were nests of miracle-mongering. Throughout the vast Eurasian continent indigenous pagan magic and incantations held their own amidst Christian rites and such doctrine as the peasant was taught. No wonder that, after reading a "plain, objective and not unsympathetic account of the Russian religion", the professor of Moral Philosophy in the University of London declared in 1934 that he could "only come to one conclusion—and it is a conclusion that all true friends of religion will share—that nearly all that religion has been, and has meant, in Russia ought to perish forever from the face of the earth and from the momory of men".[16]

Thus the erstwhile Soviet Union and East European countires had to pay a heavy price for their mechanical and dogmatic approach to the question of the role of religion in the human consciousness, notwithstanding the historical reasons which led them to this position.

In the recent years, a section of the Marxists has begun to give a fresh look to this problem. This is evident from the writings of the Russian scholars and leaders of the national liberation movements in Latin America and Africa. In his book entitled "The Religion", Cuban leader Fidel Castro has made a critical assessment of this approach.

First, analysing it from a historical perspective, nobody can deny that the Church—the Church of conquerors,opressors, and exploiters—was on the side of the conquerors, oppressors, and exploiters. It never categorically denounced slavery, an institution that is so repugnant to our condemning the slavery of blacks or Indians. The Church never denounced the extermination of the aboriginal population or any of the other crimes that were committed against those people—the fact that they were robbed of their land, their wealth, their culture, and even their lives. None of the Churches denounced those crimes, and the systems lasted for centuries.

No wonder, the revolutionary ideas that emerged in the struggle against those age-old injustices had an anti-religious spirit. There's an objective, historical explanation for the origin of these ideas within the revolutionary movement. These ideas were present in the bourgeois French revolution and also in the Bolshevik revolution. They were present in liberalism first. The philosophy of Jean Jacques Roussea and the French encyclopedists also contained this anti-religious spirit. It wasn't just in socialism; these ideas were present afterwards in Marxism-Leninism for historical reasons. There was never a denunciation of capitalism. Maybe 100 or 200 years from now, when capitalism might be completely wiped out, somebody would say bitterly, "For centuries, the capitalists and imperialist system", just as we say today that for centuries the Church didn't denounce slavery, the extermination of the indigenous Indians, and the colonialist system.

A new trend has developed, both among the liberal democrats and Marxist social scientists, that doctrinal rhetorics about religious heritage should be avoided at all costs. In fact, in some of the countries of Latin America, a new concept of "liberation theology", or "the liberation church" has been evolved. This concept implies that Christianity should go back to its "roots, its most beautiful, attractive and glorious history". This concept advocates that "logically, a religious position or theory that seeks out the best in the history of Christianity completely contradicts the interests of imperialism".

Some of the Christian leaders point out that when John XXIII became the Pope, the Catholic Church began to undergo a change in the sense that the "poor influenced and invaded the Church, and the Church in turn, as a reflection or as an echo of that suffering, also reached out to the poor". The result was that many priests and bishops began to identify themselves with the cause of the poor. This is the meaning of the "liberation theology". This also shows that even among the ardent devotees of the Christian religion, a new ferment around liberation theology has begun to take shape.[17]

This perfunctory survey of the role of religion in human consciousness reveals that the power of the prophet, the preacher, or the philosopher stems from his claim to knowledge and truth, and his ability to anticipate future events. In the past, there was a coalescence between temporal and spiritual power, or between the King and the Church. Despite Christ's injunction to "render unto Ceaser that which is Ceaser's and unto God that which is God's", the Church and the State were for long parts of the same establishment, and even now remain so in many societies. In some cases, ideology has replaced theology, and in some other cases theology is being used to maintain the old social order. Thus, the so-called religious fundamentalism is being used to disorientate the minds of the people. Such attempts can only be foiled on ideological and theoretical level, if the humanistic aspect of all the religions is revived in the consciousness of the people and religion and politics are delinked from each other.

The easteem of religious rites is based upon the attention paid to the outer symbolic expressions of religious feelings. But stereotyped symbols do not necessarily continue to express human values. The effort to recover oneself as man, therefore, implies in the first instance to imbibe the true spirit of humanism, the basic postulate of all religions. Prophetic was Kabir when he said:

"If by repeating Rama's name the world is saved, then by repeating 'sugar' the mouth is sweetened"[18]

He also wrote:

O servant, where dost thou seek me?
Lo! I am beside thee.
I am neither in temple nor in mosque,
I am neither in Kaaba nor in Kailash:
Neither am I in rites and ceremonies
Nor in Yoga and renunciation.
If thou art a true seeker, thou shalt at once see Me
Thou shalt meet Me in a moment of time
The inner veil of the temple of Mecca
Is in man's heart, if truth be known.[19]

Humanism is a trait conspicuous of the modern nation-state, largely brought about by the scientific and technological revolution. However, in Eastern countries, where the nation-state building is still in the initial stages, the various religious philosophies have clevated man to a higher status. Some religions have expressed this as being a result of God in man, while others have neglected or ceased to assume God. But the love or compassion for others is regarded as the fundamental principle for human action.

According to Tulsi Das, Rama manifests in any man who shows a perfected morality of love toward his fellow human beings:

"Thou dwellest in the hearts of those... who are dear to all, benevolent to all, equable in joy and sorrow, praise and blame...who consider other men's women as mothers and others' wealth as more poisonous than poison, those who rejoice to see others flourish and are acutely pained to see them afflicted".[20]

It is ironical that in India today, Rama and his birthplace are being used to drive a wedge among the various communities by rousing irrational passions. This shows that two parallel movements on the question of religious revivalism are developing. There are those who are giving a new political orientation to their religion and pitch one community against the other, thus undermining the social values of religion and destroying the moral and theological base of this heritage.

On the other, a distinct trend in religious philosophies is also developing, which makes man and humanism as the central piece of religious teachings.

It is for the modern Indian intellectuals—social scientists, historians, students of religious philosophies—to interpret the various religious philosophies in a meaningful way in the new historical conditions. The recent developments have, however, shown that a new ideological structure on religious philosophies divorced from the objective reality is being carefully constructed by the so-called religious fundamentalists to obfuscate the social reality. This wilful distortion of the Indian heritage on one hand and the existing reality on the other through the political use of religion, is the most despicable characteristic of the recent developments in India.

References

1. S.G. Sardesai: Progress and Conservatism in Ancient India p. iii & vi.
2. G.W.F. Hegel's Werke. Vorlesungen uber die Geschichte der philosophie, Verlag von Duncker und Humbolt, Berlin, 1933, Vol. 13, S. 135.
3. S. Radhakrishnan, *Indian philosophy*, Vol. II, George Allen & Unwin Ltd., London, 1977, p. 779.
4. D.M. Datta, "The Contribution of Modern Indian Philosophy to the World Philosophy", *The Philosophical Review*, Vol. LVII, November 1948, pp. 571-572.

5. Harbans Singh, *The Heritage of the Sikhs*, Delhi, 1983.
6. Gurbachan Singh Talib, *Sikhism* and *Democracy*, SGPC, Amritsar.
7. Major Ravi Batra, *Leadership in its Finest Mould-Guru Gobind Singh*, SGPC, Amritsar, 1979.
8. *Hindustan Times*, New Delhi; January 24, 1994.
9. Ibid; January 25, 1994.
10. Girish Mathur, *New Wave*; January 22, 1994.
11. Ibid.
12. V.D. Chopra : *Agony of Punjab*: p. 121.
13. Ziaul Haque: *Pakistan; The Roots of Dictatorship* p. 368.
14. Ziaul Haque : *Pakistan: Roots of Dictatorship* p. 370-371.
15. Rostislav Ulanovsky; *Agrarian India between the World Wars* p. 11 & 12.
16. Professor John Macmurray, in a review of Dr. Julius F. Hecker's *Religion and Communism*, in the English magazine *Soviet Culture*, February 1934, p. 15.
17. Fidel Castro: *The Religion* : p. 204 to 207.
18. Carpenter, *Theism in Medieval India*: p. 459.
19. Ibid, p. 462.
20. Wm. Th. De Bary, S.N. Hay, R. Weller, and A. Yarrow: *Sources of Indian Tradition* p. 356.

COMMUNAL CHALLENGE TO INDIA'S SECULAR NATIONALISM

D.R. GOYAL

India's secular nationalism is under siege. It is facing onslaught from not only those who oppose secularism as a political doctrine and policy but also from those who consider it a useful umbrella for protection of their communal interests, as well as from those who proclaim it to be a precondition for national unity and advance.

Organisations like the Rashtriya Swayamsewak Sangh (RSS) and the Jamaat-e-Islami condemn secularism as anti-thesis of religion and therefore unacceptable to the believers. The Bharatiya Janata Party (BJP) derides it as anti-Hindu and the Muslim League says it does not assure the political, economic, cultural and social rights of the Muslim community.

The communists find the operational practice of secularism by the ruling Congress party halting and inadequate and, therefore, consider it no more than an innocuous slogan, often used by the Congress to protect its monopoly of power. They, of course, are not for rejecting secularism either as a principle or as policy. Rather, they aspire to emerge as the main standard-bearer of secularism and, to achieve this end, concentrate more on finding fault with the present main standard-bearer, that is the Congress, rather than waging a consistent battle against forces inimical to secularism.

The Congress, which can legitimately claim to be the harbinger of secular nationalism in India, is too ready to own up its weaknesses in upholding secularism, but tends to explain them away with the plea that they have no choice but to make compromises in a political milieu where considerations of retaining or snatching state power override every other consideration. As justification of their conduct they pose the question: "If we are removed from power our place will be taken by those who would blot out the very principle from the statute book and make the most blatant anti-secular discrimination the basis of state policy. That is why we make tactical compromises in the larger strategic interest of safeguarding the principle."

In short, secular nationalism appears to have become a political orphan and needs to be salvaged from this tangled web of confused thinking and short-sighted political competition. The case, however, is not as hopeless as it appears. One has only to recollect that it survived the challenges of partition which were far stronger than the one that we see today.

Even now, despite all the setbacks and weaknesses of the political leadership, the popular support to communal politics is not such as to be considered insurmountable. Wherever the opponents of secularism have succeeded it is not because of disenchantment with secularism but on account of the follies, foibles and weaknesses of the parties that claim to be secular. Whenever and wherever the communal parties have registered success whether in 1967, in 1977, in 1989 or in 1990—they have achieved it under the protective cover of secular politics. Only in 1991 did the Bharatiya Janata Party sail to success under its own banner of *Hindutva*. But each time the disillusionment with the communal ruler has been faster than with the secular ones.

What we need to examine is why and under what circumstances does secularism go down. That, in my opinion, is the motive for discussing challenges to India's secular nationalism.

Challenge from Three Sources

Challenges to Indian secularism emanate from three main sources—ideological confusion, political opportunism and external subversion. It has to be defended on all these fronts if unity of India and its democratic character have to be preserved.

Ideological attack on secularism takes three forms:

— That secularism is the fad of western-oriented liberal intellectuals and therefore alien to the Indian genius;
— That secularism is a departure from Indian tradition and ethos which are essentially Hindu; and
— That secularism is antithetical to religious belief.

None of these propositions is supported by facts.

Even a cursory glance at the writings and pronouncements of the opponents of secularism would bear out that their observations are based not on any analyses of Indian reality but on European experiences/and/or on western versions of Indian history and philosophy, distorted and mutilated with less than honourable motives. The pity is that even contemporary practitioners of Indian secularism are viewed through glasses coloured by western views of secularism and India. Thus, Gandhi and Abul Kalam Azad are put in the non-secular category, while Jinnah and Savarkar are extolled as secular and Jawaharlal Nehru is berated as a "compromiser" because, though an avowed agnostic, he showed respect for religious sentiments of the people.

To understand Indian secularism one should turn to those who have shaped modern Indian polity rather than to the philosophers and thinkers of Renaissance and Reformation in Europe. And if we do that it would be found that it is distinct from the secularism which evolved in Europe and that it has its own indigenous characteristics. The concept that emerged in Europe was the outcome of resistance of religious dogma, to recognising the validity of scientific discoveries and the conflict between the Church and State for supremacy in affairs of the people. Those antagonisms often took violent form and caused much misery so that as the democratic spirit asserted itself, religion got relegated to the background.

No such antagonism has been seen, at least not on a similar scale, in any period of Indian History, whether the rulers belonged to one religious faith or another. Even the view sedulously fostered by orientalists of the imperialist era that the Muslim rulers were ruthless, fanatical proselytisers has been roundly repudiated by historians. Dr. Tara Chand, for instance, has pointed out:

> "Almost every one of the Muslim monarchs of India from the 13th century onwards expressed his inability and indicated the impossibility of conducting government in accordance with the Shariat. Iltutmish, Balban, Allauddin Khilji and Mohammad Tughlaq were among the pre-Mughal sovereigns of India who questioned the suitability of applying Muslim law in India. Their spokesman, strangely enough, was one of the Ulama, Zia-ud-Din Barni, the historian. In his *Fatwa-i-Jahandari*, which is a work dealing with the principles of politics, he says, true religion consists in following in the footsteps of the Prophet...But royal government, on the contrary, can only be carried on by following the policies of Khusrau Parvez and the great emperors of Iran."

He admits, "Between the tradition (Sunnat) of the Prophet Mohammad and his mode of life and living, and the customs of the Iranian emperors and their mode of life and living, there is a complete contradiction and total opposition." But he points out that the *Shariat* which is the command of God, could be followed in State matters only in exceptional times. Mohammad succeeded in enforcing *shara* because he was directly inspired by God; the first four Khalifas did so because they had been the associates of the Prophet. But their successors were faced with two irreconcilable alternatives—traditions of the Prophet and the policy of the Iranian emperors. But "Prophethood is the perfection of religion and kingship is the perfection of worldly fortune. These two perfections are opposed and contradictory to each other, and their combination is not within the bounds of possibility."[1]

Prof. Mohammad Habib of the Aligarh Muslim University, reviewing the role of Muslim rulers, concluded: "It is true that Muslim kings, mostly of foreign extraction, sat on Indian thrones for some six or seven centuries. But they could only do so because their enthronement was not the enthronement of 'Muslim rule'. Had it been otherwise, they could not have lasted for a single generation."[2]

Religious tolerance thus has been the main tradition of India although the rulers may not always have been responsive to public opinion or benevolent. It is on that that the modern day Indian secularism has been based and cannot, in any way, be described as falling outside the Indian tradition or ethos.

In India, the concept evolved in the context of the need for political unity of diverse communities with the aim of overthrowing the foreign imperialist rulers and attaining self-determination and independence. It is necessary to bear in mind that unification on secular issues was not the idea of western-oriented intelligentsia as is commonly believed. Prominent among the progenitors of the idea were Muslim ulema, deeply drunk in religious lore but equally strongly averse to imperialist exploitation. Just recall the anti-British movement, led by the Ulema even before 1857.

Ulema and Secularism

The first to articulate these ideas was Shah Waliullah of Delhi. He had witnessed the decline and degeneration of the Mughals in post-Aurangzeb years and had learnt from fellow Haj pilgrims in Hejaz about the degeneration of their respective societies and the depradations of advancing European imperialism. From his experience and observations he came to the conclusion that the monarchical system of Government had outplayed its role and, therefore, the existing system should be replaced by a new system of governance.

The rudimentary outline of the new system which he advocated has revolutionary elements of entirely secular character although there is nothing derogatory towards religion. What he condemned was unequal distribution of wealth, heavy taxes, suppression of workers and peasants and the degenerate ostentatious principle which he enunciated as that "labour generates wealth".

He has also outlined some basic human rights which include (i) right to food, clothing, shelter and adequate income to raise and maintain a family; (ii) right to get justice and protection of life and property; (iii) right to honourable living and citizenship; and (iv) right of each community to protect its language and culture. And these rights were to be guaranteed in the new scheme of things irrespective of religion, race and colour.

His grandson Syed Ahmed tried to organise the tribal areas of north-west on these lines to build a secure and stable base for an armed struggle against the British in early 19th century. It was called the *Jehad* movement, but it was given the bad name of Wahabism and disinformation was spread that the movement was pan-Islamist and intended to restore Muslim rule over India.

That it was a wilful distortion intended to mislead the people is clear from the letter addressed by Syed Ahmed to various rulers of Indian states: "God is witness that we intend neither to amass wealth nor to establish our rule. We only want to drive out the foreigners who came as traders and have become rulers of our land." A special messenger was sent to Maharaja Ranjit Singh with a letter saying: "We do not covet either your territory or your wealth. Nor do we seek to harm your life and honour. We have no intention of waging war against you. We only seek your cooperation and want you to be our comrades-in-arm. After successful *jehad* against the enemy, we shall restore your territories to you.

But if you do not accept this invitation, we shall have no alternative but to engage in battle with you.''[3]

It is another matter that Syed Ahmed's movement and effort to enlist wider support did not succeed, but his secular approach was unmistakable.

To the same tradition belonged Maulana Mehmood-ul-Hassan, who was incarcerated in Malta during World War I for attempting to "wage war" against the British rule in India. To oppose imperialism he made common cause with all anti-imperialists, irrespective of religion and creed. Alongwith Gandhi he built a mighty movement of boycott and civil disobedience on the basis of the British attitude to Khilafat. This common movement was a major advance of Indian nationalism which shook British imperialism to its roots.

The Khilafat Movement has been wrongfully condemned by the intellectual secularists as input to communalisation of the Muslim mind. History shows that those who were with the movement espoused secular nationalism, and those opposed it became prophets of communalist two-nation theory. Among the former were Khan Abdul Ghaffar Khan, Dr. Saifuddin, Kitchlew, Hakim Ajmal Khan, Dr. M.A. Ansari, Maulana Mazharul Haq, Maulana Abul Kalam Azad, the Ali Brothers and Hussain Ahmed Madni, while the opponents were led by M.A. Jinnah. It was Hussain Ahmad Madni, a disciple of Mehmood-ul-Hassan, who propounded the theory of composite nationalism and declared that "in our time nationalism is determined on the basis of territory, not religion".

I have dwelt on this at some length to clarify some prevalent misconceptions like (i) that secularism is a western concept imported by western educated elite; (ii) that the religious people are anti-secular, and (iii) that the Muslims cannot come to terms with secularism. These misconceptions are at the root of much of the trouble that Indian secularism faces and that are trotted out as justification by protagonists of Hundutva and Hindu *Rashtravad*.

Nehru Explains

The term "secular" does not convey the exact implications of the Indian phenomenon which has been described as secularism. It has been repeatedly clarified by Jawaharlal Nehru that it is quite different from the European concept of secularism. In a circular sent to the Pradesh Congress Committees, in his capacity as AICC President, he wrote:

> "We call our state a secular one. The word 'secular' perhaps is not a very happy one. And yet, for want of a better word we have used it. What exactly does it mean? It does not obviously mean a state where religion as such is discouraged. It means freedom of religion and conscience, including freedom for those who may have no religion. It means free play for all religions, subject only to their not interfering with each other or with the basic conceptions of our state. It means that the minority communities, from the religious point of view, should accept this position. It means, even more, that the majority community, from this point of view, should fully realise it. For, by virtue of numbers as well as in other ways it is the dominant community and it is its responsibility not to use its position in any way which might prejudice our secular ideal.
>
> "The word 'secular', however, conveys something much more to me, although that might not be its dictionary meaning. It conveys the idea of social and political equality. Thus, a caste-ridden society is not properly secular. I have no desire to interfere with any person's belief, but when those beliefs become petrified in caste divisions, undoubtedly they affect the social structures of the state. They prevent us from realising the idea of equality which we claim to place before ourselves. They interfere in political matters, just as communalism interferes. We have opposed communalism and continue to be stoutly opposed to it. It is, in fact, a negation of nationalism and of the national state. Communalism means the dominance of one religious community. If that community is in a minority, this is opposed to all ideas of democracy. But if that community is in a majority, even so its dominance over others as a religious community would be wholly undemocratic.
>
> "...Therefore, we have opposed communalism not only in minority communities, but also in the majority community. This argument applies to caste divisions and their functioning on the political plane...It exists and encourages fissiparous tendencies and maintains divisions in our society, which undoubtedly weaken and prevent the growth of a real democratic spirit. Many of us perhaps

do not attach enough importance to this. But I have no doubt that casteism is as dangerous as communalism, and both are effective barriers, if they are strong enough, to the development of true democracy and equality.

"We are not to take pride in our tradition of tolerance. It is always dangerous to have this complacent attitude about oneself because it hides the truth from us. Few people can see their own weaknesses and failings, although they are wide awake to the failings of others."

This statement of Nehru can be taken as the most comprehensive enunciation of the concept and approach which can be called India's ideology of secular nationalism.

It is not altogether a coincidence that Jawaharlal Nehru is the target of all those who would like to reverse the secular approach to nationalism and give it a communal complexion. He needs no advocacy or defence, and I do not presume to hold brief on his behalf. But I do commend his exposition of Indian secularism as the most appropriate technology for nation-building. He was an agnostic but he did not seek to impose his views on others, thus setting an example for peaceful coexistence and mutual cooperation in promoting the welfare of the Indian segment of humanity so that it may be able to contribute to the well-being of the entire humanity.

If we carefully understand his view and adopt it in practice, we will be able to steer clear of many confusions caused by the hair-splitting disputations about the relationships between religion and state, between religion and individual and between religion and social reform. The pastime of armchair inellectuals is no contribution either to the promotion of scientific temper or to national integration which is, and should be, the aim of any policy or approach. From him we can learn the proper approach to history and tradition; that they have to be treated as light for finding the path ahead and not as shackles to thought and action.

To talk of Indian secularism and not take account of Gandhi is like staging Hamlet without the Prince of Denmark. Indeed, his is a major contribution to moulding the mind of Jawaharlal Nehru.

Contribution of Gandhi

Gandhi, as is widely acknowledged, brought about qualitative transformation of the national freedom movement by bringing it out of middle-class drawing rooms and pushing it closer to the common people, to the workers and peasants. He gave philosophical depth to this political concept. Instead of negatively separating religion from politics, he provided to both a spiritual content which linked the two in terms of universalisation of sympathy. Describing the India of his dreams, he wrote: "I shall work for an India in which the poorest shall feel that it is their country, in whose making they have an effective voice, an India in which there shall be no high class or low class of people, an India in which all communities shall live in perfect harmony."

In his presidential address at the Belgaum session of the Indian National Congress, he said: "A Swaraj Government means a government established by the joint free will of Hindus, Mussalmans and others. Hindus and Mussalmans, if they desire Swaraj, have perforce to settle their differences amicably."

Deeply religious though he was, Gandhi did not conceive of religion as a sectarian belief but as a universal and unifying force. He told the Federation of International Fellowship in January 1928: "After long study and experience I have come to these conclusions that: (1) all religions are true, (2) all religions have some errors in them, (3) all religions are almost as dear to me as my own Hinduism". Of Indian culture, he wrote that it "is neither Hindu, Islamic nor any other wholly. It is a fusion of all."

We, the People of India

What we call the mainstream Indian nationalism or secularism is thus, not non-religious or antagonistic to religion. Only it refuses to exercise discrimination in secular affairs, in matters concerning state or its governance, on the basis of religious faith. The most important feature of this approach is that affairs of state are run and guided not according to the dictates of any religious priest, precept or scripture but in accordance with a constitution which has been adopted in the name of "We, the People of India".

"We, in the Constitution, does not denote distinction from "they" in terms of religious communities, Hindus and non-Hindus, as in some communalist theoretical writings (like Golwalkar's *We or our Nationhood Defined).* Here it means all the people of India. The Indian state derives its legitimacy from the people and not from any extra-social or supernatural authority or power. Sovereignty in this state is posted not in a God or Gods, not in any person or group claiming to be superior on any account whatsoever to the rest of society, but in the entire adult population living in the territory called India. It should be noted that India is the first country in the world where national independence has been translated into democracy based on adult franchise almost immediately after foreign rule ended.

In an adult franchise democracy like India, the danger of a religious majority riding roughshod over the minorities cannot be ruled out although that would, as pointed out by Jawaharlal Nehru, mean replacement of democarcy by fascism. That is why Jawaharlal Nehru pointed out that what is called the communal problem "was one of adjusting the claims of the minorities and giving them significient protection from majority action." Keeping this in view, specific provisions have been made in the Constitution to protect the religious, linguistic and cultural rights of the minorities.

The broad strategy for making secular values prevail in free India has been outlined in the Constitution. Article 25 and 26 of the Constituion guarantee individual and collective freedom of faith, while Article 30 grants to religious and linguistic minorities "the right to establish and administer educational institutions of their choice." Articles 16, 17 and 29 ensure equality of opportunity in matters of employment and provide protection against discrimination. Separate communal electorates have been abolished vide Article 325. The principle of the separation of state and religion is manifested in Article 27 and 28; the former provides against any taxes for promotion of religion, while the latter forbids religious instruction in educational institutions run by the state.

Those who assert that *Hindutva* constitutes Indian nationalism, that the culture and ethos of India are only Hindu or Muslim or Christian or that the inequities and discriminations, real or imaginary, practised in the past, have to be avenged by repetition of the same in reverse, that socio-cultural conformity to the practice of the majority is the test for a person's or community's patriotism are working contrary to these principles of the national movement enshrined in the Constitution. Defence of secularism should mean uncompromising, unwavering and continuous struggle against these forces.

Virus of Communal Violence

The most potent and manifest challenge to Indian secularism is posed by communal violence. When blood flows in streets, smoke rises from burning hamlets, the shrieks of suffereing women and children shake the high heavens, tenets of civilisation get the go by, society gets divided into communities and nation is torn asunder. Communal violence or communal riots as they are called, are the most effective instrument in the hands of those who seek to turn politics from secular to communal issues. Justice Madon, who enquired into Maharashtra incidents of 1970, aptly remarked: "Communal tension does not spring up overnight. It is built up over a period of time, suckled on communal propaganda, nursed on communal incidents and fed on rumours, until men's hearts are filled with hatred and their thoughts turn to violence."

The methodology and propaganda for organising riots have been analysed by justice Vythayathil (who analysed the incidents of Tellicherry) as follows:

> (a) Rousing communal feeling in the majority community by the propaganda that the Muslims are disloyal to the nation; (b) Deeping the fear in majority and playing upon that fear complex; (c) Infiltrating into administration and inducing the members of the civil, police and army serivces into adopting communal attitudes; (d) Training young people of the majority community in the use of such weapons as daggers, swords and spears; (e) Spreading rumours to widen the communal cleavage and giving to any incident or movement a communal colour."

Justice Madon has listed 27 common themes used in communal propaganda, e.g.

> 1. The decrying of the religion, customs and traditions of the other community; 2. The charge that Muslims, with a few exceptions,

are anti-national and harbour extra-territorial loyalty to Pakistan; 3. The appeasement of the Muslims by the Congress government with a view to secure their votes by upholding their so-called unreasonable demands in detraction of the rights of the Hindus; 4. The atrocities committed by the Muslims at the time of partition of India; 5. The atrocities committed by Pakistan against Hindus residing in that country; 6. The destruction and desecration of Hindu temples and idols of Hindu Gods by Muslim rulers in the past; 7. The forcible conversion of Hindus to Islam by Muslim rulers; 8. The claim that had Shivaji not lived, all Hindus in India would have been forcibly converted to Islam; 9. An exhortation to the Muslims that as they were all converted to Islam from Hinduism, they should return to the Hindu fold; 10. The charge that the Muslims alone are responsible for all communal disturbances which have taken place in the country; 11. The charge that a Muslim has publicly slaughtered a cow; 12. The charge that a Muslim has desecrated or offered insult to a Hindu temple or the idol of a Hindu God; 13. The charge that a Muslim has kidnapped or raped a Hindu girl or outraged her modesty; 14. Advocating the sending away of all Muslims to Pakistan; 15. A claim that India is the land of the Hindus only; 16. Advocating the Indianisation of Muslims, by which is really intended the Hinduisation of Muslims; 17. An exhortation to the Hindus to unite and stand up to and fight the Muslim menace; 18. The charge that some Muslim or Muslims have shouted pro-Pakistani slogans; 19. Applauding and praising for their valour and courage the Hindus of a town or city where communal disturbances had broken out and in which the Muslims had suffered more; 20. The charge that the Hindu majority is out to crush the Muslim minority and to wipe out its religion, language and culture; 21. The charge that the Muslims being in minority can get no justice or fair play in India; 22. The charge that since the Hindus are in a majority, all governments in India are Hindu governments, and will not protect the Muslim minority against the oppression of the Hindus; 23. The charge that the Muslims being in a minority, are discriminated against in service, employment and other matters; 24. The charge that the grievances and complaints of the Muslims are not heeded by the administration or the police of which the majority consists of Hindus; 25. The charge that the Muslims are being persecuted in India; 26. The charge that a Muslim cannot get any redress in India; and 27. An exhortation to the Muslims

> that as the government and the police will not protect them, they should unite and fight the Hindus in self-defence and that the best form of defence is attack.

If we even cursorily examine the attitudes and statements of political parties and persons during the last two decades which have witnessed the rise of communalism or revivalism, we would note that the first 19 of these constitute the sum and substance of the Hindu variety of communalism while the subsequent eight items are the hallmark of their counterparts in the Muslim community.

Mischief by Communalists

Protection of secularism and preservation of communal harmony, like liberty, need eternal vigilance. A review of the situation before and after the various waves of communal violence in the 60's, the 70's and the 80's would show that the communalists have succeeded in their mischief only when the protagonists of secularism have relaxed either because of the smug complacence that there is no threat of communalism or because they have indulged in mutual recrimination allowing the communalists to use it as an alibi or cover.

After the death of Jawaharlal Nehru, in the wake of the Indo-Pak war, the secular formations flew at one anothers' throat on secular issues like planning, devaluation and food imports and subsidised public distribution system. Into this conflict the communalists threw in the question of what they called the suspicious role of the Muslims and the emotive issue of ban on cow-slaughter.

The communalists of the majority community got indirect support from the news of anti-Hindu atrocities in the then East Pakistan. And there were communal riots in Calcutta, Rourkela, Chaibasa, Ranchi, Patratu, Allahabad, Meerut, Ahmedabad, Bhiwandi, Jalgaon and Tellicherry. That was the first major sweep of communal violence after partition. The minority community added fuel to the fire by moves to set up their separate political organisations giving loud calls for organised self defence.

The political result of the phenomenon was that the advocates of Indianisation found entry into the corridors of power in most of the north

Indian states. That marks the watershed in the attitude of police and bureaucracy. Recruited mostly from among the majority community and, in many cases nurtured on the ideological diet of the communal approach to history, culture and administration (still fostered in educational institutions), their dormant communalism surfaced when they saw the possibility that communalists could become the rulers. As long as this prospect was not on the horizon and leaders like Nehru consistently carried on anti-communal tirade with the crusading zeal, the Government personnel either concealed their communal proclivities or tried to cast themselves in secular mould.

What we have witnessed since 1965 is a new political culture in which dethronement of Congress from power became the main agenda of all non-Congress parties. We need not go into the motivations for this new stance or the circumstances which provoked this anti-Congressism, but the consequence was a measure of respectability to the formations which were opposed to the secular view of nationalism.

Far be it from me to accuse Dr. Lohia, the father of this new strategy, of communalism. Nor can other Left parties or leaders, by any stretch of imagination, be called communal. But they somehow arrived at the conclusion that the Congress (which had been the platform of secular nationalism and the party responsible for ushering the Constitution embodying the concept and values of Indian secularism) had deviated from its basic faith, that its political practice had been responsible for the growth of communalism and decline of secularism.

No doubt, the Congress has to bear major responsibility for weaknesses and distortions in the national polity, it being the vanguard of the nationalist movement. But its acts of omission and commission would not justify alliance, adjustment or compromise with those who are opposed to the very basis of Indian national life. Special efforts to protect the socio-economic and cultural rights of the minorities, Scheduled Castes and Scheduled Tribes which the Congress Governments made could not, and should not, be put at par with the stance of the RSS, the Jana Sangh and the BJP which challenge the very right of these sections to have distinct cultural identities or to special measure for overcoming the disadvantages they suffered for historical reasons.

This political distortion emanated from the purely political perception that the Congress was able to repeatedly win elections and stay in power because it was supported by the vote bank comprising the minorities, STs and SCs. The appeal of Congress to these sections was not seen in terms of the historical relationship that had developed between them on account of the efforts the Congress and Congressmen had put in to secure for these sections their rightful place in national life, but as a result of the so-called appeasement of minorities and the weaker sections. This precisely had been the stand of those who stood for Hindu *Rashtravad*, it was also the implication of the advocates of separate Muslim or Sikh nationalism who viewed Congress policies only as price to win over non-Hindus and not as an expression of commitment to the ideal of secular nationalism.

The communalists jumped on to the anti-Congress bandwagon. It provided them an alibi that they were not any more communal than the Congress, and that the responsibility for communal violence was to be laid primarily at the door of the ruling party. In these circumstances the Muslims became vulnerable to the enticement of the leaders who advocated formation of a separate political bloc to bargain with other political parties which became a provocation for the unwary in the majority community to veer round to the point of view of those who had been attempting to convert Hindus from a community of eclectic philosophical tradition into a political group.

The final outcome of this process is that

1. Secular profession of all parties have come to be suspected in the eyes of common people;
2. The RSS and organisations spawned by it have, for the first time in history, come from fringes to the centre-stage and boldly advocate Hindutva or Hindu *Rashtravad* threatening minorities that they can claim right of citizenship only if they conform to the culture and ethos of what they call the "national culture and ethos" and that they should be prepared to atone for whatever sins or atrocities their forefathers are perceived by the RSS to have committed against the Hindus;
3. The sense of insecurity among minorities and the weaker sections had reached a point where they feel they cannot trust the compatriots belonging to castes and religious communities other than their own;

4. The political parties seeking to dislodge Congress from power have developed a strong propensity for developing sectarian constituencies.

The above analysis brings us to the conclusion that what we call "Indian secularism" was an approach to nationalism which did not reject the validity of religion but ensured freedom to believe or not to believe, and to preserve and proliferate the culture of one's preference with the only proviso that the freedom of one individual or community did not transgress similar rights of other individuals and communities. Basically cooperative and non-competitive, positive and not negative, promoter of all-round welfare and non-predatory, it was opposed to such tendencies as imperialism, communalism and casteism which share the basic characteristic that they thrive on the exploitation of others.

References

1. *History of Freedom Movement,* India, Vol. 1, p. 110.
2. *Medieval India Quarterly,* Vol III, Nos, 1st 2, p. 5.
3. Syed Mohammed Mian's *Tehrik-e-Sheikhul Hind,* pp. 52-56.

ECONOMICS OR COMMUNALISM IN INDIA

GIRISH MISHRA

India is said to have a regular visitation of epidemics of deadly nature only after 1700 when it came into contact with European capitalism (first merchant capitalism and then industrial capitalism).[1] Similarly, the virus of present day communalism was introduced in the country after the British rule became a reality. It, however, does not mean that there were no frictions and conflicts among various religious groups or communities earlier. In fact, old Sanskrit texts are replete with attacks on and ridicule of the Buddhists. Similarly, there is no dearth of evidence of attacks on Brahminism by the Buddhists. We also know how Sasanka, the king of Bengal, tried to uproot the Bodhi tree at Bodh Gaya and persecuted the Buddhists.

Even during the medieval times, there were violent clashes and conflicts between the members of the two important communities. Had they not been there, Kabir would not have been prompted to condemn religious fanaticism. These were, however, temporary and strictly localised conflicts with not much impact on the society at large. These conflicts had much to do with religious attitudes and beliefs rather than having any serious economic dimensions or implications for production and exchange of goods. Both Hindus and Muslims remained integral parts of one socio-economic system. Inter-community fraternisation and mixing up went on uninterrupted and Bhakti poets and Sufi saints did much to cement the bonds between the two. Notwithstanding recent attempts at communalising historiography, the fact remains that the clashes between Rana Pratap and Akbar or Shivaji and Aurangzeb were, in essence, politico-economic, which could be between any chieftain or local ruler wanting to have greater freedom and revenue resources and the central or imperial power, resisting the move. Indian history is replete with clashes among the members of the same ruling family or clan for power and property. Was not the great battle of *Mahabharata* fought on this basis? Did not one of the wives of Asoka try to blind one of her stepsons to keep him out of the way of her own son ? Did not Muslim chieftains or local rulers rise in revolt against the imperial power of the Mughals?

Coming to *jaziya* it was a tax on wealth and income, imposed by a government in a situation where the economy was not so diversified as it is today and the options available for raising revenues were extremely limited. With increasing military and administrative expenditures, the Mughal government had to bring in this kind of taxation. If the incidence of this tax fell more on the Hindus, it was in keeping with medieval attitudes and values, and this must not be brought to have a bearing on Hindu-Muslim relations towards the end of the 20th century. Similarly, it will be utterly ridiculous to read much in the ancient and medieval practice which lingered on till recently to charge nominal or no rent at all from Brahmins to whom land was allotted. In the course of my research work, I have found that "on an average the upper caste people paid 50 per cent less than others for the same type of lands.[2] The system of *lakhiraj* and *brit* holdings was widely prevalent during the medieval times and even earlier, under which Brahmins and other upper caste people were granted rent-free lands or tenures. If these facts are given casteist colour in the present context of Mandalisation and interpreted accordingly, nothing but disastrous consequences will ensue. The point which needs to be emphasised here is that incidents and practices must not be presented after being torn out of their contexts to buttress one's communal or casteist designs.

Enter British Rule

Now, we come to our contention that communalism which we confront at present is a phenomenon coming into existence from the last quarter of the 18th century onwards.

After the establishment of the British rule in Bengal, following the Battle of Plassey, far-reaching changes started taking place in political and economic spheres. Politically, the court of the Nawab of Murshidabad entered a phase of rapid decline and similar became the fate of the Mughal imperial court at Delhi. Gradually, they were deprived of the sources of revenue and they became unable to sustain their old levels of expenditures. Consequently, a large number of people attached to these courts were rendered unemployed and deprived of their privileges and sources of livelihood. Among them there were substantial proportion of Muslims who had been serving the rulers in various capacities. Their plight became miserable. They were unable to adjust to new political realities like the *Kayasths* in Bihar, U.P. and elsewhere who acquired the knowledge of English and went in for modern education.

Economically, the setback to the Muslim community was more serious than it was to the Hindus. The Muslims were, traditionally, mostly artisans, though they had large landowners and tenure-holders among them.

Till the beginning of the 19th century, India was famous for its handicrafts all over the world. They consisted of textiles, metal wares, artistic pottery, arms, carpets, woodwork and so on. They provided employment opportunities and sources of income to a large number of Muslims and helped develop their artistic skills. They reached such a high mark of excellence that they earned the praise and admiration of the people abroad and foreign visitors to India, besides native aristocracy. These handicrafts catered largely to the needs of export, aristocrats and other urban dwellers and the army.

In the rural areas, Muslims worked as weavers, cotton-carders and quilt-makers, oil-pressers, barbers and washermen, besides being dyers. The products of the rural cottage industries catered mainly to the needs of the local population and were not very artistic or of high quality. They were based on locally available raw materials and skills. The artisans engaged in them were indispensable for the rural economy. There was a unity between agriculture and village industries. While agriculture supplied food and raw materials to the artisans, the latter supplied and repaired implements, ornaments, pottery, cloths, shoes, furniture, etc.

Fine cotton textiles and woollen goods were largely the products of Muslim craftsmen, be they in Dacca or in Kashmir and Punjab. Banarasi *sarees* always demonstrated the excellence of the workmanship of Muslim weavers. Varanasi, Mirzapur, Moradabad, Nasik, Pune, Hyderabad, Sialkot, Lahore and so on were famous for metal wares of various kinds, and most of the workers engaged in their production were Muslim.

All these handicrafts entered an era of decline in the second half of the 18th century. The collapse of the Mughal rule and weakening of social prestige and economic power of the regional rulers meant the cessation of the demand for artistic goods and other urban handicrafts. Handicraftsmen lost their patrons who used to give them material help and encouragement. The remnants of old aristocratic stratum of the society lingered on for quite some time, but they tried to ape the living styles of the Europeans.

The disappearance of the ruling families and their courtiers, alongwith a radical change in the nature of arms and ammunitions and the technology of warfare, rendered blacksmiths and those who manufactured equipment for horses, elephants and camels to be used in battles unemployed. After 1858, when a measure of law and order was restored in the country, it became unnecessary for individuals to possess arms for their own protection while at home or on journey. In addition, the British government banned the possession and carrying of certain types of arms by private persons.

Industrial Revolution and After

The Industrial Revolution in England and the development of roads and railways flooded the rural areas of India with cheap goods, especially textiles, turned out by British factories. Consequently, rural weavers had to give up their age-old occupations. While impoverished Hindu craftsmen and artisans became dependant on agriculture as sharecroppers and/or labourers, the Muslim craftsmen engaged themselves in low-paid menial jobs in urban areas, and rural artisans became agricultural labourers. Between them, Muslims, particularly urban-dwellers, faced greater misery because they could not migrate to the rural areas and engage themselves in agriculture.

The frustration and anger of the Muslim community found expression in several rebellions and movements against the British during the second half of the 18th century in Bengal and Bihar. The most important among them was the Wahabi Movement, with its headquarters at Patna. It continued to cause headache to the British for 40 years from 1828 to 1868. Lord Mayo's assassination in the Andamans by a Wahabi convict heightened the mistrust of the British. The unity displayed by both the communities in the 1857 uprising further perturbed the British rulers and they adopted a carefully devised policy of playing one against the other.

It may be mentioned here that while the Hindus tried to come to terms with the new realities that had arisen as a result of the British rule, the

Muslims did not do so. While the former were attracted towards English education and modern Western ideas and values as a result of reform movements like the Brahmo Samaj, the Muslims failed to do so; nay, they turned towards revivalist movements. In spite of being "indefatigable as missionaries, careless of themselves, blameless in their lives, supremely devoted to the overthrow of the English infidels, adroitly skilful in organizing a permanent system of supplying money and recruits," the Wahabi leaders tried "to stir up thousands of their countrymen to purer life and truer conception of the Almighty[3]. In fact, they wanted to revive some kind of fundamentalism among the Muslims. They did not do anything to help the Muslims take up the challenge, thrown by the British rule.

Sir Syed Ahmed Khan tried to propagate the benefits of English education among the Muslims, but he was not able to transcend the limits of Islamic scriptures. Sir Syed confined his attention mainly to the upper strata of the Muslim society. "His interpretation of Islam emphasized the validity of free enquiry (*ijtihad*) and the alleged similarities between Koranic revelation and the laws of nature discovered by modern science. Yet the theology classes in Aligarh were directed by orthodox *mullahs* and the modernistic elements in the Aligarh movement came to be considerably toned down over time, particularly under Muhsin al-Mulk."[4]

The Aligarh Movement was blessed by the British and received a handsome financial grant by the Viceroy, Lord Northbrooke. According to Sumit Sarkar, "As Francis Robinson has pointed out, it was through British support, above all, that 'a man whose religious views were so unorthodox that the majority of his co-religionists branded him an infidel was raised up as the advocate of his community'."[5]

As has already been noted, Sir Syed's efforts were oriented towards the upper class Muslims who were mostly big landlords and tenure-holders and wanted to have their separate identity. To quote Sumit Sarkar again: "separatism developed initially not for reasons of 'backwardness', but because a traditional elite felt increasingly threatened by Hindu trader, moneylender and professional groups buying up land, capturing municipalities and obtaining jobs at its expense."[6]

It may be noted here that the support to the Aligarh Movement initially was not dictated by the need to counter the nationalist challenge posed by the Congress to British imperialism. In fact, it was to counter Muslim revivalism whose base consisted of small landholders, village mullahs, petty officials, shopkeepers and artisans whose religious passions could be easily played upon and mobilised in the name of any campaign to save Islam.

Deoband school, also founded in 1867, attracted the Muslims from the poorer strata who were unable to afford English education. They were trained as Urdu and Persian teachers and they generally stood for the unity of Hindus and Muslims in the fight against British rule. The influence of this school was confined only to a small minority among the Muslims.

For a long time, the Aligarh Movement opposed and resisted the move of the Indian National Congress to bring all the Indians on the single platform in support of its demands. To quote from the report of the Congress Enquiry Committee in the Kanpur Communal riots, headed by Dr. Bhagwan Das: "Sir Syed Ahmed abstained from commenting on the Congress for two years, but on the occasion of the third session, he openly declared himself against the Congress movement. A Mohammedan Educational Conference was held at Lucknow during the Christmas week in 1887. There, at a special meeting of delegates, Sir Syed spoke against the Muslims joining the Congress. In August 1888, the socalled Patriotic Association was formed in opposition to the Congress."[7]

This kind of attitude came in for severe criticism by Maulana Mohammed Ali in his presidential address to the 1923 session of the Indian National Congress.[8] In fact, seeds of isolationism were sown and the Muslim community was made to think only of its interests and became indifferent to the sufferings of India and the Indians collectively.

Pattern of Education

A comparison of the pattern of education imparted at the Banaras Hindu University and at the Aligarh Muslim University reveals that while the former put strong emphasis on scientific and technical education, the latter did not do so. In the totality of things, teaching of Hindu theology at the BHU occupied a minor place, and most of the students did not go in for it. The influence of Hindu obscurantist elements was almost negligible and the BHU remained connected with India's freedom struggle. The situation at the AMU was different.[9]

The Report of the Congress Enquiry Committee into Kanpur riots carried a supplementary note by Dr. Bhagwan Das and Pandit Sundarlal, which demanded the appointment of a separate committee to look into the question whether the Muslims were poorer and less educated than the Hindus, "class for class and occupation for occupation". "If they are, whether the causes of this state of things are internal, such as, special laws of inheritance, ways of life, the growth of weaknesses corresponding to the Hindu degeneration, standing aloof from the new education for many decades, relaxation of enterprise because of the hope of preferential treatment by the foreign capital."[10]

Unfortunately, such an enquiry was not undertaken. Had it been done, it would have revealed a great deal.

While the lower classes among the Muslims, by and large, had little access to Western education and ideas and remained confined to their menial jobs and artisan activities, the upper classes took to English education in order to secure government jobs, security, influence and honour. While the Hindu bourgeoisie had taken birth during the second half of the 19th century, the Muslim bourgeoisie had not emerged. Hindu merchants and money-lenders had started entering cotton textile industry and other industrial activities, but the Muslims were almost totally absent from such vocations. To quote Jawaharlal Nehru, "The Muslims were still wrapped up in a feudal, anti-democratic ideology, while rising middle class among the Hindus had begun to think in terms of the European liberals. Both were thoroughly moderate and dependent on British rule. Sir Syed's moderation was the moderation of the landlord class to which the handful of well-to-do Muslims belonged. The Hindu's moderation was that of the cautions professional or businessman seeking an outlet for industry and investment. These Hindu politicians looked up to the shining lights of English liberalism—Gladstone, Bright, etc. I doubt if the Muslims did so. Probably they admired the Tories and the landed classes of England."[11]

Before we proceed further, it may be pointed out that the British government had adopted a policy of discrimination against the Muslims after the 1857 rebellion and the Wahabi Movement. The British, while trying to keep the two major communities disunited, thought the Muslims to be "more aggressive and militant, possessing memories of recent rule in India, and therefore more dangerous. The Muslims had also kept away from the new education and had few jobs under the Government. All this made them suspect. The Hindus had taken far more kindly to the English language and clerkly jobs, and seemed to be more decile."[12]

Gulf Widens

With the beginning of the 20th century, and especially after the World War I when tariff protection gave a big boost to industrialization, the gulf between the two communities widened. While the Hindus took advantage of the new situation and entered industrial activities like sugar, jute, paper, cement and so on, the Muslims, by and large, kept themselves aloof. Perhaps, they did not have inclination to undertake such activities. A host of explanations have been given. Some say, in North India, the preference of the Muslim elite was for government jobs and professions like law and medicine. Even the traders and artisans did not show any aptitude for industrial activities of modern types because they were hesitant in engaging themselves in risky ventures. The Muslim traders and moneylenders of Western India also failed in this regard. Some say, this was because of the lack of inter-community ties and support on an all-India basis which the Marwaris enjoyed. This argument cannot take us very far when one points out the case of the Parsis or the Gujarati Hindus. In fact, Muslim traders of Western India had business contacts not only inside the country but in many countries of Africa, which were part of the British empire.

Whatever may be the factors or reasons, the fact remains that the Muslims were relatively more backward economically and the incidence of poverty among them was greater as compared to the Hindus. In the words of Jawaharlal Nehru, "On the whole the Hindus were, in the Punjab, Sind, and Bengal, the richer, creditor, urban class; the Muslims in these provinces were the poorer, debtor, rural class. The conflict between the two was therefore often economic, but it was always given a communal colouring."[13]

Whenever bills came up for discussion in provincial assemblies or councils in order to get some reliefs to rural debtors or tenants, invariably, the Hindu Mahasabha always stood in opposition. It always championed the interests of Hindu landholding, money-lending and industrial and commercial interests. In effect, "on both sides, the communal leaders represent a small upper class reactionary group, and... these people exploit and take advantage of the religious passions of the masses for their own ends. On both sides every effort is made to suppress and avoid the consideration of economic issues."[14]

In the short stories of Prem Chand, one can find vivid descriptions of the machinations of reactionary elements from both the communities in order to foment riots and widen the gulf between them so that they could not unite to fight for their economic rights and demands. In fact, the communal organisations were tools in the hands of economic vested interests. The British government encouraged the mutual suspicions by its own policies and actions, such as the partition of Bengal (which was supposed to open greater avenues of economic opportunities for upper and middle class Muslims and strengthen their power of resistance against the rapacious behaviour of the Hindu Zamindars, tenure-holders and commercial interests in the new province) and separate electorate.

The government documents reveal that the British succeeded, in some measure, in moving the Muslim masses in Bengal against the *Swadeshi* campaign and fomenting communal riots which, in reality, were revolts against Hindu Zamindars and moneylenders by Muslim tenants, agricultural labourers and artisans. In the districts of East Bengal, during 1906-1907, "the targets were Hindu *zamindars* and *mahajans,* some of whom had recently started levying an '*Iswar briti*' for maintaining Hindu images. Debt-bonds were torn at many places, and at times riots took on the colour of a general 'plunder of the rich by the poor' with even Hindu cultivators joining in at place *Maulvis* are said to have spread rumours that the British were handing over charge to Nawab Salimulla of Dacca, who was painted in the rather unlikely colours of a messiah in the communal leaflet *Nawab Sahaber Subichar*. Such religious leaders often had connections with emerging rich peasant elements, made relatively prosperous by jute, and Muslim propaganda literature like the *Red Pamphlet* (1907) or the later *Krishakbandhu* (1910) visualised a kind of *kulak* or capitalist farmer development side by side with identifying the *zamindar-mahajan* exploiter with the Hindu."[15]

It may not be out of place to mention here that before the Muslim League came into existence in 1907 one of its mentors, the Aga Khan, had assured the private secretary to Lord Minto that he had instructed the organisers not to move in any matter without taking the prior approval of the government, of course, privately. Likewise, the Maharaja of

Darbhanga, a big pillar of the Hindu Mahasabha, had openly declared that "with the Hindus the loyalty to the British or *Rajbhakti* was an article of religious faith."

It is a matter of public knowledge that while the Muslim League had, among its financial backers, the Ispahanis and the talukedars of North India, the Hindu Mahasabha received ample material help from the Birlas, the Dalmias the Narangs and a host of other emerging Hindu capitalists, and landlords. The latter wanted a Hindu India where they could be in a dominant position politically in order to prosper economically without hindrance. The British impressed upon the minds of the Muslim industrial, commercial and landed interests that they would not be safe if the Raj came to an end and India remained undivided.

The growing prosperity of Hindu traders and industrialists in urban areas created a sense of deprivation and discontent among the poorer Muslim inhabitants of neighbouring *bustis*. Sometimes, this resulted in plundering the houses of the rich Hindus when riots broke out. To cite an instance, when communal riots broke out in September 1918, houses and properties of the Marwari businessmen were looted in the Burra Bazar area of Calcutta. The pull of the demonstration effect could be seen almost everywhere when civil disturbances broke out and the deprived sections attacked and looted the property of the rich in the neighbourhood. This happened in the localities where the Muslims were well-to-do and were surrounded by the deprived sections of the Hindus. In fact, the rioters masqueraded as defenders of their faith!

During the pre-Independence days, trade unions and peasant movements failed to fight out communalism. While for the realisation of their common economic demands and the redressal of their common grievances they came together on one platform, they thereafter dispersed. Very little was done to eradicate illiteracy and superstitions from their midst and impart a secular outlook. Except the Congress, no other secular political party had a clear-cut thinking on India's communal problem and none conducted any campaign against it. Among the leaders, Jawaharlal Nehru had the clearest perception and understanding of the problem of communalism and its roots. He alongwith his mentor Mahatma Gandhi campaigned against it throughout his life. The Leftists, especially the Communists, proved to be muddleheaded and they could not decide whether the Hindus and the Muslims were two religious communities or separate nationalities, and it was this that led them to support the Muslim League's demand for Pakistan.

After 1947 Partition

After the partition of the country, most of the Muslim artisans from North India and other parts of the country migrated to Pakistan. In certain cases, Muslim traders and small industrialists were forced to go because a feeling of insecurity arose in their minds after communal riots and the menacing attitude of the Hindu refugees from West Pakistan. The Hindi movie *Garam Hawa* has depicted it very vividly.

The Hindu industrialists, be they Marwaris, Sindhis, Gujaratis or Punjabis, became hostile towards the employment of the Muslims in their enterprises. One may look at the lists of employees, drawing Rs 1,44,000 or more a year, appended to Directors' Reports under section 217 (2A) of the Companies Act, 1956 of the companies owned by Hindu industrialists to find that Muslims among such employees are few and far between. Similarly, one may conduct the survey of business establishments of the Hindus in any town or city to find that the number of the Muslims employed is insignificant, and wherever they are employed, they do the work for which Hindu replacements of equal competence are difficult to find. They work as motor mechanics, drivers and so on.

An argument is advanced by Hindu industrialists that, since the Muslims do not go in for technical and management education in a significant number, they cannot be employed. Those who acquire technical and managerial skills get absorbed in the government sector. This argument can, however, be countered by saying that since there is not much demand for Muslim technical and managerial cadres in the private sector there is no point in acquiring such skills by Muslims.

After Independence, the fact remained that the entry of Muslims into the police and the armed forces became difficult, and their number declined too. This point has been underlined several times in various reports.

During the 1960s, when a commission of the government brought forth a list of 75 big business houses of the country, not a single one of them belonged to or was controlled by Muslims. Cipla, or Geep of the Shervanis were very small in size or from the point of view of turnover. Among the 14 commercial banks nationalised by Mrs. Indira Gandhi, not a single one was controlled by Muslims. Though no firm and reliable statistics are available, yet one can safely say that the share of the Muslim community in India's industrial and commercial capital has not been commensurate with the size of their population. Among big stock brokers, one seldom finds a Muslim.

After the beginning of the era of the planned economic development, a large number of new entrepreneurs have emerged in the country, but among them the proportion of Muslims has been much less. Moreover, the Muslims have gone into only small and medium scale industries. Even enterprising Muslims have been handicapped because of the lack of connections and support in the business and financial world. Over the years, a substantial number of Muslims have gone to the Arab countries and Iran and have earned money; but most of their savings have been invested in real estate and services sector. While a number of Hindu smugglers and black marketeers have laundered their earnings and entered industrial production, Muslim smugglers in Western and Southern India have not done so. As a result employment opportunities for the Muslims in the private industrial and commercial sector have remained extremely limited.

Since Independence, teaching of Urdu and Persian has suffered a great setback and, with Hindi or regional languages becoming the first official language, job opportunities for Urdu-knowing people in the courts and government officials have declined. In spite of making Urdu a second official language in some of the States, this decline has not been arrested.

With the entry of powerlooms and the adoption of the new textile policy, the weavers, most of whom are Muslims, have suffered great hardships. It is an open secret that a large number of powerlooms are owned *benami* by textile magnates. Some time ago, it was reported that a number of weavers who were on the verge of starvation had committed suicide.

Impact or Reservation

So long as the public sector was expanding and jobs were being created in it, people could secure employment opportunities irrespective of their religion, caste and region, but, now with economic liberalisation and privatisation, it is doubtful whether the Muslims will get adequate share in job opportunities.

The policy of reservation of jobs for Scheduled Castes, Scheduled Tribes and OBCs has made a deep impact on the Muslim consciousness. It is being propagated that a substantial portion of the national cake has been reserved for certain sections of the Hindus, and a blind eye has been turned towards the deprived sections of the Muslim community. In such a situation, if the poor Muslims start turning towards their communal organisations, it should not cause any surprise. In fact, as reports indicate, certain underworld dons have started providing succour to them. S.M.H. Burney was perfectly right when he asserted: "So long as people live in penury and want, they are prone to communal influence. It has often been seen that the people when they are economically backward, tend to lean on irrational habits and rituals to find some relief or an easy way out. Gullible by nature, they are easily swayed by catchy slogans and start seeking cathartic relief in communal frenzy. In a multi-religious society, where large sections of population including those belonging to religious minorities suffer from economic privations, the question of eliminating poverty with a view to promoting the health of society becomes a matter of crucial importance. What is important is to ensure that the minorities get a fair share of the economic cake."[16]

At present, around 70 per cent of the Muslims live in the rural areas and work as farmers, marginal, small and middle, agricultural labourers and artisans who are self-employed. The remaining 30 per cent live in urban areas, out of whom around 80 to 85 per cent are skilled workers—masons, tailors, vendors, small manufacturers—butchers and sellers of fish, and poultry products or are employed in *bidi*-making, perfumery, block-making, brassware and so on. With technological changes, the job-opportunities as calligraphers in the Urdu press, tailors, etc. have been fast declining. In the urban areas, Muslim population is concentrated in slums which abound in crimes, drug-peddling and various kinds of illegal activities. Basic minimum amenities are completely absent. This environment shapes the consciousness of the inhabitants. They feel alienated from the mainstream of the society and become an easy prey to fundamentalist propaganda. In other middle-class localities dominated by the Hindus, it is never very easy for any middle-class

Muslim to find a house on rent. The integration of the two communities is far from complete.

Since a large number of communal riots from 1960s onwards have occurred in industrial areas like Ranchi, Jamshedpur, Kanpur, Meerut, Ahmedabad, satellite towns of Bombay and elsewhere, enquiries have revealed that trade union organizations affiliated to secular and left parties have failed to intervene because they were either paralysed or passive. Most workers had become victims of communalist propaganda and this state revealed the weaknesses of the trade union organisations, built mainly on the basis of economism.

Trade rivalries, and conflicts in underworld economic activities, have also been an important factor in communal riots. The riots at Moradabad, Bhiwandi, Ahmedabad and Surat resulted, to a large extent, from this factor. The growing greed of traders, and small industrialists to grab the business of their counterparts from other community has led to communal killings and riotings.

Even though the toiling masses form the bulk of the Muslim population, and they have been facing great economic and social problems, the Muslim leadership which comes largely from the upper segments of the community has seldom raised or fought for their socio-economic demands or has done anything to come to terms with fast changing conditions of life in India and abroad. They still continue to go in largely for non-technical education. According to Prof. Satish Chandra, "The question of Urdu, minority character of Aligarh Muslim University, reservation of government jobs, preservation of Muslim personal law, etc., hardly touch the mass of the uneducated self-employed, propertyless Muslims. Is it because economic slogans would tend to bring all those, not merely Muslims, who are in a similar economic position together, thereby reducing the claims of a separate Muslim leadership, or is it that the very fact of educational backwardness makes the Muslims more prone to heed to slogan alleging danger to their religion and culture ?"[17]

There is a demand for reserving jobs in the government sector for backward sections of the Muslim community. The question is: will it solve their economic problem when the public sector is shrinking and job opportunities in government departments are fast declining and bulk of job opportunities are or going to be in the private sector where there is discrimination against them ? The only way out seems to be the growing acquisition of technical and managerial skills by the community and showing entrepreneurial zeal by entering new areas of industrial activities.

Scapegoat Propaganda

Over the years, communal organisations have launched a systematic propaganda to make the Muslim community a scapegoat, and responsible for a number of economic problems. Take, for example, the spectre of fast growing population of Muslims in India, impinging upon limited availability of living space, food, clothes and jobs. The intention is to pit the poor and deprived sections from the majority community against those from the minority community. Obviously, vested interests do not want the toiling masses of the two communities to combine for the realisation of their common economic demands.

It is asserted that the population of the Muslims is growing so fast that the day is not far off when they will outnumber the Hindus, and when this happens, India will automatically become an Islamic country! It is further alleged that this is a part of a big conspiracy which the secula-rist parties have been encouraging because they want to keep the Muslims as their 'vote bank.' The government of the country, whether led by the Congress or the Janata Dal, has allowed the Muslims to have their separate personal law which permits an ordinary member of the community to have four wives at any particular point of time. With a large number of wives, a Muslim is bound to produce more children. No Hindu is legally permitted to have more than one wife at any particular point of time.

In essence, this assertion boils down to the proposition that the number of children varies directly according to the number of wives a person is allowed to have. This interesting proposition needs to be tested theoretically as well as on the basis of facts.

Second, it is claimed that Islam forbids a Muslim to practise family planning while Hinduism does not do so. The result is that an ordinary Hindu gives heed to the campaign and the need to limit the number of his children, but a Muslim, on the contrary, cannot use contraceptives or other methods to limit the number of his children because his religion does not allow him to do so.

Third, it is said that a large number of Muslims have been surreptitiously entering India from Bangladesh and have been settling for ever. Thus, they add to the existing population of the Muslims.

In a nutshell, the claim is that the higher birth rate as well as the higher immigration rate account for faster growth of Muslim population in India.

Let us examine the validity of these assertions and claims, first on the basis of the tenets of demography.

The changes in the size of the population of any country over a period of time depend on two things; namely, the balance between the total number of births and that of deaths, and the net result of the number of immigrants and that of emigrants.

Let us first take up the births. Historical studies by well-known scholars have pointed out that there has been a negative association between the level of income and economic status on the one hand and the birth or fertility rate on the other. In other words, generally speaking, the well-off and socially highly placed people have lesser number of children than the poor and socially depressed people.

For the people placed in upper income and social groups, a child does not mean an addition to the earning capacity of the family, but expenditure on its rearing, education and making it suitable for some skilled job, which involves more brain-work than mere physical efforts. In these socio-economic groups, the chances of survival of a child is much greater, and the infant mortality rate much less, because of better and nourishing food for the mother during pregnancy, good housing facilities, access to medical aid and practice of hygiene. Hence, there is no uncertainty about the survival of the children. More the number of the children, more is the prèssure on the family budget and living standards.

Religion and Family Planning

In these families, the level of education is fairly high, and both the parents are generally engaged in some productive activities. If the number of their children is more, it means the mother has to give up her job, her freedom is also curtailed and her physical beauty and health are also affected. These families thus try to limit the number of their children consciously and practise family planning methods. Here, religion does not become a constraint.

Had it not been so, the Catholic dominated countries like France, Italy, Spain, Ireland, etc., could not have shown a decline in their birth rates and the rates of natural increase in population. The same is true for Poland where even the Communist rule of more than four decades could not reduce the influence of Catholicism and of the Roman Catholic Church.

It is well-known that the Pope has been opposed to abortion and the use of other means of family planning. The Greek Orthodox Church also follows the same policy and yet, the rates of natural increase in population in both Greece and Cyprus have been falling.

In France, the average annual growth in population has fallen from 1.1 per cent during 1960-70 to 0.5 per cent during 1970-82, and is estimated to come down to 0.4 per cent by the end of this century. In Poland, it has gone down from 1.0 per cent during 1960-70 to 0.9 per cent during 1970-82, and is likely to come down to 0.7 per cent by the end of the century. In Italy, where the Roman Catholic Church has its headquarters (Vatican), it has gone down from 0.7 per cent to 0.4 per cent, and by 2000 A.D., it will be just 0.1 per cent. The '*World Development Report 1984*', (published by the World Bank) carries a detailed discussion of population change and development for a large number of countries.

In the Islamic countries, where the average standard of living and per capita incomes are very high, the average annual rate of growth in population is much lower than India's. In Saudi Arabia, which is regarded as the most orthodox among the Muslim countries, the average annual growth rate of population is projected to decline from 4.8 per cent during the 1970s to. 3.7 per cent during the 1980s and the 1990s. The decline is much more dramatic in UAE: from 15.5 per cent to just 3.7 per cent. Obviously, the rate of growth of population in high-income oil exporting countries like Saudi Arabia, Oman, Libya, Kuwait and UAE began after the boom in oil revenues, which brought about greater prosperity for their citizens. It must also be remembered that in these countries, the death rates have dramatically gone down, rather than the fertility rates going up.

Turkey is a country where the majority of the population belongs to the Islamic faith, but the rate of growth of population there is not more than what it is in India. Indonesia is another Muslim-dominated country which has shown a declining average annual rate of growth of population over the year. This has been brought about by conscious policy of the government, encouraging the people to limit the number of their children by practising family planning methods. Islam has not come in its way.

Irrespective of religious affiliations, the richer and socially and educationally advanced people have fewer children and smaller families. Religious injunction or no religious injunction, they have been planning their families.

Even the number of wives one has or is allowed does not have any significant influence on the growth of population. The fertility rate of the people having more than one wife has not been found to be exceptionally high. The famous social scientist from Latin America, Joshua de Castro, in his well-known book, *The Geography of Hunger* (which was issued in its revised version as *The Geopolitics of Hunger* has sought to prove that greater the in-take of protein-rich food, the lower the fertility rate. In other words, the poor and hungry people have more children; men and women from the higher economic strata have many other diversions than only sex.

In India, the erstwhile ruling families and the elite who had more than one wife never had a high fertility rate. In Bihar, many zamindars died issueless though they had more than one wife at a time. The last Maharajas of Bettiah and Darbhanga died issueless eventhough each of them had two wives. The same was the case with the last Maharaja of Banaras. The Doctorine of Lapse was applied by the East India Company in the case of the native rulers to grab their states because they left no natural successors. It may not be out of place to note that many of these rulers, irrespective of their religious affiliation, had more than one wife.

Thus all this boils down to the fact that only the poor have more children. Even among them, the rural poor score over the urban poor. This is because the former does not have access to modern health and medical facilities. Obviously, poverty eradication is one of the most effective contraceptive!

Poverty and Children

To quote a World Bank study; "Consider the issue from the point of view of parents and potential parents. All parents everywhere get pleasure from children. But children involve economic costs; parents have to spend time and money bringing them up. Children are also a form of investment, providing short-term benefits if they work during childhood, and long-term benefits it they support parents in the latter's old age. There are several good reasons why for poor peasants the economic costs of children are low, the economic (and other) benefits of children are high, and having many children makes economic sense.

"First, where wages are low, the difference between children's and mother's earnings will be small; income lost by the mother during a child's infancy may be easily recouped by the child later on. In poor rural areas, especially, children can help a lot.[18] Boys and girls of six to eight years of age may work eight to ten hours in rural areas, tending animals and caring for their younger brothers and sisters. They do not have to go to schools. In urban areas many children may bring in some cash by doing odd jobs at eating houses or acting as self-appointed parking attendants or sellers of something or the other. Their families are always on the verge of starvation and the death rate among the children is very high. Moreover, there is neither any social insurance nor old-age pensions. Thus, the greater the number of children, the greater the chances of survival of the family. The incidence of unemployment is so high that a large number of children is an assurance that at least a few of them will always earn something for the family's survival.

Unlike the women from the higher socio-economic strata, the women from poor families combine their traditional work (farming, handicrafts and petty retailing) with rearing of children. Other members of the family, especially the older folks and children, are ready to extend a helping hand in caring the infants.

Lack of suitable schooling facilities for both boys and girls (and more so for the latter) in the neighbourhood and the inability of the parents to send them to places away from villages is another reason for more children in poor families. If the boys and girls were sent outside for schooling, expenditure on their board and lodging and fee will only increase.

According to the World Bank, "High infant and child mortality rate are a third reason for having many children. Although morality has fallen in many parts of the developing world, it is still high. One out of five children dies before reaching the age of one in some parts of Africa; one out of seven in much of Bangladesh, India, and Pakistan. Parents may feel the need to have many babies to be sure that a few will survive. Where boys are more important than girls—say, for security in old-age—parents may need to have five children to be sure that one son survives. Yet in poor families, frequent births, especially if they are close together, increase the probability of infant deaths by weakening both the mother and the babies.

"Fourth, poor parents are worried about who will take care of them when they are old or ill... For many adults, the need for support in their old age outweighs the immediate costs of children.

"One reason for parents to look to children for help in disability and old age is the lack of safe alternatives. In developed countries there are trusted institutions banks, pensions, government bonds, insurance, and mutual aid societies) that help individuals to earn today and save and spend tomorrow.

"In poor countries, capital markets are not nearly so well developed. In parts of South Asia, there is no tradition of community support; elsewhere, community support is weakening with increasing mobility. For the rural poor, children are the best possible annuity, a way to transform today's production into consumption many years hence, less risky than are bank accounts, credit instruments, and precious metals, all of which are subject to theft, inflation, and the jealousies of neighbours. Even land has to be managed to provide income and, in any case, may require children to work on it and make it a secure asset.[19]

It has been established by demographers and economic historians that the rate of growth of population is very closely related to the stage of economic development. The theory of Demographic Transition shows that during the pre-industrial era the rate of growth of population is very low or insignificant even though the birth rate is very high because the death rate is also high.

When a country makes a transition from pre-industrial to industrial stage, the rate of growth of population picks up because even though the birth rate does not undergo any change, the death rate declines fast because of changes in socio-economic spheres.

After the country becomes sufficiently industrialised, the birth rate also declines and the rate of growth of population becomes very low or insignificant.

Obviously, there is no causal relationship between the number of wives or religion, and the growth of population. There is only a spurious relationship which a *homo illiteratus* from a communalist outfit cannot discern.

The data relating to India shows it is not only the Muslims that go in for polygamy. Notwithstanding the law against it, the Hindus are not averse to having more than one wife at any particular point of time. The data from the office of the Registrar-General and Census Commissioner show that the percentage incidence of polygamous marriages is 5.80 among the Hindus and only 5.73 among the Muslims. The official publication from the census establishment. *Polygamous Marriage in India-A Survey*, makes it abundantly clear that the communalist propaganda that bigamy and polygamy are more common among the Muslims is nothing but a white lie. It says: "In India as a whole, the incidence of polygamous marriages is the highest among persons returning their religion as tribal religion (15.25 per cent), next come the Buddhists (7.97 per cent) followed by the Jains (6.72 per cent). " The incidence of polygamous marriages among the Muslim population is thus nothing unusual.

Another pertinent data for India is that polygamous marriages do not lead to any inusual increased fertility rate. The reality of the situation and the sex ratio is such that if a Muslim marries more than one woman, he deprives at least one of his co-religionist of the pleasure of marriage. According to the 1981 census, there are only 937 women per 1,000 men among Muslims. Had the number of women been more than that of men, the argument of Hindu communalists could have cut some ice, even if superficially.

M.E. Khan in his book *Is Islam Against Family Planning* has shown that Islamic scriptures do not forbid the practice of family planning. He has quoted from the Holy Quran to substantiate this claim. He has cited a number of facts to show that all temporary methods of family planning are allowed by Islam. Even abortions and sterilisations are permitted on health grounds.

Economic Factor

Quoting from a number of surveys, a write-up in *Economic Times* has concluded that "the percentage of couples using contraceptives in predominantly Muslim countries is very high—63 per cent in Turkey, 48 per cent in Indonesia and 38 per cent in Egypt. In India too the percentage of Muslims practising family planning is quite significant—23 per cent".[20]

The birth rate among the Muslims is slightly higher than among the Hindus, but this is because the Muslims are on the whole poorer than the Hindus. According to the write-up, "The data on fertility in relation to monthly per capita expenditure is... revealing. It clearly indicates that the decline in fertility is associated with increasing income... the marginally higher fertility observed among Muslims is a reflection of their relatively lower socio-economic standing".[21]

A survey by the National Sample Survey Organisation says: "Muslims in urban India are about 20 per cent below average in per capita monthly expenditure which makes them nearly as poor as the SC and ST communities. In contrast, the average per capita expenditure for other religious groups (Jains, Parsis, Christians, Sikhs, etc.) taken together is about 18 per cent above that for the general population in the urban sector as a whole".

Unless the socio-economic position of the Muslims improves, it is difficult to impress upon them—as is the case with similar downtrodden groups like SCs and STs—the need to bring down their fertility. It is not the question of their religious beliefs, it relates to their socio-economic conditions and perception about the future. Their terrorisation by Hindu communalists will create among them a greater sense of insecurity and prompt them to increase their numbers so that their security prospect improves. Another fact to be noted is that Muslims are a differentiated lot. The fertility rate is lower among the upper and middle class Muslims, but higher only among the lower strata.

What about the future? Will the Muslims swamp the Hindus and turn India into a Muslim dominated or Islamic country? The alarm is false and far from reality.

According to a study by P.S. Bhatia published in 1990, the population of the Hindus went up by 23.71 per cent during 1961-71 and by 24.42 per cent in the next decade. During the same periods, Muslim population increased by 30.85 per cent and 30.20 per cent, respectively. This means the decade rate of growth increased by 0.5 per cent for the Muslims, which was much less than that for the Hindus.[22]

Assuming the situation does not change in the future and the rate of growth remains what it is now, a hundred years from 1981, Hindus and Muslims will have the decade growth rate of 30.71 and 30.55 per cent, respectively. In other words, the Hindus will grow at a higher rate than the Muslims. The data given by Bhatia show that there has been a significant decline in the fertility among Muslims in both the rural and urban areas. The birth rate in the Malabar region of Kerala, where there is a substantial Muslim population, is much lower than that for U.P. or Bihar. It must not be lost sight of that Goa, which has a large Catholic population, has one of the lowest birth rates in the country. Obviously, religion is not a major determinant of the population growth in our country.

The noise about the Bangladeshi immigrants is also motivated by communalism. Even if one believes the figures put forward by Hindu communalists, it cannot make any difference to the predominance of the Hindus in the Indian population. Secondly, migrants from Bangladesh are generally unskilled and illiterate, hence they cannot pose a big problem for skilled and educated Indians entering the labour market. We should search for the reasons for our food, housing, unemployment and other problems in the kind of development we have since independence and the type of policies we have been pursuing. Hitler tried to put blame for every ill and every problem on the Jews; on the same pattern Hindu communalists have found a scapegoat in the Muslims.

Wherever and whenever communal riots have taken place, these have had consequences for both local and national economies for many months. A number of industrial activities where labourers have been traditionally Muslims have come to a standstill because a number of them perished or fled. Temporarily, curfew had prevented them from reporting for work. As production halted daily wage labourers and people like handcart pullers, loaders and so on lost their earnings. As bazars did not function, not only the shopkeepers but a large number of unskilled labourers suffered. The communal riot in Bombay, Ahmedabad, Baroda and elsewhere in December 1992-January 1993 did a great deal of damage to industrial production and export trade. It was reported: "Most of the small export-oriented readymade garment units in the Lower Parel areas of Central Bombay are lying idle. The *galas* (sheds) are mainly owned by Hindus but the skilled workers here—tailors, embroiders and weavers—are mostly Muslims who are too scared to come back to work in this Shiv Sena stronghold."[23]

The report went on to add: "The scene is no different on the other side of the divide. About 80 per cent of the 2,000 workers involved in the utensil polishing trade in the Madanpura area, a Muslim-dominated locality, are Maharashtrian women; their bosses are all Muslims. Since the riots broke out, only 350 women have been coming to work, that too for just half the day.

"Then there are those caught in the middle of the divide like the *kirana* traders in the Pydhonie area. Having done business in this sensitive area with Muslims for decades, they are now thinking of moving to New Bombay.

"Fear really is the key. Muslim gangs in Pydhonie have been demanding protection money up to Rs 2 lakh from the merchants. In Tardeo, at a place called L.B.M. compound, goondas from the majority community have warned the small Muslim businessmen, engaged mainly in auto repair work, to leave or face the consequences."[24]

Not only in Bombay, but also in Varanasi, the same thing was witnessed. The production and export of 'Banarsi Sarees' came to a standstill after the riots broke out and both Hindu traders and their Muslim weavers suffered while the country lost valuable export earnings. This led to the realisation by the Hindu traders, who had elected a BJP candidate, an activist of the Vishwa Hindu Parishad, that they would be ruined if the disturbances continued. They later came out with a strongly-worded statement against making the Gyanvapi mosque the next target.

The bomb blasts which damaged the Bombay Stock Exchange in March 1993 disoriented the capital market of the country and scared investors, both Indian and foreign. The hopes of the government which has put reliance on the inflow of foreign investments were dashed for some time. Transport and communications were disoriented and both the movements of goods and men were badly affected. Prices of most commodities rose in the markets because supplies could not be reached.

The deaths of young men and women and artisans and other skilled persons in communal disturbances mean loss of valuable human capital. Similarly, the burning of factories and destruction of looms and small workshops mean the loss of physical capital.

Communal disturbances help the real estate dealers who get valuable areas cleared since the slum areas are the main targets and their inhabitants flee their huts. Likewise, profiteers earn a lot due to scarcity of goods and services created by the disturbances and curfew. Anti-social elements plunder properties and belongings of those who flee their houses.

It needs a deep study why communal tensions and disturbances mostly affected towns and cities, and relatively advanced regions like Maharashtra, Gujarat and Western U.P. On the surface it invalidates the thesis that as an area becomes industrialised, the differences of caste and community get reduced in importance and the people adopt modern values and secular outlook. It has also been claimed that the modern industrial working class, particularly under the influence of Communists, is above communalism. But the experiences of riots in industrial towns and cities point to the contrary. Why?

References

1. Kingsley Davis, *The Population of India and Pakistan*, Princeton, 1951, p. 42.
2. Girish Mishra, *Agrarian Problems of Permanent Settlement: A case study of Champaran*, New Delhi, 1978, p.133 and pp. 169-170.
3. W.W. Hunter's remarks quoted in R.R. Diwaker (ed), *Bihar Through the Ages*, Calcutta, 1959, p. 649.
4. Sumit Sarkar, *Modern India: 1885-1947*, Delhi, 1983, pp. 76-77.
5. Ibid., p. 77.
6. Ibid.
7. N. Gerald Barrier (ed.) *Roots of Communal Politics*, New Delhi, 1976, p. 189 and also see pp. 190-192.

8. Sankar Ghose (ed.), *Congress Presidential Speeches*, New Delhi, 1972, pp. 149-154.
9. One of the objects of the college founded by Sir Syed at Aligarh was "to make the Musalmans of India worthy and useful subjects of the British Crown" and it was proclaimed that "the British rule in India is the most wonderful phenomenon the world has ever seen".
10. N. Gerald Barrier, *op. cit., p. 445*.
11. *Jawaharlal Nehru, An Autobiography*, Bombay, 1962, p. 462.
12. *Ibid.*, p. 460.
13. *Ibid.*, pp. 466-67.
14. *Ibid.*, pp. 467-68.
15. Sumit Sarkar, *op. cit.*, p. 122.
16. S.M.H. Burney's "Courage and Convictions" in Radhey Mohan (ed.), *Secularism in India*, New Delhi, 1990, pp. xxiii-xxiv.
17. Satish Chandra's paper "A Protracted Struggle" in *Ibid.*, p. 39.
18. The World Bank, *World Development Report 1984*, New York, 1984, p. 51.
19. *Ibid.*, p. 52.
20. *Economic Times*, 25 January, 1993.
21. *Ibid.*
22. P.S. Bhatia, "Population Growth of Various Communities in India—Myth and Reality" in *Demography India*, Vol. 19, No.1, 1990.
23. *Times of India*, 23 January, 1993.
24. *Ibid.*

GENESIS OF HINDU REVIVALISM IN INDIA

V.D. CHOPRA

Observers of the recent political developments in India, including the 1993 election in the Hindi-speaking belt, can well understand that the Indian nation-state is at a turning point. Can India remain a broad liberal democratic country based on secularism or will it adopt the elements of a theocratic state? This is the question being asked both in India and abroad. There cannot be an easy answer to this question in simplistic terms because in a developing country like India with its ancient civilisation, it is difficult to draw a clear line of demarcation between the two concepts of nation-state—theocratic and secular. In the last decades of the present century, even theocratic nation-states are facing new contradictions and conflicts.

For instance, it is not yet clear whether the Muslim masses in these countries are experiencing a new awakening of moral consciousness within the framework of Islamic morality. In the recent elections in Pakistan, fundamentalist forces did receive a setback, reflecting that secularisation of the consciousness has begun there. But, it will be wrong to ignore the hold of religious revivalism on the Pakistani masses. Election results only partially reflect such changes in the consciousness of the people. As such, no hasty conclusions should be drawn from the election results in the Hindi-speaking belt of India.

In an ancient country like India, religious-belief system is multidimensional, and has exhibited a remarkable capacity to captivate the minds of the people for centuries. It has a distinctive character, which not only influences ethical value-system of the Hindus but has a direct bearing on their political behaviour pattern too.

The phrase, "resurgence of Hindu revivalism", implies the existence of an antecedent state of torpor or decay from which Hinduism is supposedly arising to new life. Therefore, it is pertinent to ask what that antecedent state was, and how it has been changing ? Unlike other great religions of the world—Christianity, Islam and Buddhism—the Hindu religion has no single founder, no single basic book. It has no Christ. Mohammad, or Buddha; no Bible, no Quoran and no Buddhist canon. In a manner of speaking, it has no prophet as such. But has *rishis, munis, avtars* and recognised historical figures like Shankaracharyas, as also other saints, as its religious authorities. With all the revealed nature of the most ancient *Vedas*, the *smritis* the *Geeta*, the *Mahabharata* and the *Puranas* are no less authoritative scriptures of Hinduism than the *Vedas*. In fact, it will not be incorrect to say that *Vedic* Hinduism was very different from that of the *Brahamanas* and the *Upanishads*, and the latter again from that of the '*smiritis*' the *Geeta*, the *Puranas* and the *Mahabharata*. The difference, indeed, is so great that a *Rig Vedic rishi*, if he were to be reborn today, would not be able to recognise today's Hinduism as his religion! There is no *Atma*, no *Brahma*, no *Moksha*, no idol worship in the *Rig Veda*.

This aspect of Hindu religion is being re-called to explain that Hinduism has its own peculiarities and has been undergoing change and transformation from time to time.

Some philosophers claim that Hinduism as a religious philosophy does not reflect the aspirations of the most downtrodden sections of the population, which, according to them, stands in complete contrast to other religions. However, it is a historical fact that the origin of Christianity was in the misery of the slaves in Rome. The roots of Buddhism lay in Buddha's compassion for the downtrodden castes. Islam arose as a movement for uniting the warring tribes by assuring equality to all who recognised only one Allah, and Mohammed as his only prophet.

Whatever may be the element of truth in this comparison, one thing is certain: that no other religion in the world has succeeded in synthesising a profound faith in the oneness of God with the actual worship of a myriad of deities, as Hinduism has. It will also not be incorrect to say that the entire superstructure of Hindu religion has not experienced any significant qualitative reforms like, for instance, Protestantism in European Christianity. The social structure of India would have been very different if the envelope of ideas surrounding its existence had taken some other shape, or if Hinduism had experienced its own profound reformation.

Attempts at Change

This is not intended to mean that Hindu religion did not undergo any changes. In the late nineteenth century, reformist movements in India succeeded in attracting widespread popular support, primarily because the various reformist leaders generally spoke in an idiom and utilised philosophical concepts and symbols, which were widely understood. Reformist leaders like Bal Gangadhar Tilak, Sri Aurobindo Ghosh, Swami Vivekananda, Swami Dayanand and others brought into focus that India's decline could be traced to the Hindus' separation of spiritual enlightenment from society's welfare. Aurobindo Ghosh, in the spirit of such European nationalists as Mazzino, saw a divine expression of God in the nation. Nationalism for him was not merely a form of patriotism, but "nationalism is a religion that has come from God", as he said. Both Aurobindo and Vivekanand believed that national rejuvenation would come only when Indians tapped their potential source of power and directed their energies to the service of Mother India. This reformist movement unleashed a new popular mass upsurge, and revolutionary activities increased significantly in Bengal, Maharashtra and Punjab. Gandhiji carried forward this process and gave a new sense of direction to the entire nation. Gandhiji, for instance, was the first to perceive that the specific feature of the Indian village community was that its social division of labour was caste-based, and hence hide-bound and unalterable. That is why he awakened the "dumb millions", and in the process developed a charisma. Then, Jawaharlal Nehru gave a new content to this nation-state concept. He knew more than anybody else that not all religions permit any separation of spiritual and temporal affairs. Nehru and Gandhiji created a new mass psychology in the country that religion and communalism should not be allowed to weaken and break the dialectical link between the "spiritual value system" of various religions and the social responsibilities of the followers of these religions. This was the single biggest factor which finally led to the political independence of India. And in this furnace of the national movement, the concept of the Indian nation-state became part of the popular mass consciousness. That also explains why anti-communalism was inscribed on the banner of the Indian patriotic forces. Not to oppose communalism and not to stand for secularism was considered to be downright unpatriotic.

Here, another aspect needs to be underlined which is specific to India. For centuries Indian village had remained almost isolated from the outside world, and developed as an autonomous entity. This kept our rural masses economically and culturally backward in a caste-ridden society. This explains the historical reasons for the hold of Hindu revivalism in the Hindi-speaking belt of the country. Like Prussia in imperial Germany, the Hindi heartland is by far India's largest region. Its six states, including the two largest ones—Uttar Pradesh and Bihar—and one Union territory have provided all the Indian Prime Ministers so far, except two. With 43 per cent of Parliamentary seats, it occupies more political clout than any other region. Its definition as a 'political region' starts with the common Hindi language; and extends to its heartland characteristics of cultural parochialism and social and economic backwardness.

During the Nehru era, and partly in the early seventies during the Indira Gandhi period, the success of the Congress in the elections depended on this region. The Congress won disproportionate share of its votes and seats from this region. However, a close analysis shows that this disproportionate electoral support was, in turn, based on the bloc support by India's principal disadvantaged minorities and scheduled castes and tribes, who came to believe in the nationalist era and during Nehru's time the Congress was their friend and protector. Since 1967, however, a steady decline in the influence of the Congress has been taking place, though this was reversed in 1971, 1980 and again in 1984.

Singnificantly, except for Bihar, the Indian left did not succeed in making any headway in this region; even in Bihar, the CPI lost considerable mass base particularly after the "Mandalisation" of politics. Therefore, the exponents of "Mandalisation" and communalism are waging a political struggle to dominate this region. One likely reason for this development is that this region is economically and culturally most backward, and those who wield the weapon of religion and caste succeed in creating a mass psychology in their favour. Even if this is a simplistic conclusion, it cannot be dismissed lightly.

The conclusion is that we cannot expect our rural masses to be genuinely enthusiastic about radical economic policies and the concept of a secular state without at the same time weeding out from their minds the concept of *karma*, which for generations had told them that their miserable lot was the result of their misdeeds in the previous births rather than because of their current economic backwardness. It has to be recognised that feudalism, caste loyalties and economic backwardness mould the consciousness of the people, and keep on feeding their minds. Those who claim to be secular and builders of modern nation-state cannot be expected to be any soft on these causes.

Indian intelligentsia too has been brought up in an atmosphere of communal indentity which must have influenced its moorings. This, in turn, also promoted veneration for communal indentity and caste origin. Let us not overlook the fact that even today in the most sophisticated and modern social gathering, caste affiliations do play a major role. To try to be critical of these tendencies entails the risk of incurring great social displeasure. But truth is not necessarily what we have become accustomed to imagine as true for centuries; and something that is time-honoured is no sufficient reason for its total acceptance. Were not the institution of *sati*, of prohibition of widow-remarriage and untouchability time-honoured in the country? Yet, the circumstance of waging a relentless war against these made Raja Rammohan Roy, Vidyasagar and Gandhiji the greatest among our leaders.

Birth and Evolution of Caste System

The Vedantic metaphysical concept of *Brahma* as the ultimate, formless, eternal, unchanging, unthinkable, *nirguna* developed *pari passu* with the concept of *Brahma* as the creator and regulator of the social system of *'Chaturvarna'*. Still, further down the time, the theory that every member of every *varna* attains *Moksha* (merging into the *Brahma* through a series of rebirths, by strictly perfroming his *varna* duties called *Karma* in Hindu scriptures) was worked out by the Brahmin-Kshatriya establishment in its own interests, though it is difficult to establish as to when this concept emerged. Nevertheless, the fact remains that the development of *Chaturvarna* was not only as a religious institution, but clearly a socio-economic system. It is this theory which gave birth to not only the caste system, but also to the exploitation of the lower castes by the upper castes. The key to the self-propelling nature of Hinduism in this sense lies in the self-propelling character of the caste system born out of *Chaturvarnya*, with its occupational, endogamous basis.

The historical evolution of the Indian society from the primitive stage to the modern has taken place in a manner in which tribes of the hunting and food-gathering stage evolved into that of settled agriculture, artisanship and handicrafts with the caste system intact. That is why Babasaheb Ambedkar thought that it was not possible to destroy caste division in a short period of time because it was based not only on economic factors, but also because it has its basis in religious dogma. Having studied the effects of religion on the social status of the scheduled castes in Hindu society, Ambedkar brought into focus the mechanism of exploitation in the caste system, and how the caste system was the prime impediment in the way of unity of the exploited.

In his assessment, caste for a Hindu was a certain state of mind. The Hindus clung to the caste because they were deeply religious; therefore, Ambedkar's ideological fire was directed against the Hindu religious philosophy.

Criticising Hindusim as a religion that justified untouchability, Ambedkar wrote:

> "The religion which teaches man to behave with man in an inhuman manner is not a religion but infamy. The religion which does not recognise a human being as a human being is a curse."[1]

Dr. Ambedkar also pointed out that the struggle against discrimination was made difficult because discrimination itself was supported and sanctified by religion. The common Hindu looked upon scheduled castes as part of his religion, and his behaviour with the scheduled castes proceeded "more from a feeling of attachment to his religion" than due to any premeditated cruelty. When a Hindu for some reason could not meet the demands of the observance of untouchability, he only retreated a little, but never gave them up entirely, as this would mean renouncing the basic religious postalates of Hinduism in the form in which they existed in the minds of the Hindus. Therefore, in his assessment discrimination against the scheduled castes would remain as long as Hindu religion did not undergo any transformation. He, therefore, concluded that it was not possible to destroy caste division in a comparatively short time because it had its basis in religious dogma. That is why he did not share the perception of the Indian Marxists on this central question.

To say this, does not mean that the role of Ambedkar in the national movement and his contribution to the national consciousness was no significant. The greater part of his political life was spent in the anti-imperialist struggle of the Indian people. On the question of independence of the country, Ambedkar and his supporters occupied patriotic positions. At the same time, as Prof. Hiren Mukherjee writes, "the bitterness of Ambedkar's own experiences" on the question of improving the condition of scheduled castes often threw him into a desperate position..."

Ambedkar, therefore, directed his struggle against the "exploitative essence" of Hinduism and the caste system, and did not treat the struggle of all the sections of the downtrodden as an integrated whole. Therefore, the demands for guarantees for the scheduled castes and reservations that Ambedkar had demanded were considered a temporary measure by him. Nevertheless, he still continues to symbolise the aspirations of the scheduled castes, as even after five decades of independence the scheduled castes have not been fully integrated into the national mainstream. Therefore, they again and again assert their separate identity.

There is another aspect of this problem. Almost half of the total number of scheduled caste people live in the five states of the Hindi-speaking belt—Uttar Pradesh (23.5 million), Bihar (10 million), Madhya Pradesh (7.3 million), Rajasthan (5.8 million) and Haryana (2.5 million). In the South, they are concentrated mainly in Tamilnadu (8.8 million) and Andhra Pradesh (7.9 million), and in the East in West Bengal (12 million). The highest ratio of the scheduled castes in the total population is in Punjab (27 per cent), in Himachal Pradesh (25 per cent), in West Bengal (22 per cent), in Uttar Pradesh (21 per cent) and in Haryana (19 per cent). These figures are indicators of the changes which have been taking place in the political superstructure of India during the last decade of the century.

Congress and the Minorities

Minority support has always been central to the strength of the Congress. The minorities—scheduled castes, scheduled tribes and Muslims—in the past voted disproportionately for the Congress because they regarded the Nehru era of the Congress as their special friend; and thereby helped sustain the secular orientation of the Congress. The minorities supported the Congress in Hindi-belt *en bloc*, though the Congress enjoyed good support from the upper castes too. The process of erosion in the mass support for the Congress among these three minorities began in 1967, but in 1971 this trend was reversed when Indira Gandhi's slogan of "Gharibi Hatoa" (eradicate poverty) gripped the minds of the people. In 1977, after having fallen victim to the excesses of Emergency, they again deserted the Congress *en masse*. In 1971, the Congress won 65 per cent of seats reserved for the scheduled castes in the 17 large states, but in 1977 the Janata Dal almost reversed the process and captured 58 per cent of these seats. In 1980, the Congress again re-established its 1971 relationship with the scheduled caste voters by winning 61 per cent seats. Except for 1984, after the assassination of Indira Gandhi, the Congress has been gradually losing ground among the scheduled castes and the scheduled tribes, in a zig zag manner as was confirmed by state assembly election results of 1993 end. The fact that in the two biggest states of the country, U.P. and Bihar, the congress has been voted out of power needs to be studied objectively.

The scheduled castes and scheduled tribes strata today no longer provide the essential support to the Congress in the party system. At the same time, centrist, ethnic and casteist parties and, above all, the religious revivalist Bharatiya Janata Party (BJP), are making efforts to emerge as alternatives to the Congress. In the Hindi-speaking belt, the main struggle to capture power is between the Congress and the BJP. The other centrist formation, the Janata Dal, is disintegrating and the Indian left—the CPI (M) and the CPI—have become marginal factors. However, there is another dimension to the changes which are taking place in India's political superstructure.

The Muslim Factor

In the post-Nehru period, a process of alienation of the Congress from the Muslims has been taking place, though both Indira Gandhi and Rajiv Gandhi with their own political styles had partially succeeded in halting this process.

The main reason for this decline phenomenon was the religious Muslim revivalism in the countries around India and Hindu revivalism within the country, which increased the minority consciousness among the Muslims. A study has suggested that the special relationship which the Congress had developed with the poorest strata of Muslims in India began to weaken after Nehru's death.

A significant aspect of Jawaharlal Nehru's perception was the language issue: to him even more important than the status of Hindi or English, was the future of Urdu, particularly in the Hindi-speaking belt. He knew that future of Urdu was an important component of the Muslim consciousness. He, Maulana Azad and Dr. Zakir Hussain knew it well that if the Urdu language was not given its rightful place in the language policy of India, the Muslims will learn it at *madarsas* run by Muslim revivalists. With its multilingual, multicultural and multireligious composition, it is essential in India to give constant attention to the needs and complaints of the minority community. Nehru, therefore, initiated many steps to give the Urdu language its proper place in the Urdu-speaking areas. He, for instance, drew the attention of the Chief Ministers as early as in 1958 that Urdu was being gradually eased out even in places like Delhi, where Urdu had once enjoyed a place of pride. He instructed the Chief Minister of Uttar Pradesh to declare Urdu as a regional language.

Whenever and wherever Hindu-Muslim riots took place, Jawaharlal Nehru took a firm stand. In his speeches and letters to the Chief Ministers and Congressmen, he time and again underlined that the "communal-mindedness of the Hindu majority" was clear manifestation of their backwardness. Secularism, or the acceptance that a citizen's religion was a private matter, had been explicitly formulated in the Indian Constitution, but had not been generally accepted. It was in this context that he once confessed that for this reason, he felt a sense of darkness creeping over him.[2]

Nehru was clear in his mind that the question of Kashmir was part of the general problem of the political consciousness of the Muslims in India. In fact, Pakistan's Kashmir policy, its attempts to destabilise the Jammu and Kashmir state and its organised efforts to incite separatist forces by sending armed infiltrators, have all been strengthening Muslim revivalist forces in India. Jawaharlal Nehru was clear in his mind that any weakening of the secular edifice of the country would give a handle to Pakistan. To compete with Pakistan in hatred and barbarity was to accept defeat, and sink below the human level.[3]

What Nehru regarded as the chief problem of Indian unity was the need to foster among the Muslims the feeling that they were not "second class" citizens in India. For this purpose he made secularism as the national policy. There was to be no official religion and religious belief was a private matter for each individual. Secularism was the cement of a new social contract binding together the inhabitants of India into one single political community, with religious faith having no bearing on civic rights. This, of course, was the only civilized position possible for any state in the twentieth century; and Nehru strove incessantly to ensure implementation of this policy. The need, for example, to recruit to the civil services a sufficient number of Indians belonging to faiths other than Hinduism was one of his perennial concerns. The rejection of the outrageous thesis that a good Muslim cannot be a good Indian, featured even in his foreign policy and strengthened his resolve not to hand over Kashmir to Pakistan. But a secular society had not become firmly established in India by the time of his death. Communal riots still had not become a phenomenon of the past.

Paradoxically, in his efforts to make the Muslims feel at home in India, Nehru declined to enact a common civil code and insist on monogamy and rights of divorce, property and inheritance for all Indians of whatever faith. Nehru prided himself on what he had done for the emancipation of women, which was to him the test of civilization; but he had to reconcile himself to the denial of equality, proclaimed by the Indian Constitution, to Muslim women. In the interest of unity and integration, this vital aspect of the social revolution, on which Nehru laid great store, was deliberately held back.

All these and other facets of Nehru's policies, including the manner in which he built friendly relations with Muslim-dominated countries, however, had a deep impact on the Muslims, both in India and abroad.

In the Indian political system, the scheduled castes, the sheduled tribes and Muslims will continue to play a key role in the electoral process as long as its existing secular edifice remains intact. There are around 207 parliamentary constituencies, where Muslim voters are concentrated, though the percentage of their concentration varies from constituency to constituency. These constituencies can be divided in three categories:

(i) constituencies where the Muslim population is 10 to 20 per cent;
(ii) constituencies where the Muslim population is from 20 to 50 per cent, and
(iii) constituencies where the Muslim population is above 50 per cent.

However, the voting pattern in these constituencies has been different. The secular national parties get their support in the first category; while in the second, the pattern is almost the same except for the fact that if a secular party puts up a Muslim candidate, the Muslim electorate votes for that party. In the case of the third category, a Muslim candidate with pronounced pro-Muslim bias gets the support. Higher the proportion of Muslim population, the more likely they will vote for the secular parties with orientation to defend the rights of the Muslims as a religious minority. Herein can be the strength of the left parties and the Congress, in that order.

Communalised political formations, including Bharatiya Janata Party, have no other option but to rally the entire Hindu population on a Hindu revivalist platform. The BJP can only gain power through this route; any other course will force it to adopt a political platform more secular and radical than that of the Congress.

Rise of Hindu Revivalism

The reality, against all pious expectations, is that with all their variants, Hindu, Muslim or Sikh communalism is not showing any signs of withering away with the passage of time. In fact, communalist political formations are playing a see-saw game, reinforcing each other. Hindu communalism is on the ascendency, confirmed by the following table:

Year	Percentage of votes polled by Jana Sangh/BJP
1952	3.1 percent
1957	5.9 "
1962	6.4 "
1967	9.4 "
1971	7.4 "
1977	41.3 (BLD)
1984	7.4 percent
1989	11.2 "
1991	19.9 "

In the state assembly elections in the end of 1993, the BJP lost political power in U.P. and Himachal Pradesh, but in terms of votes polled, it consolidated its strength. The number of seats won by the BJP by itself does not reflect its hold over the people. This becomes clear from the following table:

State	Percentage of votes			
	Congress	BJP	Janata Dal	Others
Delhi	34 %	49 %	12 %	
U.P.	N.A.	33 %	N.A.	BSP & SP 28%
Rajasthan	39 %	38 %	6 %	—
Himachal Pradesh	49 %	35 %	8 %	—

From these cold statistics, it is clear that a change has come about in favour of Hindu communalism.

Though on the surface there was no "wave" for or against any political party in the Hindi-speaking belt in the state assembly elections in October 1993, the demolition of the "Babri Mosque on 6 December, 1992 by some "volunteers" gathered at Ayodhya in Uttar Pradesh at the call of the BJP, the Vishwa Hindu Parishad, the Bajrang Dal and several other organisations associated with the Rashtriya Swayam Sewak Sangh (RSS)—collectively called the *"Sangh Parivar"*—marked the beginning of a new phase in the Indian polity.

There is sufficient evidence to prove that this demolition had a grand design behind it and was undertaken with long-term objective of driving a permament division between the Hindus and Muslims of India, and between the upper caste Hindus and those scheduled castes which were drifting away from the concept of *"Hindu Rashtra"*.

Such a development is a clear proof that the process of modernisation of our socio-economic structures and great expansion in technical and scientific education have not made any basic change in our outlook. What has been most disturbing is that since the midsixties, secular political formations had been entering into political alliances with communal parties in varying degrees in the game of power politics. This tendency was not confined to the non-Congress secular parties: it had its powerful exponents within the Congress itself. In the late sixties, for instance, a powerful section of the Congress leadership had made determined efforts to come to some understanding with the Jana Sangh and the Swatantra Party, leading to a split in the Congress. However, this is not the place to analyse this development here. What needs to be understood today is that the wobbly stand on such a central issue created a mass psycho-logy, which strengthened communalism, parochialism and casteism. Again, as political consciousness rises and each stratum of the population begins to search for its identity and asserts itself, religious and sectarian beliefs become an effective channel of social communication. At the superstructural level, as the Indian state rides towards economic develop-ment, and in the process emerging a new political elite, various political formations have begun to mobilise the masses through communal, regional and casteist slogans. This trend became more marked in the post-Nehru period. In the initial stages, communal, regional and casteist political formations directed their fire against Jawaharlal Nehru and his thought structures. Anyone who claimed that he or she inherited Nehru's legacy became their target. And there were reasons for this.

Jawaharlal Nehru knew more than anybody else that not all religions permit separation of spiritual and temporal affairs by agreeing to render unto Caesar what is Caesar's, and giving unto God what belongs to Him. He was also aware of the fact that a vast majority of the votaries of Hindu, Muslim and Sikh religions did not understand that by giving a new "political" orientation to their religions, the communal leadership was undermining the social values of the teachings of the various religions, thereby destroying their moral and theological base. Communalism was breaking the relationship between what is known as the "spiritual value system" of various religions and the social responsibilities of their devotees. That is why religion, as Nehru saw it "practised, and accepted even by the thinking minds" did not attract him. He believed that religion was closely asso-ciated with superstitions and practices and dogmatic beliefs, and behind all this lay a method of approach to life's problems which was certainly not scientific. Yet, he did not impose this rational approach on others, though he practised the philosophy in his personal life in letter and spirit. Nehru was clear about the fact that religion merges into mysticism and metaphysics, and yet believed that metaphysics and metaphysical philosophy had greater appeal to the mind. That is why he or his close associates were never seen performing *'Yagnas* or consulting *Tantriks* and astrologers. Alas! today most politicians, including Congress leaders, draw their inspiration from mysticism and mystic figures, both dead and alive. They, naturally cannot inspire the new generation to follow modern and scientific outlook or look afresh into the rich Indian heritage, including in the realms of metaphysics and philosophy.

On the other hand, political formations based on religious loyalties are not only politicising religion, but using every opportunity to rouse irrational emotions to the exclusion of social responsibilities *vis-a-vis* the national mainstream. This has given boost to hypocrisy and obscurantism. Externalised religiosity, therefore, provides a defence mechanism for the new Indian rich to insulate themselves from the growing indignation of the people against social and economic problems faced by them. This new linkage between religion and contemporary Indian polity has its own variants—one in Jammu and Kashmir, another in Punjab and yet another in the Hindi-speaking belt of North India. The common factor of all these variants is that all of them are objectively creating an atmosphere of instability in the country, which in turn, is making our nation-state vulnerable to external pressures. Thus, the rise of communalism and intertwining of politics with religion are posing new threats to India's independence and sovereignty.

RSS—The Saffron Brotherhood

During the last two decades, the Rashtriya Swayam Sevak Sangh (RSS) has been the main driving force behind the so-called Hindu revivalism. Some Hindu revivalist leaders believed that the interests of the Hindu community were not adequately protected by the Congress. The RSS founder had his doubts whether the Congress, which included Muslims, could bring about the desired revival of "*Hindu Rashtra*".

The RSS was established in 1925 with the objective to train a group of Hindu youth who, on the basis of their character-building experience in the organisation, would work to unite the Hindu community so that India could again become an "Independent" country and a creative society. Its founder was convinced that a fundamental change in social attitudes was a necessary precondition of a revived India, and that properly trained cadre of nationalists could be the cutting edge of that change.

The two leaders of the RSS, during the pre-independence period—its founder, Keshav Baliram Hedgewar (1925-1940) and Madhav Sadashiv Golwalkar (1940-1973)—laid a firm foundation, supervising the training of the full-time workers who thereafter spread the organisation outward from its original base in eastern Maharashtra. This is proof enough that the RSS was conceived and evolved as a semi-fascist organisation.

Linked to the RSS in India are several affiliated organisations, referred to in the RSS literature as the '*Parivar*' working in politics, in social welfare, in the media, amongs students, industrial workers and Hindu religious outfits and groups. If the BJP—and in the past the Jana Sangh—was the political platform of the RSS, the Vishwa Hindu Perished was the ideological platform for Hindu revivalism.The pattern of the RSS organisation has resulted in a high degree of loyalty on the part of its cadre. The recruitment process employed by the '*Parivar*' organisations has enabled the RSS to remain insulated from the day-to-day affairs of its affiliates, thus protecting its self-defined role as a controlling body which functions through various instruments in almost all walks of life.

The far-sighted leadership of the RSS adopted a cautious, non-confrontational approach towards the political authority to reduce the chances of governmental restrictions in the post-independent period. After independence in 1947, however, the RSS came under political attack of the government. Though Gandhiji's assassination isolated the RSS from the national mainstream, the RSS leadership did not dilute its operations. The RSS was banned twice—first in 1948 after Gandhiji's assassination and again in 1975.

Till the sixties, the RSS could not integrate itself into the national mainstream. In the post-Nehru period when the Congress mass influence declined, the RSS and its political wing, the Jana Sangh, began to grow in strength. The main reason for this was that in a number of states coalition governments were formed between 1967 and 1969, in which the Jana Sangh shared power with the non-Congress political formations, including the Indian Left. Blind anti-Congressism prompted certain secular forces to make common cause with the Jana Sangh. The formation of the Janata Dal government at the Centre gave a new credibility to the RSS and the Jana Sangh, though, later, this government disintegrated on the controversy over "dual" membership—one of the RSS and the other of the Janata Dal.

The Jana Sangh merged into a new governing party, the Janata Party, and former Jana Sangh leaders were included in the national cabinet and served as Chief Ministers in several states during the 27-month period that the Janata Party remained in power. Never before had RSS worked so closely with such a broad spectrum of groups, many of which had previously demanded curbs on its activities.

After the defeat of the Congress in 1989, and the formation of the Janata Dal government headed by V.P. Singh at the Centre a new phase began in the evolution of the RSS. The V.P. Singh government depended for its existence on two crutches—one of the BJP and the other of the Left Front; of the two, the BJP was the stronger. Naturally, the RSS and the BJP began asserting themselves in shaping the policies and finally, as was expected, a break took place between the BJP and the Janata Dal.

Now, this Hindu revivalist force is far more self-confident about its place in the Indian society than at any time since India's independence. The unprecedented growth of the RSS and its affiliates may also be traced to the upsurge of militancy among a section of the Hindus. The main reason for this was that the Indian political forces, including Congressmen, the non-Congress formations and the Indian Left, grossly under-estimated the potential of the rise of Hindu revivalism in the Indian society.

As a result, many Hindus came to believe that the Congress and the Indian Left were "pampering" the Muslims for political gain. The government's decision in March, 1986 to enact a legislation negating a court order that did not adhere to the traditional Islamic law on the question of alimony, was seen as one such favouritism.

In the eighties, Hindu militancy as represented by the RSS became more active than ever before because at a number of places temples used as mosques were restored. The RSS and its *'Parivar'* had been in the thick of many of these activities.

Of a far-reaching significance is the fact that the various front organisations of the *'Parivar'* are controlled by the RSS cadre. The front organisations have a highly centralised authoirty structure, very similar to the RSS. All of them recruit their cadre largely from the RSS, and the RSS-trained cadres occupy main organisational positions. Thus, the RSS plays a key role in moulding the policies, ideology and orientation of the various front organisations of the *'Parivar'*.

In recent years, the RSS has changed its tactics. RSS leaders have come to realise that close association with the political power evokes envy and oppósition, which complicate their efforts from a long-term point of view. With the massive increase in its influence, the RSS leadership now controls these organisations from behind, though most of the front leaders had undergone RSS training some time or the other.

These trainings are carried out in the RSS '*Shakhas*' which meet daily ostensibly to teach character-building exercises to the 'Swayam Sevaks.' The founders of the RSS had devised a training system which was intended to establish what is described as the "Saffron Brotherhood".

The RSS training ideally starts at the pre-adolescence stage and ideological training takes place at a time when the youth generally work out in their own experiences, satisfying a relationship between themselves and the society. This is the period when the individual is particularly susceptible to ideological brainwash. He seeks, a person, a cause, to which he can give uncompromising obedience. The RSS appeals to this impulse by advocating sacrifice of the self for the *Hindu Rashtra*, and this impulse is expressed organisationally in the RSS and reverence for the RSS leaders. The society envisaged is not the one that objectively exists, but the one which is perceived by the RSS ideology.

However, the various movements sponsored by the RSS are not religious in character. Religion is only a signboard; the real goods in the communalists' shops are essentially of a non-religious character.

What, for example, have the campaigns of the RSS-sponsored Vishwa Hindu Parishad got to do with the religious beliefs of the Hindus? There does not, and cannot, exist any threat to their religion and culture in a secular state, 85 per cent of whose population is Hindu. And yet, the RSS and the VHP are trying to convince the lay Hindus that they are "under siege" and that there is an international conspiracy to reduce their number through conversion! The whole propaganda is to intensify a perception of threat among the majority community with a view to inciting aggressive hatred against the adherants of other religions. The high watermark of this demagogy is the assertion that India should be declared a Hindu state because then alone would secularism, democracy and non-alignment be safe.

One is reminded of the Nazi propaganda which made the Germans believe that extermination of the Jews was essential to protect the German race and the nation; that the German race provided the only guarantee for civilised existence of mankind; and that Germany had the divine mission to rule and civilise the rest of the world.

The Zionist Jews who today dominate Israel are inspired by similar feelings of being the "chosen people" of God. So are the followers of the Ikhwan, whose Indian form is Jamaat-e-Islami: they declare themselves the "party of God—Hizb-e-Allah. They do not confine themselves to the propagation of mere faith; according to the Ikhwan belief, "Islam considers the enforcement of law and order as important as propaganda and percept", and insist that "God prevents and stops through state power what the *Quran* cannot accomplish". It is interesting to note that these movements accept and admire each other despite their apparent contradictions. All of them hold fascism and racism in high regard. This is what Golwalkar had said about Nazi Germany in 1938: "German racial pride has now become the topic of the day. To keep up the purity of the race and its culture, Germany shocked the world by her purging the country of the semitic race—the Jews. Race pride at its highest has also manifested here. Germany has also shown how well-nigh impossible it is for races and cultures, having differences going to the root, to be assimilated into one united whole, a good lesson for us in Hindustan to learn and profit by."

The RSS leaders are not generally known for commenting on events beyond India's borders. As a rule they avoid making international sympathies and possible contacts known to public, because they are extracareful about the veneer that they have no links outside India. If and when they choose to make an exception to this rule, it is obviously under complusion of circumstances, but are indeed flashes that expose reality.

Nearly two decades back, the then RSS chief, Golwalkar, had sent a message to US President Johnson extending support to his Vietnam policy. That was a time when the US Administration had been totally isolated in the region; and opposition to the escalating aggression in Vietnam was growing even within the USA. Golwalker had then written that in the worldwide confrontation between *Dharma* and *Adharma* the USA was leading the forces of *Dharma*.

For the Zionists, the RSS has had as much admiration as for Hitler's Nazi Germany. In his first book, *"We and Our Nationhood Defined"*, Golwalkar has paid glowing tributes to the race spirit, both of the Nazi Germany and the Zionist Jews. That was the time when the Indian National movement was opposing fascism and condemning the induction of Jews into Palestine "under British bayonets."

These facts underline the political character of the RSS. Both Mahatma Gandhi and Jawaharlal Nehru were aware of this fact. Gandhiji even refused to give RSS a good chit when somebody praised the discipline and hard work of the RSS men and pointed out that those qualities were found in Hitler's Nazis too. Jawaharlal Nehru, when repeatedly pressed by Golwalkar for an interview, informed the latter that it was no use because what the RSS people said was not the same as what they did. That is why various attempts by the RSS to secure entry into the Congress did not succeed.

As early as on September 10, 1949, in a letter to Mohan Lal Saxena, Jawaharlal Nehru had warned the nation, "All of us seem to be getting infected with refugee mentality, or worse still, the **RSS mentality**. That is a curious finale to our careers". This warning by Jawaharlal was given after the assassination of Gandhiji when the RSS-engineered tension in the country had led to a serious communal situation.

Though the first ban on the RSS was lifted in 1949, the ban had been a serious setback to the RSS. Its dreams of playing a major role in independent India was shattered as has been the case after the Ayodhya tragedy. The RSS leadership then had come under heavy attack both from within and without. The RSS was treated as a pariah organisation and the leadership was ridiculed in the press and by politicians. Its membership dropped and the number of *pracharaks* too decreased. Morale within the organisation was at an all-time low.

Between the lifting of the ban in 1949 and 1953, Golwalkar was confronted by an organisation beset by internal division. However, in 1952 the RSS leadership again became active and started as agitation against cow slaughter. This enabled the RSS to partially rehabilitate itself. At the grass-root level, the agitation depended heavily on RSS volunteers. Nevertheless, till the early fiftees, the RSS remained in a bad shape. It was faced with serious financial problems because it could not pay off loans arranged during the ban. In fact, at one stage Golwalkar seriously considered selling off the RSS headquarters in Nagpur to raise money. It was not until 1956 that the RSS was able to pay back its debts.

Given the continuing problems in the mid-1950s, the central leadership decided that a further consolidation was needed. Eknath Ranade, appointed general-secretary in 1956, ruled that the RSS could not afford to loan *pracharaks* to the affiliates when its own work continued to languish. The RSS would devote its resources almost exclusively to character-building. This policy came as a blow to the affiliates and their leaders lobbied against it. Some activist *pracharaks*, such as the Deoras brothers withdrew from RSS work.

The consolidation phase ended in 1962. Two years earlier, Golwalkar had called an assembly of full-time workers at Indore to review the future orientation of the RSS. For the first time, *pracharaks* working in the affiliates strongly recommended that the RSS should again allow some of its own full-time workers to work for the affiliates. They pointed out that the future of the affiliates would be bleak unless they could get the help of RSS *pracharaks*. Their arguments had the desired impact. Ranade, assigned to a long-term project aimed at popularising the revivalist message of Swami Vivekananda, was replaced in 1962 by Prabhakar Balwant Dani, who held the position between 1946-56, and who was more sympathetic to the activists' views. After 1962, RSS workers were again allowed to shift to the affiliates. Perhaps the most prominent on this score were the Deoras brothers. Balasaheb was appointed assistant general secretary, and Bhaurao was given the position of northern zonal *Pracharak.*

The main reason for the 1962 change in the policy was that following the Sino-Indian border conflict, the Congress received a serious setback and for the first time direct political attacks on Jawaharlal Nehru had began. Since then, the RSS and its various front organisations have been expanding their influence.

Farsighted as the RSS leaders were in the sixties, they evolved a well-designed policy of "mind management." In the initial stages they created an informal communication system based on verbal messages carried by RSS cadres. The RSS in this period, created trusts for publication of newspapers and journals. The publication, *Organiser*, was started on July 3, 1947, a month after Lord Mountbatten announced the decision to partition the country. Later, weeklies *Panchjanya* in Hindi and *Rashtra-Shakti* in Marathi started their publications. In 1970, the *Hindustan Samachar* News Agency with a network of over 1000 correspondents began to function. By the 70's the RSS and its front organisation had nearly 41 newspapers and journals in the country. After the emergency period (1975-1977) the RSS newspapers experienced an upward surge in circulation.

Though the Vidyarthi Parishad was started in 1948, it was in the 50's and the 60's that it became an important factor in the youth movement particularly in Delhi, Punjab, Uttar Pradesh, Madhya Pradesh and Maharashtra. By the early 1970s, the Vidyarthi Parishad had become a significant force in various Indian universities. In the mid-seventies, it had a membership of 1.6 lakhs in 790 branches, with 24 full-time workers. In the 1974-75 agitation in Bihar and Gujarat, the Vidyarthi Parishad was most active. In Bihar, for instance, the Vidyarthi Parishad fully backed the students' agitations behind Jai Prakash Narayan.

Surprisingly in the 50's, the RSS worked out a plan to penetrate the working class movement. In the sixties, the RSS-led Mazdoor Sangh became another important organ. Following the 1977 electoral victory of the Janata alliance, the influence of the RSS in the working class movement began to increase rapidly. The Bharatiya Mazdoor Sangh, according to its claims, has 1725 unions with a total membership of 18.79 lakhs. According to its claims it has already become the second biggest trade union organisation in the country.

However, the most important component of the multifaceted activities of the RSS was that it began to organise Hindus on a religious basis. In 1964, it established the Vishwa Hindu Parishad with three main objectives.

1. To consolidate and strengthen the Hindu society;
2. To protect and spread Hindu values, ethical and spiritual, and to make them relevant in contemporary society; and,
3. To establish and strengthen the links among Hindus living in different countries.

Till the early 70's, the VHP concentrated its resources in the Hindi-speaking belt with the main focus on the tribal people. It was in the early

80's that the VHP started organising the Hindus at the national plane. A month-long *'Ektamata Yagna'* was organised all over the country to raise resources for its activities. According to an estimate of the RSS leaders, 60 million people participated in this *'Yagna'*, with the various processions converging at Nagpur, the headquarters of the RSS. The processions were accompanied by portraits of 'Bharat Mata and large urns containing water from the Ganga river. The Ganga water was distributed among the Hindu temples for use in the worship of the temple gods.

It was after this success that the VHP, in the late 1983, became an active participant in the campaign to restore the birthplace of Lord Rama, and with this began the Ram Janmabhoomi-Babri Masjid controversy. In its campaign to get the Ramjanmabhoomi at Ayodhya converted into a temple, the February 1986 court decision permitting the performance of *'pooja'* at the Ramjanmabhoomi gave the VHP new credibility. In this movement the VHP received help from the Hindu religious establishments, including the four *Shankarcharyas*. The VHP then decided to raise Rs. 250 million for building this temple, and simultaneously raised the demand for conversion of two other historic sites in Uttar Pradesh—Krishnajanmabhoomi, the birthplace of Krishna at Mathura, and the Kashi Vishwanath Temple at Varanasi. In addition, the VHP identified 25 other mosques to be converted. Since then, the cleavage between the Hindus and the Muslims had been widening which reached its climax on December 6, 1992. But there is much more to it than meets the eye.

In 1970, RSS members residing in the United States met in New York City to form the Vishwa Hindu Parishad of the United States of America. The American and Canadian units of the VHP published a bi-monthly magazine. These two units have been organising camps in various parts of America and Canada and several RSS leaders from India have been regularly touring these countries. Besides the US and Canada, the VHP has spread to other countries, especially England and several East African and South Asian countries. In Great Britain the VHP now claims 14 branches.

This amply shows that the Vidyarthi Parishad, the Mazdoor Sangh, the VHP, the BJP and other front organisations are run exclusively by the RSS. From all angles, the "Saffron Brotherhood", namely the RSS, has emerged as an important force in India, and has been pushing forward to build a theocratic state by demolishing the secular edifice built over the last one century—during the freedom struggle and in the post-independence period.

The Defence of India's secular edifice has both regional and international significance. India constitutes five per cent of South Asia. India's size and geography is such that what happens to this ancient nation will have a chain reaction in the entire Asia-Pacific region. Indian nation-state based on secularism has been a model for this region, for that matter for the entire developing world. What happens to India and in India can change the course of history in the coming decades. In this sense all the liberal democrats throughout the world should realise that by encouraging communal, revivalist and terrorist forces, they are only destabilising the entire region.

References

1. Writings and speeches of Dr. Ambedkar 1925-1936 Vol. 4, Bangalore, 1979 p. 62.
2. Speech at Patna, 30 April, 1959 the *Hindu*, 2 May, 1959.
3. *Abdullah to Ayub*, 1 September, 1967 p. 81-82.
4. S. Gopal, *Jawaharlal Nehru, A Biography* Vol. iii p. 281.

ISLAMIC FUNDAMENTALISM

ASGHAR ALI ENGINEER

The recent upsurge in the Muslim world has thrown the question of Islamic fundamentalism into bold relief. The Western media—our major newspapers take the cue from the Western news agencies or simply reproduce their stories—have shown great interest in the events, especially the developments in Iran. However, one would be greatly disappointed if one expected unbiased and objective reporting by these agencies. Edward W. Said, Professor of English and Comparative Literature at Columbia University, who is also well-versed in West Asian affairs, in his article on Iran has given a provocative assessment of U.S. coverage of the Iranian crisis. "Why was it that political events seemed reducible in so Pavlovian a way to the peculiarities of Islam ?" asks Prof. Said and goes on to reply: "Mainly because the news media, as well as governmental and academic experts, seemed to have agreed implicitly not to recognize political developments as political but to represent them as a cosmic drama, pitting civilization as we like it against the uncivilized and the barbaric. In such a way history could be simplified, alongwith social processes, everyday reality and the humanity of other people whose interests did not happen to coincide with ours."

It is necessary to understand the role played by the media before we get down to discuse the phenomenon of Islamic fundamentalism, as our concepts about it (i.e, Islamic resurgence or fundamentalism) owe their origin to the media reports. For an objective analysis, therefore, we must make ourselves fully aware of the subtleties, prejudices and distortions of the media. Some Western newspapers have used screaming headlines such as "Militant Islam on the March" or "The Soldiers of Allah Advance", while scarcely mentioning the upsurge in Judaism and Egyptian or Lebanese Christianity. Referring to the subtle ways of the Western media, Edward Said says:

> "There were subtle ways to incriminate 'Islam'. One was to put an expert before the public and have him or her suggest that Khomeini was not really 'representative of Islamic clergy' (this was

> L. Dean. Brown, former U.S. Ambassador to Jordan and Special Envoy to Labanon and now President of the Middle East Institute)..., that the 'iron-clad' mullah was a throwback to an earlier, obviously 'Islamic', age and that the mobs in Tehran were reminiscent of Nuremberg, just as the street demonstrations were signs of the 'circus as principal entertainment' habitually provided by dictators."

I have quoted from Edward Said at some length only to show that all is not well with the reporting about the Muslim world in the Western press, which is so often quoted in our Indian press. However, with equal emphasis, I wish to assert that it does not mean that everything is in order in the Muslim world and that the religious revivalism reflects the genuine aspirations of the peoples of the Muslim countries. If the developments in the Muslim world are to be seen in the proper perspective, religious revivalism or the emergence of fundamental Islam (as it is often referred to) cannot be divorced from political motives. I wish to emphasise the fact that it is not religion that is in command but politics. Any careful observer of the socio-political scene in the Muslim world can understand that it is not religion which inspires the politicians, but the politics of the ruling classes which determine the instrumentality of religion. Whether it is the Nizam-e-Mustafa of Zia-ul-Haq in Pakistan, or the fundamentalism of Khomeini in Iran, or the unrelieved orthodoxy of the Saudi family, none has remained untainted by the politics of the ruling classes in these countries.

Islamic Resurgence

Anwar Moazzem calls Islamic resurgence a "semi-political development". He asks: "Can these semi-political developments be described as Islamic resurgence? What is Islamic resurgence? If this term is to mean the strengthening of Islamic fundamentalism, then it is not at all a new trend. What is new is the state-sponsored Islamic revival and a political and social system through partial implementation of Sharia." The words "partial implementation of Sharia" are quite significant. The ruling classes implement only those parts of Islamic Sharia which suit their political purpose. Islam is sought to be used by them to preserve and strengthen *status quo*. Everyone knows that the penal measures like cutting off a thief's hands or lashing a drunkard or stoning an adulterer to death are not the essence of Islam. In no religion do penal measures occupy central position. As a religious vision, Islam stresses the concepts of brotherhood and equality. However, while the penal measures which do not disturb the *status quo* are sought to be enforced by the rulers, teachings of Islam stressing equality and brotherhood are seldom talked about as they would tend to change the direction of the current repressive and exploitative social structure towards a more just and equitable one.

It is noteworthy that in none of these countries has "Islamisation" of the society been the result of a people's movement. There was no popular demand in Pakistan, nor in Iran, and much less in Saudi Arabia to enforce the Islamic Sharia. Even in Iran the popular upsurge began as a revolt against the Shah who came to be hated for his highly repressive rule. One has only to read the Iranian papers and pamphlets to understand the depth of the anti-Shah feeling among the people of Iran. He is invariably referred to as *'Janayatkar Shah'* (the criminal Shah). It was only later that Ayatollah Khomeini gave it a religious turn. The popular upsurge against the Shah had dangerous implications for the upper classes as militants like the Mujahidin-e-Khalqi-Iran and Fidaiyan-e-Khalqi-Iran were quite influential among the people and they wanted to give a decisive turn to the movement in favour of social change. The ruling classes of Iran and the clergy led by Ayatollah Khomeini were fully aware of the revolutionary potential of the movement, and so, Khomeini's first task was to enforce mediaeval Islam. In my opinion it would certainly be wrong to view the ironclad 'mullah' as merely a religious fanatic.

Fanatic he was, but there was a definite method in his fanaticism. Had he been inspired by pure love of Islam, he would not have trained his guns against the militant Mujahidin. Mujahidin are committed to Islam—but radical Islam—as their literature convincingly shows. They reject mediaeval Islam and believe in its reinterpretation so as to establish a just society, ending exploitation of man by man. Their official organ, *'Mojahed'*, carries as its motto, "Onwards towards the annihilation of exploitation and oppression of every kind and the realisation of the classless society in *Towhid* (Divine integration)". In an article, "How to study the Quran", published in *Mojahed*, it is said: "The founders of the PMOIL (People's Mojahedin of Iran), in seeking an approach which would provide the best mode of assuming the functions of a revolutionary social school of thought and action, chose Islam. Thus, along with the organisation's 'ideological approach', efforts were made to become as familiar as possible with the *Towhidi* worldview of Islam and its systematic structuring."

These pronouncements should leave no one in doubt that the Mujahedin are committed to Islam. But the Ayatollah came down on them heavily precisely because they see Islam as a revolutionary force, and not merely as a mediaeval ideology for preserving the *status quo*.

Iran and Saudi Arabia

According to an *A.P.* report from Iran, Ayatollah Khomeini had frequently said that Iran's revolution was essentially for God's sake, not for the economy. These and other statements of the Ayatollah, and his trenchant criticism of organisations like the Mujahedin which are committed to revolutionary change through radical reinterpretation of Islam, clearly show that the patriarch was determined to keep Islam mediaevalised for *status quo*. He used Islam as long as it served his purpose through its mediaeval accretions. Islam was used by mullahs like Khomeini and some other rulers like Zia-ul-Haq of Pakistan and the ruling family of Saudi Kingship, or 'Islam minus democracy' notion of Khomeini on the grounds of religion. The politics of Islamic fundamentalism varies according to political conditions from country to country. Thus, the Saudi rulers—supposedly enthusiastic supporters of Islamic fundamentalism—were shaking with fear when the Islamic fundamentalist revolution was sweeping through Iran. The Saudi rulers sympathised with the Shah despite the fact that he had done everything to revive Iran's pre-Islamic past and to put down not only the clergy but also other lay Islamic revolutionaries. Peter Mansfield, an expert on West Asia, points out:

> "Here, the Saudi leaders were outspoken in their support for the Shah until the moment he left his country, and they openly criticised the conduct of Khomeini and his followers."

Further, explaining the reasons for the Saudi rulers' fear of the Islamic revolution of Iran, Mansfield says:

> "There is corruption (since there are over 400 royal princes, it would be surprising if there wasn't) and, while there is no urban or rural proletariat as in Iran, there are wide disparities of wealth. Then there is the question of consultation, or *'Shura'*—a very important principle adhered to by the Prophet himself and the first Caliphs. No *'majlis al-shura'* or consultative council, has been set

up, although one has been promised on several occasions during the past 20 years."

Thus, the crux of the matter is political power, and not the concern for religion. Religion is, to use a current journalistic term, mere cosmetics. Saudi Arabia is a known supporter of America which was strongly denounced by Khomeini. In every respect, thus, Iran and Saudi Arabia, are opposed to each other, although both swear by Islamic fundamentalism.

Saudi Arabia wants Muslims all over the world to believe in its "faithful adherence" to Islam. It has been spending huge sums of oil money to project this image as also to strengthen reactionary regimes in Muslim countries like Pakistan. Criticising those who hold Saudi Arabia as a model of Islamic fundamentalism, Professor M.S. Agwani says: "In fact, Saudi Arabia was not the fundamentalists's model even before the oil boom of the seventies when the variance between the Saudi rulers' Islamic pretensions and practices had not yet become so wide and conspicuous as it is today."

It would also be equally wrong to believe that the Islamic 'cosmetics' of the Saudi rulers have deceived their people. Knowledgeable circles believe that the stability of the regime is more apparent than real. An investigative report, "Countdown in the Desert" published in the *Middle East Currency Reports*, a journal from London, is an eye-opener for those who believe in the myth of stability in Saudi Arabia. Various methods have been used by the Saudi rulers to suppress information about the disaffection among the people and, more seriously, among the armed forces as well. Commenting on the methods of suppression, the report says: "Methods employed range from payments to individual journalists and publications, to the sponsorship of specialist media and the provision of heavy advertising support for special supplements which are supposed to contain 'objective information'—which, invariably, include 'loaded' reports—not to mention other, more subtle methods of persuasion and even collusion.

Major Hassan Hosni, a co-conspirator in the plot to overthrow the Saudi rule, said while being interrogated that "It was high time for the country to be ruled by the young and the educated, rather than by people who were old and illiterate." The officers, he claimed, objected to the blatant corruption in high places, and to the evident dissipation of members of the ruling family and its hangers-on. He also strongly objected to the extensive American presence in the armed forces and in the country as a whole.

People and Islamic Appeal

Let us now consider the appeal of Islamic fundamentalism among the people of the Islamic countries. Whereas the rulers have used Islam as an instrument of legitimising their power, the same cannot be said of the masses. In the third world countries, due to economic and technological backwardness, religion is a force to be reckoned with. The masses are steeped in ignorance and superstition. The scanty resources are monopolised by the elite of the society, more often than not in collaboration with multinational companies, and the entire educational system is designed to serve the needs of these elite groups. Gains of economic development only widen the gap between the rich and the poor, giving rise to acute social tensions. Various groups and communities thus feeling insecure—depending on their perception of the situation, the feeling of insecurity may be real or imaginary— seek refuge in religion. Increasingly in the Afro-Asian countries, religion is being sought to be used as a militant weapon for fighting privileged groups or to defend certain privileges. Thus, religions have become an ally of the left or the right, depending on whether it is fighting for or against the privileged groups. These roles can be reversed also, as happened in Iran in an amazingly short period. Khomeini and his followers fought militantly, with religion as their main weapon, against the exploitative regime of the Shah and his American ally, but after the overthrow of the Shah, their role got reversed, and religion was used by them to reinforce *status quo*.

Gunder Frank sees the whole thing as a consequence of the world economic crisis and its impact on the economies of the backward countries. He says:

> "The apparently most widespread and powerful moving force in this development crisis and crisis (of) development is nationalism, sometimes combined with religion. Varieties of nationalist, ethnic and religious interests and allegiance seem to define and move the superpowers, their challengers, and the other States in their mutual

> rivalries to participate in world development. Tensions and conflicts that often have their sources in the constraints and readjustments imposed by the world economic crisis and their political most viable expression, through combinations or coalitions of national regional, ethnic and religious movements within 'nation-states' and their zones of influence."

He also points out that "nationalist, regional, ethnic and religious movements are also defining factors in the Philippine Mindanao, Tamil Sri Lanka, in all three corners of India, through Pakistan and Afghanistan and Iran, thanks to the Baluchis and others, among Kurds and other minorities in Iran, Iraq and Turkey (not to mention the former Soviet Union), and of course throughout the Israeli-Palestinian Arab conflict."

Of course, of all these nationalist, ethnic and religious movements, the Islamic fundamentalist movement is much more noticeable for two sets of reasons: One, inner, integral, i.e., the nature of religion, and the other extraneous, i.e., political, having impact on the world political scene. Islam, of all the world religions, is the most totalitarian. "Indeed, in principle", says Rodinson, "it dominated every act and every thought of the faithful... All actions, even those arising out of the most elementary biological needs, such as excretion and coitation, were regulated by the ideological system." Therefore, any movement based on Islam seeks to encompass all the areas of life, including the most trivial ones. Zealots on the fringe stretch it to an extreme, and thus, tend to attract much wider publicity, especially in the Western media. It has certainly went to its extreme in Iran where the Islamic guards indulged in vandalism, inspired by the thoughts of Khomeini. The lumpen elements, uprooted from the rural areas, doing odd jobs or remaining unemployed in industrial towns, become vehicles of such fanaticism.

Also, a section of the "semi-intelligentsia", who can be more accurately termed "proletariod" (term coined by Geiger to describe the social origins of the storm troopers of the Nazi Party) too, comes in handy for this purpose. According to Kishore Jethanandani, with the proletariat, the "proletariod" stratum shares its condition of destitution but ideologically it identifies itself with the petit-bourgeoisie. Under the ideological guidance of the Iranian clergy, this section of the society played a most abominable role in Iran. This is not to deny that a section of the intelligentsia, especially university teachers and students, is also committed to the Islamic revolution. The Jamaat-Islami in Pakistan and Ikhwan-al-Muslimin in Egypt and some other Arab countries draw their cadres mainly from amongst the university teachers and students.

The second reason for Islamic fundamentalism attracting particular attention is the strategic nature of the region because of its oil reserves. The Western countries whose economies are largely dependent on oil, are very sensitive to any developments there. Khomeini, whatever his attitude to internal change within Iran, continued to be militantly anti-American. Naturally, therefore, the American press adopted, subtly or crudely, a hostile attitude towards him. However, on the other hand, the American papers' attitude towards the injunction of the Sharia to the Saudi society is entirely different, as Saudi Arabia happens to be an American ally.

Apart from political considerations, sociological and historical problems are also involved. The Arab society is partly tribal and pre-feudal. Any attempt to push it into the modern technological era throws up highly complex and challenging problems. Many people who are still in a primitive stage get uprooted by the technological changes, and hence react adversely by trying to rally round those forces which promise the historical continuity of the old social patterns. Also, they strongly disapprove of the reckless Westernisation of the privileged classes which totally shatters the old morality. Here, we must distinguish between Westernisation and modernisation. Westernisation is nothing but copying superficially the ways of the Western countries which, in the case of elite groups, means drinking, gambling, indulging in extramarital sex, and so on. This naturally causes deep revulsion among the masses, and often takes the form of militant religious movements. The sense of deprivation (compare the stark misery of the masses and the highly luxurious ways of the rich) is as much a motivating force for such fundamentalist movements as religion itself. Modernisation, on the other hand, is a far more serious project and involves intellectual reorientation and an acceptance of the rational and scientific way of thinking. These battles are fought on the intellectual plane, and hardly ever assume the form of a militant movement. Islamic fundamentalism is bound to fail if it challenges modernisation, but may continue to enamour the masses in its role as an opponent of Westernisation.

Muslim Fundamentalism and Modern Nation-States

V.D. CHOPRA

To understand the social, economic and political factors which have boosted Muslim fundamentalism in the 1990's one must take into consideration certain aspects of Muslim population in various countries. In the developing world where the Muslims are either in absolute majority or constitute a substantial minority, the process of modern nation-state building began only since the end of World War II and the dawn of the era of decolonisation. In fact, most of them are yet to start building a democratic structure.

Outside Europe, modern nation-states have developed in three ways. One was the authoritarian political structure with bourgeois economic values. Examples of this can be found in Latin America and a few of them elsewhere, and one can only hope that these state structures will evolve themselves into more liberal regimes. The second was the authoritarian model of Marxist states. And the third was the Indian way.

No developing nation has been able to overnight become a democratic state, reduce income disparities and launch on a path of economic development based on liberal democratic values. For quite some time after independence, there were strong hopes of building India into a modern democratic nation-state and, with centralised planning, also of reducing income disparities. That dream has not materialised, and a significant portion of our population (whether 40 per cent or more) still remains below the poverty line while income disparties have grown wider. On the political side, the growth of healthy political traditions has been disappointing. Parties have fragmented on the basis of personality cults; inner-party democracy is missing, as revealed by the absence of intra-party elections, while black money and corrupt practices dominate elections. The lack of assertion of autonomy of the judiciary, dominance over it by the executive, tyrannical abuse of power and authority and inadequate protection to citizens against such abuse have become the[1] order of the day.

Population and Poverty

Out of nearly 120 developing nations, about 55 are estimated to be ruled either by the military directly or have military-dominated regimes. The majority of the rest have various forms of authoritarian governments, some of them laying claims to being native to the genius of the country or the people, which very often is a euphemism for tribalism. All of them—kings, sultans, military rulers, chieftains or single-party rule—claim they are practising their own particular brand of democracy.

Estimates of world Muslim population at the end of the third quarter of the 20th Century vary between 600 and 900 million.[2] The distribution of population as presented reveals that while two-thirds, (548.5 million) of them live in Muslim-majority countries, one-third (244.9 million) live as a minority in several non-Muslim states. Among those Muslims who live in Muslim-majority countries, more than 92 per cent (506.2 million) enjoy a majority status of over 80 per cent in their national population. On the other hand, among Muslims who live as minorities in non-Muslim states, 202 million constitute a minority of 12 per cent or less of their national population. It is thus apparent that most Muslims enjoy either a dominant majority status of over 80 per cent or a small minority status of 12 per cent or less in their countries of residence.

Countries in which the Muslims constitute at least 80 per cent of the population are: Afghanistan, Albania, Algeria, Bahrain, Bangladesh, Egypt. Indonesia, Iran, Iraq, Jordan, Kenya, Kuwait, Libya, Mauritania, Morocco, Niger, Oman, Pakistan, Saudi Arabia, Somalia, Sudan, Syria, Tanzania, Tunisia, Turkey and Yemen Arab Republic.

Countries with 50 to 79 per cent Muslim population are: Benin, Ethiopia, Ghana, Guinea, Ivory Coast, Lebanon, Liberia, Malaysia, Mali, Sierra Leone, Togo and Upper Volta.

Countries with 13 to 49 per cent of Muslim population are: Cameroon, Central African Republic, Chad, Cyprus, Malawi, Mauritius, Mozambique, Nigeria and Zaire.

Thus there are 26 countries where the Muslim population is at least 80 per cent, and another 12 where the Muslim population is between 50 per cent and 79 per cent. There are 6 countries which have a Muslim population ranging between 13 and 49 per cent. These figures bring into sharp focus the concentration of the Muslim population in the developing and the least developed countries on our planet.

In the following countries, the Muslim population is up to 12 per cent of the total population: Bulgaria, Burma, China, France, Greece, India, Israel, Madagaskar, Philippines, Sri Lanka, Thailand, Uganda, the erstwhile U.S.S.R., Vietnam, Yugoslavia and Zambia.[2]

As such, there are 44 countries where the Muslim population constitutes the overwhelming majority of the population. Thus, these Asian and African countries, stretching from the Atlantic Ocean to the Pacific, across North and Central Africa and South Asia, constitute an important geopolitical factor. Of the estimated total world Muslim population of about 800 million, the Sunnies, one of the two main branches of Islam, constitute 80 per cent, the remaining 20 per cent are Shi'ites.

Political Structures and Orientations

The Muslim countries differ greatly in terms of their political structure and orientation, as well as their level of social and economic development. There are states possessing huge amounts of petrodollars (e.g., Saudi Arabia, the UAE, Kuwait), and also those which are counted among the world's poorest (Bangladesh, Zambia, Guinea, Mali, Niger, Sudan). A certain lack of uniformity, even a degree of internal contradictoriness, is typical of Islam itself which, to a certain extent, stems from the absence of any centralised organisation.

Unlike, the Roman Catholic Church, Islam has no single religious or political centre. Nor does it have a single globally organised church hierarchical system. Saudi Arabia is considered the most authoritative political centre of Islam, and close relations with that country enable the United States to use its influence in the Islamic world to promote its own aims. However, Saudi Arabia, despite all efforts made by its regime, does not enjoy undisputed authority among the Muslim states. In general, Saudi influence is determined not so much by religious or political hold, but by economic factors.

However, despite all their differences, the Muslim countries are united by Islam, which is not only a religion, but also a code of conduct and repository of rules for everyday life and a code of ethics and philosophy. There are two very contradictory aspects in Islam: one, that is conservative, opposed to new trends and social progress, almost desiring to push mankind hundreds of years back in time, to the situation that existed during the emergence of Islam itself; and, the other, an inherent protest against a system that dooms the people to poverty and ignorance.

Centuries of domination of these countries by colonial powers has kept them economically most backward. The measure of dietary energy supply, as expressed in per capita kilo-calorie consumption per day, indicates that most countries in Africa and Asia, have a per capita consumption ranging between a low of 1,800 and a maximum of 2,500 kilo-calories. And over two-thirds of predominantly Muslim population countries fall far below the 1975 world's average of 2,470 kilo-calories per person per day. Only Turkey has a per capita consumption level of over 3,000 kilo-calories. The gross national product (GNP) is low in almost all predominantly Muslim countries which do not have oil revenues. The high GNP of £ 4,090.00 in Kuwait and £ 1,830.00 in Libya reflects principally the recent wealth from oil. About half of the 27 Muslim countries have a GNP of less than £ 200.00, and two-thirds are under the £ 400 figure. Furthermore, it is widely recognized that these figures tell us nothing about how income is distributed among the people of a given country.

With the exception of Lebanon and Malaysia, countries with Muslim majorities of between 50 and 79 per cent are all in Africa. Excluding Ethiopia, the other eight countries are in West Africa, which is the region of overall high fertility and low levels of socio-economic development. The average birth rates for the 1970-75 period were around 50 per thousand in six of the nine African Muslim countries. The death rates were also high, generally over 22 per thousand. Only Lebanon and Malaysia have birth rates in the 30s and death rates as low as 10 per thousand and both have achieved relatively high levels of development in their group.

Iranian Revolution and After

It is in this socio-economic background that the hold of the religious fundamentalist forces in the Muslim world needs to be examined. While

Islam is common to all the states; the stress laid on it by political establishments varies. By and large the ruling elite in these countries emphasise Islam, but this is more assertive in societies where tribal values are predominant—states of the Arabian peninsula—than elsewhere. Only in recent years, in some oil rich Arab countries, have a secular-minded modern elite begun to emerge.

Egypt under the leadership of Nasser, Syria and Iraq under the leadership of the Arab Baath Socialist Party and Algeria were the first among the Arab countries to embark on the path of modern nation-states. The Palestinian Liberation Organisation and its various components also made a valuable contribution in creating a secular consciousness among the Muslims in the Arab countries.

That being the position, to paint all Muslim countries with the brush of Muslim fundamentalism would be historically wrong, and a very unfair conclusion.

The view that Islam had a key role to play in the social and political processes in a number of Eastern countries became widespread in the USA after the victory of the Islamic revolution in Iran. The revolution was regarded as the biggest ever defeat for the USA not only for its geo-political reasons but most specifically because what had collapsed in Iran was a whole system of social development intensively imposed by the USA on a number of developing countries.

The theoretical basis of this US approach to Islam has become the notion of the "Islamic revival". At the same time it is maintained that on the world scene Islam could be a link capable of ensuring a certain degree of unity among the nationalist ideologies in the developing countries with a predominantly Muslim population. On this basis, certain US officials conclude that it is possible to work out a common approach to the Muslim countries. Much has been written and said with particular concern in the USA about the "explosion of Islamic neo-fundamentalism". The term is understood in the USA, first of all, as close adherence to the precepts of the *Quran* i.e., proclaiming Muslim institutions unshakable and in opposition to any form of modernisation.

According to American analyses, the growing fundamentalist trend in Islam, which is the reaction of the Islamic clergy and the poorest sections of the population in the Muslim countries to the Western model of "modernisation", is an attempt by the centrists and some conservative sections to get away from it, and find their own "third" way of reshaping the society. The men in Washington consider all these as negative. In addition to some other negative aspects of Islam, US analysts emphasise that Islam, as a religious and political movement, is hampering the development of capitalism in the Eastern countries. Islamic ideas, with emphasis on the "equality" and unity of all Muslims, hold back development and the spread of the individualistic psychology inherent in capitalism. The Islamic dogmas oppose the establishment of an effective credit system, and in general, modern capitalist relations in production.

As the 20th century ends, are the African and Asian countries dominated by the Muslims witnessing any new awakening to the Islamic beliefs and its moral and ethical axioms? Though much has been written about Islamic justice, equality, tolerance and free-will by the scholars of the *Quran* and *Sunna*, it is not yet clear whether the Muslim masses have been positively affected by the framework of Islamic morality.

Genesis of Religious Conflicts

What most exponents of Hindu revivalism in India fail to understand is that the political map of the contemporary Islamic fundamentalism is largely the product of European imperialism. When Europe finally established its political superiority over the Islamic world, it posed threat to its cultural traditions and social institutions in the same manner as it did to other people under colonial bondage, including the Hindus. In the Indian sub-continent, the plight of the Muslims was at its lowest at the turn of the century because the final collapse of the Mughal Empire, and its replacement by the British imperial authority, brought the downfall of the Muslim privileged classes and the *ulema* who performed religious, judicial and administrative functions under the Mughal courts.

This is how a section of the Muslim leadership joined the national mainstream, while another section consisting of feudal aristocracy and obscurantists became the props of the British rule. It also becomes necessary to distinguish between the communal divisions and the special political forms it assumed following the development of the Muslim League and the demand for Pakistan. The so-called "communal" problem, or the question of relations between different religious communities,—Hindus (two-thirds of the population), the Muslims (one-fourth of the population) and other minor religious groupings (about 10 per cent of the population)—had special significance for pre-independent India.

Under certain conditions, the mingling of diverse races or religions in a single country can give rise to acute difficulties, sometimes leading to riots and bloodshed. Orangemen and Catholics in Northern Ireland, Arabs and Jews in Palestine under the Mandate, Slavs and Jews in Tsarist Russia, the so-called "Aryans" and Jews in Nazi Germany; these are familiar issues of the twentieth-century world. Anti-semitism in Europe in the 30's was the sharpest expression of this type of race-religion division and antagonism. Event today racial conflicts are taking place even in the most developed countries.

Under what precise conditions do such types of problems arise? In Palestine before the British Mandate, Arabs and Jews lived peacefully together for centuries. Since the British rule was established, and since the forcible introducttion of Zionist immigration by imperialist armed power with Western finance capital, violent conflicts have arisen. These are at times described as racial or religious conflicts, but in reality are national struggles for independence against invasion and alien domination.

In Tsarist Russia, especially during its decline and eventual fall, pogroms of the Jews blackened the pages of its history, and sickened the conscience of the world. These pogroms were widely attributed to uncontrolled outbreaks of the ignorant and savage Russian masses. Only subsequent publication of secret police records finally proved that the government and the "Black Hundreds" or the hooligan "patriotic" organisation, had a tie-up and that the pogroms were directly inspired, and initiated by the government. The day the Russian people became their own masters, the pogroms completely ceased and in the Union of Soviet Republics most diverse races and religions lived happily together.

In Germany under the Weimar Republic, Germans and Jews lived peacefully together. But under the Nazi Germany, the pogrom regime transferred its old base from Tsarist Russia to Central Europe. Thus, there is no inevitable difficulty for the cohabitation of differing races or religions in a country. The difficulties arise from socio-political conditions, in particular wherever a reactionary regime endeavours to maintain itself against the popular movement. However, these are also the surest signs of the impending downfall of such a regime.

The Indian Scene

Prior to the British rule in India, there were no trace of the type of Hindu-Muslim conflicts seen in later years. There had been wars between states, which might have had Hindu-Muslim antagonism. But Muslim rulers freely employed Hindus in the highest position of their set-ups and vice versa. This traditional character of pre-British India could be traced in the Indian states, where the Simon Report had the occasion to refer to "the comparative absence of communal strife in the Indian states today". What had occasionally been attributed as "communal strife" in certain cases, as in Kashmir in 1931-32, had been a misdescription of an entirely different struggle. In Kashmir, the issue was that of a popular uprising of a four-fifths Muslim population against a ruler who happened to be Hindu; and the British Press was compelled to admit of a "paradoxical position" of "a 'communal rebellion' in which not a single Hindu has been killed" (*Daily Telegraph*, February 8, 1932).

As far back as 1821, a British officer writing under the name of "Carnaticus" in the *Asiatic Review* of May 1821, was declaring that "*Divide et impera* should be the motto of our Indian administration, whether political, civil or military". Lieutenant-Colonel Coke, Commandant of Moradabad, laid down the principle in the middle of the nineteenth century:

> "Our endeavour should be to uphold in full force the separation (for us fortunate) which exists between the different religions and races, not to endeavour to amalgamate them. *Divide et impera* should be the principle of Indian government."

In 1888, Sir John Strachey, a leading authority on India, wrote:

> "The truth plainly is that the existence side by side of these hostile creeds is one of the strong points in our political position in India."[3]

Gandhiji has related how Hume, the joint founder of the Congress, frankly confessed to him that the British Government was "sustained by the policy of Divide and Rule."[4]

In 1910, J. Ramsay MacDonald wrote with reference to the foundation of the Muslim League:

> "The All-India Muslim League was formed on December 30, 1906. The political successes which have rewarded the efforts of the League... have been so single as to give support to a suspicion that sinister influences have been at work, that the Mohammedan leaders were inspired by certain Anglo-Indian officials, and that these officials pulled wires at Simla and in London and out of malice a forethought sowed discord between the Hindu and Mohammedan communities by showing the Mohammedans special favour".[5]

Subsequent evidence has since become available which more than confirms the "suspicion". In the post-war period, particularly after a large number of the Asian and African countries liberated themselves from the colonial rule, the "Muslim Policy" of the West underwant certain basic changes. It is in this period, that the religious revivalist movements became an important political and ideological instrument in the hands of the imperialists to subvert the newly-liberated countries.

Factors of Western Anxiety

A new movement of Afro-Asian solidarity had begun to unfold itself. This new feature of the developing world was illustrated at the Bandung Conference of the Afro-Asian countries on April 18, 1955. As many as 29 Afro-Asian countries attended the conference with as many as 340 delegates from countries totalling 30 million square kilometres in area—about a quarter of the world's land surface—with a population of nearly 1,500 million, about two-thirds of the world population. Jawaharlal Nehru, supported by other heads of government gave a new sense of direction to the Afro-Asian nations at the meet, laying down a basis for unity and solidarity among them.

The need then arose for a new policy of the West, of the American administration in particular, to make "Asians fight Asians". The various military alliances of that time had this as one of their objectives, though they were also directed against the so-called threat of communism from the erstwhile Soviet Union.

All these factors have been at work for quite some time. However, from the second half of the 1970s did Washington begin to show a special interest in Islam. This, to a large measure was caused by the unprecedented energy crisis of 1973-1974. The Muslim countries of West Asia, and North Africa at that time provided as much as 55 per cent of the oil for the capitalist world, and as much as 75 per cent of the oil was exported. Another important factor was that these Muslim countries had built up huge financial reserves from sale of oil, which enabled their ruling classes to exert greater influence on the economy of the entire capitalist world. The USA also took into account the growing political and economic weight of the Muslim oil-producing countries in the non-aligned movement, among the developing countries in general, and in international organisations and the world as a whole.

In January 1979, Zbigniew Brzezinsky, then Assistant to the US President for National Security Affairs, had even instructed the relevant departments to arrange for an intensive study of Islam and its political role in the world, and prepare a detailed report on the situation in a number of Muslim countries *vis-a-vis* their religious movements. Thus in the 1970's and 1980's the problems posed by Islam figured prominently in the activities of the US government, its institutions and scientific circles, and Washington began to integrate the studies as important parts of its foreign policy.

In the mid-sixties, Saudi Arabia initiated a move to set up an Islamic Alliance with a view to uniting all the Islamic countries and sponsored a programme for the revival of orthodox Islam at home and abroad. Simultaneously it accelerated the process of expanding and modernising its armed forces and intelligence in active cooperation with the West. Thus, a new power centre opposed to Nasser's Egypt began to take shape.[6]

This has to be seen in the context of the fact that Nasser had become the hero of the Arab masses, particularly after his involvement in North Yemen's civil war against British imperialism. In West Asia the Saudi monarch hit back at Nasser with the announcement that Saudi Arabia had concluded an arms deal with Britain and America worth 360 million US dollars.[7]

In the early eighties, the Carter Administration decided to establish a joint task force of 50,000 for safeguarding the Gulf oil supplies and to build up the American fifth fleet, operating from the Island of Diego Garcia near Mauritius, in the Indian Ocean. Soviet intervention in Afghanistan and the proclamation of the Carter Doctrine added urgency to the newly-formed force, called Rapid Development Force. Plans were laid to expand it to 300,000 by the mid-1980's, and increased efforts were made to secure American military bases in and around the Gulf.

The Reagan administration went a step beyond Henry Kissinger's public recommendatons: it tried to involve its allies in its military plans for the Gulf. Addressing a conference of military experts in Munich in late February 1981, American Deputy Defence Secretary, Frank Carlucci, asked NATO allies to "station troops in the Gulf". He secured the immediate support of the British Under Secretary for Defence. Early next month, during her visit to Washington, British Prime Minister Margaret Thatcher backed the idea of a multinational RDF. "There is an urgent need for a new defence policy beyond the North Atlantic", she said. "As a loyal ally, Britain will help (the American RDF) to the very maximum of her ability." Her statement coincided with a report that the Reagan administration was seriously considering placing the RDF under its European Command, with its headquarters in Brussels, which is also the headquarters of NATO. A few days later, the US Secretary of Defence publicly called for permanent American military bases in Egypt and Saudi Arabia.

The outbreak of the Iran-Iraq war in September 1980 gave additional urgency to their proposals. Prince Navef, the Saudi Interior Minister, toured the Gulf states later in the year to win support for the plan, and discuss the structure of the proposed Gulf organisation. The third Islamic summit, held under the auspices of the Organisation of the Islamic Conference in Saudi Arabia in late January, 1981 provided a chance for the heads of the six Gulf states to meet. The result was a decision to form the Gulf Cooperation Council. A meeting of the Gulf foreign ministers, held a week later in Riyadh, decided *inter alia* to establish a coordination committee to unify "the military potential of the Gulf region" by recommending ways of rationalising arms procurement, and developing inter-Gulf cooperation in "training and the use of weapons".[8]

These historic developments establish the fact that the so-called resurgence of Islamic revivalism was not an autonomous development. In the past, colonial rulers had used religious revivalism to subjugate the Asian and African people; in the recent years, this instrument is being used to retard the process of modern nation-state building in these countries. That is why some of the leaders of the Muslim revivalist movement have always had moral and material support of the West.

Carter's Adviser on National Security Brezezinski declared during a visit to Islamabad: "We in the United States neither fear nor deplore Islamic resurgence, we see in it a new element of strength and a new contribution to the cause of peace." The sudden US support to Islamic resurgence may appear surprising, particularly in the background of American hostility to Khomeini's revolution in Iran. In the post-cold war period, the US and the West did get upset about the rise of Muslim fundamentalism, particularly when it took anti-West turn, but they also had something to welcome the revival. These two conflicting approaches surface again and again, depending the way Muslim revivalism asserted itself in the global geopolitical situation, especially after the disintegration of the Soviet Union and East European countries.

Muslim revivalist movements had been there in the past too. But the current phase arose when the Muslim countries were confronted by challenge of not only the imperialists, but its domination over their economy. The situation was further compounded by the Western cultural invasion. A significant section of the Muslims, including in India, felt the need to return to Islam. They wanted to unite under a big Islamic confederation, and this movement was called Pan-Islam. However, this Pan-Islamic movement could not gather momentum because every Muslim country was passing through a different stage of development, and because of national characteristics, including traditions, history, culture and ethnicity.

The Indian Trend

In India, for instance, this movement took the form of an anti-British movement, and many of its leaders later played important roles in the anti-imperialist campaigns. Maulana Azad was one of the most eminent leaders of this Pan-Islamic movement. Later, in the 1920's he moved to the ideology of the Indian National Congress even as the revivalists accused him of 'betraying' Islam. There were other streams of Muslims too who joined the national movement, such as Ahrar leaders in Punjab and some leading Ulemas from other parts of the country.

It would be a mistake to attribute that the Ulema or their organisations before or after independence were associated with the Islamic revivalist movement. On the contrary Ulema, in spite of the nature and character of their theological background, disagreed with the revivalists and opposed them. The Ulema have made a contribution second to none in the struggle against British imperialism in India. They have adhered to secularism and democracy in spite of fierce attacks from communal and revivalist parties and groups.

In independent India, Islamic revivalist movement has been represented mainly by the Jamaat-Islami-Hind. The attraction for Islamic revivalism is much greater in a country with Muslim majority than in a country where Muslims are in a minority. That is the reason why the Jamaat-i-Islami could attract greater attention in Pakistan, the Muslim Brotherhood in Egypt and the Islamic revolutionaries of Khomeini in Iran, than in other countries.

The basic premise of Islamic revivalism is to convert the state into an Islamic state; and this appears possible in a country where the majority is of Muslims. This is apparently impossible in a country like India, whose constitutional and political set-up is based on secularism and democracy. Whereas in Pakistan, the Jamaat emphasizes the need to Islamise the state and its laws, in India it confines itself only to purification of the Muslim society and building of a Islamic personality.

Jamaat-i-Islami was born in 1941, almost a year after the famous Pakistan Resolution of the All India Muslim League. The Jamaat was opposed to both the Indian National Congress and the Muslim League. The Congress, according to it, believed in 'one nation', which would mean the absorption of the Muslims into the Hindu nation. The Muslim League, wanted a Muslim national state, which would not as such be an Islamic state. The founder of the Jama'at-i-Islami, Maualana Anul Ala Maududi, was opposed to nationalism based on territory, race, language, colour or economic factors. All the Muslims were one nation, irrespective of country, caste, colour or race, according to him. His 'Islamic nationalism' was different from 'Muslim nationalism' represented by the Muslim League.

Actually, the Muslim League and its leaders had never spelt out what policy Pakistan would adopt. They had used Islam as a slogan to mobilise the Muslims behind the demand for Pakistan. When Pakistan actually came into being, the Muslim League leaders did not know what political system to adopt. The League leadership consisted mainly of feudal landlords, bureaucrats and the urban rich, and they were satisfied with running the country on the British colonial pattern. This was an opportunity for the revivalist Jamaat-i-Islam to jump into the field by claiming that since Pakistan had been achieved in the name of Islam, the Islamic state, as understood by them, must be established.

In India, Muslim revivalists have not been able to create a mass base for themselves so far because of the democratic and secular character of the political system. Nevertheless, the emphasis of the Muslim revivalists on Islam as a "complete code of life" governing all aspects of human life, its unique character and exclusiveness, creates a gulf between the Muslims and other communities. And the activities of Hindu revivalists, their slogans, also reinforce the chasm.

On social problems, Muslim revivalists defend the Muslim personal law. Though in theory they are against the formation of political parties within an Islamic state, in actual practice they participate in political activities to strengthen the Muslim revivalist forces. Their economic outlook being most conservative, the revivalist ideology and programme is hardly relevant to the problems which the Indian Muslims face today. Still, the revivalists keep on nursing the minority consciousness among the Muslims, and their economic backwardness becomes a political instrument in their hands. Thus, Indian secularism cannot be talked about in abstract terms. The genuine grievances of the Muslims, their economic backwardness, their low percentage of representation in the services, the neglect of the Urdu language, protection of their places of worship and above all the growing aggressiveness of Hindu revivalism, all these issues need to be dispassionately examined by all those charged with ensuring secularism in India.

Conclusion

It is naive to believe that all the Muslim countries are today witnessing what is called "Muslim Fundamentalism". Secularisation of politics, political superstructures and the consciousness of a modern nation-state are emerging in all the developing countries, and Muslim-dominated countries are no exception. However, this process has its own variants. Hindu fundamentalists in India are playing up the so-called rise of Muslim fundamentalism for their narrow political gains, forgetting that with globalised politics and economy, and the specific Indian conditions the process of modern nation-state should not be thwarted in the national interest.

Most religious philosophies are being given two diametrically opposite interpretations, and Islam is no exception. On the one hand Islam is being given an orthodox and reactionary interpretation, and on the other a liberal and modern one. Periodically, these are cited as ideological guidelines for action to pull up the believers from socio-economic decline. The first set of interpretations emphasizes in varying degrees, reconstruction, renovation, *tajdid* and adaptation.[9]

The intensity of the Hindu fundamentalism to bring about a synthesis between religion, nationalism and Indian nation-state matches in degree its counterparts in Pakistan. Any synthesis of traditional religion and modern polity, and a blend of religion and science on the intellectual plane, is a formidable challenge, if not an impossible task, for several reasons. First, construction of a viable and dynamic social order requires an adequate command of the modern natural and social sciences and their related methods and techniques of application, in competition with a powerful and fast developing international industrial society. Second, linking the social order and science to a religion with a strong medieval tradition tends to impede original thinking and progress of both science and society, because any idea or practice 'repugnant' to religion is to be shunned and what is repugnant to religion is difficult to define and open only to the arbitrary judgement of the ruling classes and their apologists.[10]

Like other religions, Islamic theology has been interpreted differently by different people. The traditional literature of Islam relates to various historical periods—the pristine period of the Prophet (peace be upon Him) and uprightly-guided Caliphs. The Muslim community of that time was a cohesive fraternity of believers and their Islam was a revolutionary social principle. Later, under the Umayyads and Abbasids, Islam developed as a part of general social formation in the context of a feudal mode of production. All institutions, ideas and theories elaborated during these later periods bear a deep imprint of the feudal epoch.[11]

There are Islamic scholars who do not hesitate to describe Islamic ideology, in its theory and history, in a historical category in the social institutional sense. There are Muslim scholars who have examined Islam in its historical context, though they, underline that in essence, the *Quran* is a 'Book of Action', a declaration of war against all exploiters of the weaker human beings, and against all vested interests.

References

1. K. Subrahmanyam: India's Unity and Security, p. 63 & 64.
2. Journal of Institute of Muslim Minority Affairs, King Abdulazziz University, Jeddah, Vol 1, No. 2.
3. Sir John Strachey, "India", 1888, p. 255.
4. J.T. Sunderland, "India in Bondage", p. 232.
5. J.R. MacDonald, The Awakening of India, 1910, pp. 283-4.
6. Dilip Hero : Inside The Middle East, p. 81 & 82.
7. Ibid: p. 254.
8. Ibid: p. 346, 347, 348.
9. Hassan Gardesi: Pakistan Roots of Dictatorship: p. 354.
10. Ziaul Haque : Pakistan: The Roots of Dictatorship: p. 367.
11. Ibid: p. 368.

IDEOLOGICAL ASPECTS OF CONTEMPORARY SIKH REVIVALISM

NIRMAL SINGH

Religious revivalism is a complex societal phenomena of resurrecting selected parts of historical past, real or imaginary, connected with the founders of the religion, their life works, scriptures and commentaries, traditional heroes and their deeds and symbols which may be potential to mobilise the masses. The past is always seen through the prism of contemporary needs. The present-day context thus is decisive in selecting the specific past to be revived, and consequently, in different phases of revivalism, it is seldom the same past which is attempted to be relived. Even if the scriptures, events, heroes and symbols are apparently the same, newer meanings are read into them. Revivalism necessarily involves revisionism and exigencies, even if return to the fundamentals, the original faith, is cited as the reason. Old institutions are revived and newer ones are foisted in the name of the old. The behavioural orientation of the adherents of the faith in the past and their institutions are projected as the result of being imbued with certain concepts and ideologies. These reinterpreted concepts and ideologies are advanced to motivate contemporary behaviour to uphold the selected religious values and meet the present-day spiritual and temporal needs of the religious community. Paul Brass writes: "It must be stressed, however, that Sikh historians and politicians have been engaged in a process of symbol selection from the events of the past, adopting those that would best support contemporary Sikh self-consciousness and rejecting those which would not."[1] Not only are the selected symbols support the contemporary self-consciousness, but they also effectively alter the course in the direction desired by the revivalist elite. Contemporary Sikh revivalism is no exception to the general characteristics of religious revivalism mentioned above.

The Foundation

It is asserted that Sikhism is a revealed religion. But it cannot be denied that it has also evolved through the preachings of its 10 Gurus and the historicity of the community professing faith in these teachings and swearing by the *Guru Granth Sahib*, serving as the Guru thereafter. The *Granth Sahib* has a collection of hymns sung in praise of the creator by the first five Gurus and the ninth, as also by Farid (a Muslim Sufi), Kabir, Namdev and many other Saints from different parts of India united by no other faith than devotion to God. As the number of the followers grew, a certain institutionalisation was provided by the fifth Guru, who compiled the *Adi Granth*, set up common places of worship and hymn singing and established regular communication and exchange for communitarian life for the Sikhs. *The Granth* and the Gurudwara Harimandir Sahib at Amritsar was the culmination of the process of institutionalisation of the faith.

Yet, all this was continuation of the basic faith founded by Guru Nanak round the key concepts of 'Sabad', 'Nam', 'Guru' and 'Hukum'. Moreover, Guru Arjan Dev, done to death in 1606 by an order of Emperor Jahangir, epitomised non-violent resistance to unjust prosecution. The same value was ingrained in the martyrdom of Guru Tegh Bahadur in 1673, when the Guru agreed to be beheaded on Aurangzeb's orders rather than succumb to forced conversion to Islam. Guru Hargobind, the son of the fifth Guru, established the Akal Takht and the concept of 'Miri-Piri', and extolled the Sikhs to take to arms and arms training to defend their faith. The tenth Guru concretised militancy and the martial tradition through his own example and by carrying on a relentless war against the treachery and tyranny of Hindu princes of the hill region and the representatives of the mighty Moghul Emperor, indulging in religious persecutions. He proclaimed the birth of the Khalsa in 1699 by building an institution of initiation ceremony called *Pahal*. The followers became the Khalsa, volunteering to sacrifice their lives for the faith, acquires the name of Singhs, took a vow to live in accordance with the prescribed code— never to cut their hair, always carry a sword and the three other symbols of having been initiated. In Zafarnama he preached the morality of taking to the sword to uphold the right, destroy sin, evil and tyranny when all other options fail. "Thus, the creed of the Sikhs remained the pacifist one of Nanak and the Gurus, whose writings appear in the holy book, whereas the practice of the Khalsa became the martial tradition of Guru Gobind with their justification in the stirring message of the many lines composed by Gobind."[2]

This brief sketch of the development of Sikhism does explain that the traditions associated with religion are varied, yet constitute a complex whole from which different selections are made by the revivalist elite. The first phase of revivalism started with Banda Bahadur in the face of Moghul repression against the martial traditions, militancy and valour of the Sikhs. Apart from the political aspect of the struggle against religious persecution, the urge for greater state power became part of the Sikh psyche with victories and defeats in various battles. The disintegration of the Moghul Empire and its failure to provide protection against the marauding invaders from the North-West had two consequences for the Sikhs of Punjab. It encouraged some local warlords to aspire for political power and in the process fight against each other; and, secondly, the need was felt for a coordinated force against the receding empire of the Moghuls and also against the new invaders. The fact that both the Moghuls and the invaders were Muslims influenced the character of Sikh revivalism. The '*misl*' period right upto the Maharaja Ranjit Singh's rule, was marked by militancy, reckless valour, sacrifices and an urge for state power. '*Hukumnama*', the edict issued in the name of the Guru and the collective consciousness of the community, '*Sarbat Khalsa*' the periodic gatherings to take collective decisions, and the '*Akal Takht*' the seat of temporal power, were revived and the institutions were made effective. The desecration of the Sikh shrines by the invaders resulted in retaliatory destruction and desecration of mosques by the Sikhs by slaughtering pigs in them or simply looting their treasuries. Such acts have no justification in the Guru traditions or their sacred writings. In fact, the reverse is true. The spread of the catchment area of the faith among the Jats only added to the non-doctrinaire thrust of Sikh revivalism towards more militancy and sacrifice, rather than towards compassion.

Anglo-Sikh Wars

The second phase of Sikh revivalism began with the annexation of Punjab by the British after the defeat of the Sikhs in the Anglo-Sikh War. The pursuit of state power was abandoned, and the martial tradition got reduced to serving the British in their army. The humiliation of defeat in the war was explained away to Dogra 'betrayal' and Maratha 'infidelity'. As part of the deliberate British design, the decline in the fortunes of the Khalsa after the annexation of Punjab was ameliorated by preferential recruitment of the Sikhs in the British India Army, and injecting a feeling of separateness of the Sikhs from the Hindus, both in faith and in social institutions, and a fear of being absorbed by the Hindus.[3]

Symbols emphasising uniqueness and separateness of the Sikhs were resurrected. Hindu revivalism in the form of Arya Samaj in Punjab in the 70's of the last century with its aggressive anti-Sikh tirades, strengthened the feeling among the Sikh elite that Sikh revivalism should centre around (i) loyalty to the British rules, (ii) assertion of separate identity against absorption by Hindus, (iii) primacy of the Khalsa identity, strengthening the institution of *Amrit Prachar* with a view to increasing the numbers and congregations (Darbars) in the presence of the *Granth Sahib,* and (iv) research in Sikh history, spread of modern education among the Sikhs and propagation of Punjabi in Gurmukhi script. Thus, in this period which culminated in the *Singh Sabha* and *Khalsa Dewan* movements, the selected instruments were influenced by the perception of the reviving elite of the historical context. There was greater concern with the issues of religious doctrines and discovery of history and traditional institutions; even the old tradition of militancy was retained. Distancing from the Hindus and loyalty to the British were thought most appropriate. The period lasted till World War I.

The third phase of Sikh revivalism is associated with the Gurudwara movement after the War. The general awakening in the country because of the national movement, the growing disaffection of the Punjab peasantry with the British rule, the government repression to meet the independence movement and the awareness brought to the Sikh peasantry by the soldiers returning home after the war, qualitatively created a new scenario altogether. Sikh revivalism developed round the demand for democratic control over the management of their Gurudwaras, and ending the non-Sikh practices of the corrupt Mahants who ruled the Gurudwaras as their feudal possessions. The British rulers sided with the Mahants with repressive violence, imparting an anti-imperialist character to the Gurudwara movement. This phase of Sikh revivalism was marked by (i) assertion of the community's right to manage its Gurudwaras by democratically elected representatives, (ii) participation of ordinary peasants in the movement, (iii) a broad alliance with the national movement for Independence and consequent toning down of separatism, (iv) non-violent resistance against Government's repression involving renewal of the value of supreme sacrifice exemplified by the martyrdom of the fifth and the ninth Guru and Sahibzadas, and (v) continuation of aspects of the Singh Sabha-Khalsa Diwan movements with emphasis on the Khalsa form, *Amrit Prachar* research in Sikh history, propagation of *Gurbani* and the cause of Punjabi in Gurumukhi script.

The success of the movement to wrench the Gurudwaras free from the British-propped Mahants resulted in the emergence of the Shiromani Gurudwara Prabandhak Committee (SGPC) as a statutory body functioning as the supreme parliament of the Sikhs, and the Akali Dal, the political party representing Sikh communal interests. It also resulted in renewed interest in historic Gurudwaras and a general acclaim for the Sikhs and their faith among non-Sikhs. The original rejection of caste-based disabilities in religious and social affairs propagated by Guru Nanak got a new shot in the arm. With power flowing from the SGPC and its enormous funds and institutional establishments, the Akali Party gained more and more of communal orientation with an eye on political power, so much so that Sikh spokesperson began talking of "inseparability of religion and politics" almost echoing the Muslim League ideology of "Muslims being a separate nation", and started feeling for an exclusive territory for their political operation. In the absence of any area with a Sikh majority, they took the first hesitant steps towards a Sikh sovereign state.[4]

Now comes the fourth phase of the contemporary Sikh revivalism of the 1970's and 1980's. This needs detailed analysis.

Partition and After

The traumatic experience of the partition of India in 1947, with millions of Sikhs—also Hindus—uprooted from their homes in West Pakistan with the loss of lakhs of lives, property and prestige, was no conducive time for any massive Sikh revivalism in the early post-Independence period. The enthusiasm for the new Indian State was not shared equally by those who suffered the most in the communal frenzy let loose in the wake of Pakistan becoming a reality. The confused Sikh masses were driven to a state where eking out a living and rehabilitation efforts left little time or resources for religious revivalism. The self-image of being "God's chosen people" destined to rule was shattered, and replaced by that of a persecuted people from whom not only Nankana Sahib, the birthplace of Guru Nanak, and other Gurudwaras in Pakistan were snatched away, but were also made to run for their lives across the border. Punjabi Hindus, who also suffered a similar fate, could not be painted as the demon. Even the feeble symbolic protest by the Akali representatives to refuse to sign the Indian Constitution in the Constituent

Assembly went almost unnoticed. However, the demand for a separate electorate for the Sikhs or carving out a province within India with Sikh numerical dominance, advanced as Punjabi Sabha, and projecting the punjabi language as a Sikh privilege, were not given up by the communal elite. Gandhi and Nehru were denounced for "going back" on their promises to the Sikhs of a privileged position in Independent India. These, however, did not find a ready response among the Sikh masses: they were content to participate with others to build a new democratic state, peasant productivity through developmental activities like road building, electrification and irrigation facilities and refugee rehabilitation under the state initiative.

The call by the Punjabi Hindu communal leadership during the 1951 and 1961 Census to the Hindus to declare Hindi as their mother tongue, opposition to Gurmukhi on religious grounds and denial of a Punjabi-speaking state by the States Reorganisation Commission in the mid-fiftees with Nehru's concurrence did add grist to the Sikh separatist mill. The Sikh masses were, however, too engulfed in their secular pursuits to pay much attention to these.

In the mid-sixties, planned development along capitalist lines had been deadlocked: having achieved success in building an infrastructure it was unable to bear the burden of the wars with Pakistan and China. There was widespread dissatisfaction with the Congress leadership at the Centre, demonstrated by non-Congress governments being installed in all the North Indian states, and Kerala and Tamilnadu in the South. Prime Minister Nehru had died, and the Congress was not averse to opportunistic alliances even with communalists of different hues. The merger of Pepsu states with Punjab and the separation of the Hindu-majority areas as Haryana and Himachal, created for the first time a state in India with Sikh majority. The delayed formation of a Punjabi state, and with Shastri and Indira Gandhi conceding it as an Akali demand, projected Sikh separatism as a viable plank for Sikh religious revivalism. This found a complementary support in the growth of Hindu separatism in the form of the Jana Sangh. The gains of the 'Green Revolution' ushered in a rich peasantry, mostly Sikhs, in Punjab, seeking greater share in political power and other non-economic matters. This created a class base for Sikh revivalism. Akalis, who had come to power in Punjab along with the Jana Sangh, lost the elections in the post-Bangladesh war and could not reconcile to this. In 1973, the SGPC passed the Anandpur Sahib Resolution which later became the rallying point for the present-day Sikh revivalism. Giani Zail Singh, the Congress Chief Minister of Punjab, in order to appropriate the Akali platform, officially organised a big show of Guru Gobind Singh's relics brought from abroad. These were taken to different Gurudwaras in the state, while roads were built to link these Gurudwaras. This and other state-organised functions gave a big boost to revivalist sentiments amongs the Sikhs. The installation of the Akalis back to power in Punjab in 1977, in alliance with the Hindus communalists after the Emergency, convinced the Sikh masses that competitive politics in order to succeed can legitimately be articulated in the name of separate religious communities. The Akalis in power, however, did not vigorously pursue the Anandpur Sahib Resolution demands. Akali chief Jagdev Singh Talwandi for factional consideration, and Jarnail Singh Bhindrenwale, propped up by Zail Singh and Sanjay Gandhi to keep the Badal Government engrossed to evade punishment for Emergency excesses, queered the pitch for the Akali government by taking an extremist stand. An Akal Takht *Hukumnama*, endorsing an earlier SGPC position, declared the Nirankaris as "renegades" and called for their social boycott by the Sikhs. On April 13, 1974, Bhindrenwale led a procession of his supporters to a gathering of Nirankaris, demanding their dispersal which resulted in the death of 13 Sikhs at the hands of the Nirankaris. Many Nirankaris, including their Guru, were later systematically killed by Bhindrenwale's men. Thus, Bhindrenwale came to be recognised as representing the new phenomenon of Sikh revivalism.

Sikh revivalism of the late 1970's and 1980's was the result of a number of national and international forces impinging upon the field of activity of a number of competing elites among the Sikhs. The revivalist elite, clamouring for a sovereign Sikh state of "Khalistan", indulged in large-scale violence with most sophisticated weapons smuggled from Pakistan, and treated as enemies not only the representatives of the so-called "Brahmin-Bania Hindu Government" in Delhi, but also moderate Akalis and other dissenting Sikhs. This could have been avoided, if only the numerous factors within the revivalist elite and outside it had taken to an alternative course. The Akali leadership formally coopting the Bhindrenwale movement in their *'Dharam-yudh'* SGPC chief Gurcharan Singh Tohra allowing Bhindrenwale to take residence in Akal Takht and collect arms inside the Golden Temple complex and convert it into a varitable headquarters for terrorist activities, and the anti-Hindu and anti-Government tirades could all have been otherwise, had the Akali leadership so wanted. Indira Gandhi then decided upon 'Operation Blue Star' in June 1984 to flush out Bhindrenwale and his supporters from the Akal Takht and the Golden Temple. She was murdered, and about 3000 Sikhs were slaughtered in Delhi as a sequel with the Government leadership merely looking on. If only alternative action had been resorted to by the principal actors.

As Khushwant Singh has noted: 'It is a strange coincidence that about the same time as there was revival of religious fundamentalism in the Islamic world, came the revival of aggressive Hinduism, which, in turn, triggered off revivalism among the Sikhs...With the Sikhs, the challenge did not come from Islam but from Hinduism, and the Sikh revivalist movement dwelt on differences between Sikh traditions and the Hindus.[5] Emphasis was laid in the contemporary Sikh revivalist movement on the primacy of the *Khalsa* form, *Amrit Prachar* and Sikh initiation ceremony, building alternative customs like immersion of ashes of the dead at Kiratpur Sahib instead of at Hardwar as done earlier, pilgrimages to Takhts and other historical Gurudwaras—or even founding of new ones like the mythological Humkunt—*Anand Kara* marriages that differentiates Sikhs from the Hindus, etc. Demands like renaming the Flying Express to Amritsar as "Golden Temple Express" or broadcasting of *Kirtans* from the Golden Temple or the enactment of an All-India Gurudwara Act are expressions of Sikh revivalism in the modern technology-oriented state, so also the proliferation of audio cassettes of *Gurbani* and *Shabad Kirtans*. The demand for declaring Amritsar as a 'holy city', huge '*Bhog*' ceremonies, daily '*Prabhat Pheris*' and processions to celebrate events important in Sikh history are the Sikh response to the demonstrative Hindus religiosity. This aspect of contemporary Sikh revivalism is shared by all revivalist elites.

Numerous concepts and revived institutions are indicative of the new direction. The Akal Takhat, Kesgarh Sahib and Damdama Sahib, all situated in Punjab (Patna Sahib is in Bihar and Hazoor Sahib in Maharashtra) and representing the collective Sikh consciousness, indicate the importance of territorial attachment of revived Sikhsim. Revivalism relies on '*Punjabiat*', for the Punjabi language in Gurmukhi script and 'Indian Punjab' for territorial affinity. Primacy of the Sikhs in Punjab is asserted in two senses: (i) Sikhism is primarily Punjabi and (ii) Punjab is primarily Sikh. New terms—*Hukumnama, Singh Sahiban, Jathedar, Tankhaiya, Sarbat Khalsa, Dharam Yudh, Marjiware, Kharkoo, Shaheed,*

Shamshir, Kar Seva, Raj, etc. are more often in use than *Nam, Krit Gurmukh, Shabad, Sarbat da Bhala, Nimanian da man, Seva* etc. In short, it is militancy, marital spirit and aspiration to leadership and state power, that dominate.

Bhindrenwale's campaign against Nirankaris' alleged 'subversion' of the faith, or the endorsement of the campaign by a *hukumnama* from the Akal Takhat, or the reiteration and resurrection of the 1973 Anandpur Sahib Resolution in 1978 by the Shiromani Akali Dal when it was in power in Punjab, or the *Gurmata* on January 26, 1986 in a *Sarbat Khalsa* calling for "Khalistan" were all connected with one basic question. The role of the Sikh community in State power and the historical role of the Sikh doctrine or mission involving relationship with other religious communities in politics, social institutions and religion. Another question was the management of internal dissent.

The original Anandpur Sahib Resolution was drafted by a committee in which Kapoor Singh, an ex-I.C.S. man, played a dominant role. It's diverse interpretations hovered round the question whether the call was for (i) a polity wherein Sikhs were to enjoy a privileged position and responsibility in the historical fulfilment of the original Sikh mission, or (ii) it was meant as a compendium of Akali demands on behalf of the Punjabis in general and Sikhs in particular. Both the interpretations have been advanced, depending upon the immediate expediency of the power struggle and the targeted audience.

Ideologues like Kapoor Singh have stuck to the position that Sikhism from its very inception was a separate, unique and revealed mission, whose fulfilment and fruition lay in sovereignty of the Khalsa polity. His *Sachi Sakhi*[6] was originally written in 1960. He was dismissed from the Civil Service on charges of misappropriation on funds meant for refugees. Apart from providing justification for his own case, he depicts the history of Sikh thought, institutions and communitarian struggles in his writings, by underlining his central theme of separateness, uniqueness and struggle for political power for the community *(Panth)*. In his interpretation of Sikh history, negative references consistently point to Hinduism, Brahminism and the individual political elite from the Hindu communities. In his tirade to carve out a sovereign space for the Sikhs, he paints with black everything that is Hindu. He also depicts many Muslim feudal rulers as protagonists of heterogenity and pluralism. He whitewashes the repressive colonial British rule, praising the underlying sense of perceived justice. He objects to Bhagat Singh, hanged by the British, being called *Shahid-e-Azam* (Great Martyr). Jinnah, according to him, was committed to the cause of justice, specially to the Sikhs. He eulogises Jinnah's British sense of 'justice', and his justified adherence to the single cause of a sovereign territory for Muslim rule. The author of the Anandpur Sahib Resolution has only pity and contempt for the Akali leaders, for not clasping the hand of friendship and justice extended by the British and the Muslim League supremo at the time of Partition. He describes Dr. Gopal Singh, translator of the *Granth Sahib* in English, as a "despicable character" looking for rewards from Nehru. Gopal Singh is alleged to have betrayed the trust placed on him to carry an Akali proposal to Jinnah during the Cabinet Mission negotiations.

Kapoor Singh's writings shows explicit loyalty to the British rulers. His denial of any continuity between the thoughts of Guru Nanak and the Hindu thought after *Rig Veda*, and emphasis on armed struggle for political supremacy being in line with the Sikh tradition, together with the good words for Jinnah provided ideological props for sanctifying the Khalistan demand, including collusion with Pakistan. He had no good words for the leaders of the freedom movement.

Studies in Sikh History

A number of talented and committed academics, specially Punjabi litterateurs and teachers of English literature, took upon themselves the sacred duty of studying the authentic writings of the Sikh Gurus, semi-historical and poetic narrations about the Guru's lives and the Sikh struggle. Some of them have provided interpretations that justify the extremist position of separateness, commitment to armed struggle and yearning for a sovereign Sikh state and refusal to live as equals in a multilingual society.

Harinder Singh Mehboob's *Sahje Rachiyo Khalsa*[7] is claimed to be the result of decades of reading into Sikh and other religious thought. This to me tooks eight years to write, sources having been reportedly read in the origional. The central idea of the book is the uniqueness (*nyara*) of the Sikh Mission. Even Kapoor Singh has been taken to task for conceding some geneological relationship of Guru Nanak's thoughts with ideas of *Rig Veda*, though Kapoor Singh was careful to write that Hinduism was a post-*Rig Veda* phenomenon. Mehboob has expounded a methodology of history which forecloses any questioning on an empirical-rational basis. Thus, his separatist and violence-oriented interpretation cannot be faulted on factual or logical grounds. In order to understand and interpret any work of religion (and poetry), he says, one cannot but give auxiliary place to empirical facts. The meaning has to be seen in the light of the overarching meaning (purpose) of the work, to avoid superficiality. His outright rejection of empirical-rational methodology of authentication and interpretation by historians leaves him free to first announce the overarching principal meaning, and then enter into a discoursive process to prove the same meaning. He uses both normal logic and facts to support his interpretation, but the final (unquestionable) argument is the extralogical rejection of the counterview. Facts not in consonance with the fundamental meaning have no relevance. His rejection of Karam Singh's evidence for '*vasah sudi teej*' as Guru Nanak's birthday and his acceptance and rejection of parts of the *Dasam Granth* or of Bhai Gurdas' writings and other *Sakhis* follow his methodology of convenience.

According to him, the Sikh Mission was built round the overarching meaning: full light of the Eternal, unity with His Creations, with human beings carrying out His command etc. All revelations and religions before Guru Nanak were partial; and nothing that may come later can ever approach the fullness of Nanak's Mission. Uniqueness and fullness have been declared, and the reader has to take it from Mehboob. His comparative study of all other religions has shown, he writes, that *Khalsa* was "perfection personified" and that all revelations have been completed. One can notice a soft corner in him for Islam; although its concept of *Jehad* etc. was imperfect, it was better than other religions. The book relentlessly points at Hindu Brahminism as evil incanrate, with redemption laying in the *Khalsa*, and the *Khalsa Raj* taking to the sword. The chapter carries the heading *Shamshir* (sword) and it is quite explicit. Dipankar Gupta writes that militancy, martial tradition and struggle for state power as the only part of Sikh tradition, has no resonance in Guru Nanak's teachings. He quotes Kahn Singh Nabha's *Guru Sabad Ratnakar Mahanakos* to list the three essential articles of faith of the Sikhs as (i) mystical union with *Waheguru*, (ii) all men are brothers irrespective of caste, race or belief in "*Sarbat da bhala*', and (iii) to accept *Nanak Panthis*, irrespective of the external form.[8] Has Mehboob not warded off such rational-empirical methodology, and come to counter conclusions ?

Guru Nanak had Bala and Mardana as his two constant companions in his travels. The latter, a Muslim, has been picked up by Mehboob as the one who spread the Guru's message and Mission, whereas the former was merely a travel companion. He also absolves Sheikh Ahmed Nakshabandis' involvement in Guru Arjun Dev's persecution, and declares Jahangir's guilt as of secondary level, the real culprit being Chandu Shah. Thus, the author has attempted to rewrite history to build Sikh revivalism on an anti-Brahmin, anti-Hindu base, removing traces of anti-Muslim separatism as non-historical. It is difficult to assess whether the *'Khalistani'* political strategy has influenced Mehboob's interpretation, or vice versa. While he writes of hazy heroes of history like Ram, Krishna, Buddha or Christ failing to produce full vision, Islam from Omar to Ali does provide colour of the sword to pure nature, and incompletely-achieved higher consciousness (*uchchi surah*) and eternal victory *(Akal fateh)*

Many popular articles and learned papers by some other academics fall under the same category. One can read Gurbhagat Singh[9] or Gurdarshan Singh Dhillon[10], Gurbhagat Singh's writings form a series of propositions, though couched in moderate terminology, and are repeated piecemeal by many outside the intellectual circle. He starts with the proposition that development of the Punjabi language is a must for cultural consciousness to flurish, and urges changes in keeping with the changing times. A conscious understanding of the uniqueness of the Punjabi culture in the context of the prevailing Indian and world culture is emphasised. Certain bodily and mental characteristics of Punjabi culture are recounted as leadership urge, initiative for life, courage for just distribution of life's goods, flare for enjoyment, premium on friendship, etc. But, then, these stable traits acquired through long historical experiences become in Gurbhagat Singh's writings traits of commitment to the sword, armed struggle and violence to usher in justice, punishment for the unjust, fearlessness before death, willingness to die a martyr on the battlefield, etc.—all acquired through the Sikh struggles led by the Gurus against the Delhi Sultanate and Brahminical priesthood. Specific Punjabi traits become traits of only the warriors; and the carriers of these traits from Punjab become the Sikhs, to the exclusion of the Hindus and the Muslims. The non-Sikhs, through their alleged propensity to betray, are declared to have lost the benefits of these Punjabi traits.

What starts as a normal discourse on awareness, intellectual persuits, language, culture, class analyses and the role of productive systems soon degenerates into Sikhs alone being true Punjabis. His is one-sided reading of Sikh history and traditions, centering round wars, violence and aspiration for monopoly over state power. Only those who follow the Gurus and accept *Guru Granth Sahib* as a document of political revolution, are said to have the self-awareness of the Punjabi culture. The Punjabis are the Sikhs produced by the '*bani*' and Sikh Youth organisations are lauded for the violence practised in persuit of the egalitarian and "higher" socio-political model of the Sikh Gurus as the "poetry of history". He demands that the avant-garde Punjabis be recognised as a nationality with Punjab as their territory. Thus, we have a version of Sikh revivalism wedded to war and violence, fighting for political and cultural hegemony in the territory of Punjab to the exclusion of, or reduced status for, non-Sikh Punjabis. Talking of heterological model, the hegemony of the Hindus and the Centre is denounced, but homogenisation of the Punjabi culture is attempted by one-sided emphasis on violence as a Sikh tradition, and granting only secondary status to non-Sikhs. The Central Government is denounced as "capitalist", then as "anti-Punjabi" and finally as "Hindu Brahmin"!

Dhillon writes: "This (separate Sikh) identity was the creation of an ideology, new institutions and of a 400-year old tradition of martyrdom and unparalled sacrifice". He refutes the contention that the separate Sikh identity was solely a British creation: it was also the creation of repeated assertions that "Sikhs were first in everything", a myth Dhillon supports. According to him the first rebellion against the British was the Namdhari Sikh rebellion, so also the Ghadar rebellion, and that three-fourths of the sacrifices against the British were made by Sikhs. He forgets that the very Namdharis, Ghadarites and even Shahid Bhagat Singh were denounced as unworthy of being accepted as role models by the Sikh orthodox identity fixers.

Another treatise in the same vein is Sukhbir Singh's *Tej Dharak Guru Khalsa Panth Darshanik Such*[11] with foreword by S.G.P.C. chief Tohra and Punjabi University *Sri Guru Granth Sahib* Study Deptt. chairman. Tohra underlines the uniqueness and separateness of the *Khalsa* and brings out his thrust as "for this *quom*, politics is under religion; and any attack on Sikh policies, therefore, is considered as an attack on Akal Takht". The author, in the chapter on "Religion and Politics" has advanced many cogent ideas but has attributed all wrongs to the Brahmins and the Khatris with redemption coming only through the *Khalsa Quom*, despite its smallness in number. He rationalises the actions taken by a minority of the people by saying that they are the "selected ones" to deliver the rest. The text, otherwise, is a good expression of some of the strong points of Sikh value orientation, derecognition of *varna* and caste hereditary privileges, moral and ethical upliftment of man being within human capabilities without the "brokerage" by the priests. It does not situate ritualism, elitism and priesthood as brokers between the creator and the humanity in the practices of the Sikh community. It also creates as ideological cushion for those who see all the noble values in the Sikh form, and evil incarnate in the Hindus. The right to self-appoint themselves as executioners of the eternal *(Akal)* Will is only a logical step, according to Sukhbir Singh. He justifies the call *'Khalsa ji ka Bolbala'*.

Violence Through Gurmatas

Writings by militant outfits propagating violence on one pretext or another include the so-called *Gurmatas* (Resolutions passed in meetings convened as *Sarbat Khalsa*) and an open letter to the President of India by (or in the name of) Sukha and Jinda. These first state the Gurus' writings, mission and history of the Sikhs more or less on the same lines as discussed earlier. The Khalsa Mission was ordained to dispel the prevailing wrong ideas about the relationship between the creator and His creation, to undo the human institutions and agencies which downgrade human capabilities to build a moral world, and to strive for political power to enforce this moral order. The writings also try to show by an appraisal of Sikh history the continued armed struggle against Brahmin-Hindu hegemony, emphasising the spirit and practice of martyrdom. Violent means to seize power is claimed to be derived from Sikh precepts and history. All those who advocate negotiations, compromise or even participation in the democratic processes under the Indian Constitution are denounced as "traitors" who should be eliminated, as also those suspected to be aiding or abeting the enemy i.e. Indian government. Brahmin-Bania Hindus are denounced as the main enemy, alongwith the communists and the mainline Akalis.

The *'Gurmata'* adopted by *Sarbat Khalsa* at Akal Takht on January 26, 1986 published by Bhai Mohkam Singh can be an appropriate example. "To destroy the voice of the spirit, Sikhs were under fatal attack from many sides", it said. A call was given to destroy the malicious with the double sword—secular and religious—unfolded by Guru Har Gobind after Guru Arjan Dev's martyrdom. The challenge to "Delhi Darbar" was epitomised by the erection of the Akal Takht to establish "Khalsa Raj" on the earth, eliminating falsehood, fraud and deception, and supporting truth, kindness, knowledge, love etc. The resolution recalled the glorious traditions connected with the Akal Takht and *Sarbat Khalsa* in later Sikh history to overcome crises. The state that came into existence in 1947 in India, it declared, was 'Brahmin-Bania Raj', with some greedy Sikh collaborators. It alleged that the communalist Bania of Punjab disowned the Punjabi language, and supported by Sikh Congressmen like Darbara Singh, pleaded to keep Sikh areas out of Punjab, and water and energy resources in Delhi's control. The Punjab Arya Samaj and the Banias betrayed Punjab by supporting the Army attack on the Golden Temple and Bhindrenwale.

It called for a total social boycott of all such anti-Sikh and anti-Punjab elements. It condemned the "Delhi Darbar", the Chandigarh Government and Rajiv Gandhi for patronising "Goondaism" and spreading anti-Sikh lies. It named Mrs. Indira Gandhi, General Vaidya and many Government leaders, officers and generals, and all known communist leaders of Punjab, as 'guilty men' for the attack on Harmandir Sahib, as also many journalists and media agencies for their alleged Brahmin-Bania, communalistic and anti-Sikh tendencies. Amrinder Singh, the Akali leader, was mentioned as 'enemy within'. The *Gurumata* declared the present status of the Sikhs as slavery and named its own men to preside over the SGPC and all the Sikh Takhts. The document betrays absolute intolerance to all dissent within the Sikh community.

The Sukha-Jinda letter was a masterpiece of draftsmanship and presented the militants' ideological stance in most explicit manner. The "sacred violence" it preached was connected with examples from historical and current international scenes, but under the overarching religious exegency of Sikh tradition. "Defiance of the judicial processes of the 'enemy' (Indian State) is absolute and the company of the most-revered Gurus and former martyrs is the 'true realism'." Commitment to violence for ushering in the just and pure regime of the *Khalsa* was proclaimed, as was the determination to 'settle score' with enemies like Zail Singh and other traitors in the manner punishment already meted out to Indira Gandhi and Gen Vaidya. The document wanted the militant outfits purified of errors, and avoid harm to the innocents, but justified such harm when attacking the targets makes it unavoidable. Thus, the attack on Gen Vaidya's wife was rationalised. The militants were answerable for errors only in the next world. The *Tribune* editor was terrorised into publishing the letter in full, in both Punjabi and English editions of the paper on July 27, 1990.

A number of Sikh intellectuals have brought our publications in the name of the Punjab Human Rights Organisation, the Punjab Sikh Vakil Council, the Punjab Study Circles, the Sikh Ex-Servicemen and Intellectual Forum—all dishing out the same ideology but not avowedly transgressing legalities. A quote from a pamphlet: "The Betrayal of the Sikh's" by ex-Servicemen is illustrative. It says; 'Sikhs are a separate nation and are different from Hindus as white from black. Sikhs suspect that Hindus want to assimilate them in their fold and destroy their separate identity. Nehru and Patel had declared Sikhs as 'criminal tribes' and issued instructions to District Officers to shoot them dead so that they, the Sikhs recognise the political realities as to who are the masters and who are the slaves". In terms of ideological stance, there seems to be no difference: only open violence and defiance of law was not preached.

Other Versions

A number of liberal, democratic and left intellectuals are also engaged in the study of Sikh traditions and history[12]. They have tried to advocate ideologies against violence and secessionism without much success for two reasons. First, being liberal and democratic, they produced pluralist statements and not homogenous hegemony; and secondly, they did not control legel structures like the SGPC and religious institutions like the Gurudwaras and the '*granthies*' to propagate their views at the popular level.

When Prof. Kishan Singh and Jagjit Singh study Sikh history writings of the Gurus and their life stories, they situate them in the then prevailing social context. Many a time they apply scientific analysis which does not easily result in texts with one-sided conclusions like "total opposition" to anything Hindu. Thus, their findings do not evoke mass emotional acceptance. Both of them are careful to point out that even 'Hindu' or 'Brahmin" are terms to describe certain historical situations which do not apply to the modern scientific world. Such scientific analyses cannot easily lend themselves to be used as ideologies, inspite of (or, perhaps, because of) the complex truths contained in them.

As Sarhadi[13] had said: "Ahluwalia has very analytically probed into reasons that promoted the industrial and corporate self-expression of the Sikhs, which originally was only religious, linguistic and cultural in chara-cter, but later turned political. The Sikhs have always been an integral part of Indianism...The Sikhs have always pursued their corporate identity, but this has never led itself to, and cannot lead to, separation and secessionism". Ahluwalia writes: "In Sikhism, the relationship between religion and politics, between religious authority and secular polity, cannot be organised in terms of unity-separation dictotomy. It is of the nature of neither monistic unity nor simplistic separation...Unity in separation...Differentiated unity". Too subtle for popular consumption. He wrote that recent *Sarbat Khalsa* congregations with accent on numerical mass-mobilisation have tended to result in lumpenisation of the *Sarbat Khalsa* tradition. His demand for working out a proper relationship between modern democratic institutions and emphasis on the essentially 'pluralist character' of Nehruite conception of secularism was unacceptable to simplistic hegemonising separatists. Moreover, there are few institutions to back or popularise liberal pluralistic secularism. The placing of modern individual protest within the religious corporate self-expression adds to the complexity of the situation, and scientific discourse makes its ideological conversion all the more problematic, which demands either "for-or-against" position.

Khushwant Singh[14] emphasises the *'Sarbat da bhala'* ideal. He writes that just as Sikhism is itself an edifice of Hindu bricks and Muslim mortars, so also the Sikh's holiest shrine bears witness to its Hindu-Muslim geneology and the most elaborate of all celebrations (at the Golden Temple) is of the Hindu festival of Diwali (Sikhs celebrate all Hindu festivals). According to him, Guru Nanak's study of the two religions showed him that there was much in common between Islam and Hinduism, and therefore, he was acknowledged by both Hindus and Muslims to be a devinely inspired prophet. Khushwant's history told him that the English rewarded the Sikhs for supporting them in 1857 by granting them large estates in the new colonies and making special provisions for their recruitment in the army and the police. His statement that the seeds of Sikh separateness were sown by the Sikh's own gurus when they gave them their own temples, their own scriptures, their distinct appearance, the common casteless name, Singh, and the British nurtured the feeling of separation across the ideological divide. Though he supported, with Master Tara Singh, the 'Punjabi Suba' demand, but he writes that the linguistic argument was only a sugar-coating for what was essentially a Sikh majority state. He has condemned Bhindrenwale for preaching hatred and violence; for him it was most important to see that Sikh Gurudwaras retained their sanctity and are not allowed to become sanctuaries for fugitives from justice or platforms for politicians; and there can be no compromise with the principle that where there is a criminal, the police has the right to enter. He is most vociferous in condemning '*Operation Blue Star*' and letting guity men of the 1984 massacre of Sikhs in Delhi go unpunished. But authors like Khushwant Singh, who take a stand in accordance with their conscience or reading of history, do not produce usable ideology for militant Sikh revivalism, or any other simplistic image of Sikhism.

In a review of Jaspal Singh's thesis, *Raj da Sikh Sankalp*, K.S. Duggal, a wellknown Punjabi litterateur (*Hindustan Times*, Sept. 9, 1990) writes that there was no doubt that the Sikhs were conceived as a political, entity. He also says that there was no reference to '*Sikh Raj*' in the Holy Granth, but only in Sikh historical writings. The Sikh concept was not of a theocratic state with sacred laws and order of priesthood. The establishment of the *Khalsa Panth* by Guru Gobind Singh was not designed to constitute a communal outfit: instead it was all pervading, a religious, social and political brotherhood, giving opportunity to the downtrodden and the oppressed to find their own expression. The concept of State, according to Duggal, was marrying the Divine Truth with human good. He sees no reason in converting the Sikh shrines into a refuge for the outlaw and an arsenal for unlicensed arms. Earlier in an article[15] he had cited Puran Singh to support the position that the Sikh is in no sense an alien: he is born in India, he has the glorious heritage of Indian culture, he cannot be without Prahlad and Mira: Guru Gobind Singh sent his Sikhs to Benaras to study Sanskrit. He is said to have translated *Krishna Lila* himself. It was mischievous to suggest that we are not Hindus, and not equally Muslim. It is mischievous to multiply the points of difference with the Hindus, which are not fundamental."

These assorted references are only to indicate that there exists a lot of democratic, secular, liberal and scientific literature on Sikh history and traditions running counter to the separatist ideology of contemporary

Sikh revivalism. The politico-social context today seems to be unfriendly to these liberal-democratic or scientific self-images of the Sikhs and Sikhism. So much so that historian G.S. Grewal who, writing about *"The making of Self-image before Independence"* has said that it would be naive to look upon the Sikh community as a monolythic whole in its entire history. It was possible, in fact, to identify more than one self-image among the members at a single point of time. In his comprehensive review, *"Guru Nanak's Mission in Western Scholarship"*,[16] he quotes approvingly only those authors who talk of 'nation of Sikhs' not to imply similarities so much as to understand his (Nanak's) distinction, 'from the Origin of the Nation to the Battle of Sutlej, 'predominance of Jats in the Sikh Panth', a third course which sould supersede both (Hinduism and Islam)', 'formation of a new nationality', 'retain distinct identity' etc. The image of a separate, unique nationality comes out of this historical review of Western scholarship and, incidentally, it dovetails the dominant ideology of contemporary Sikh revivalism. There is room for alternative reviews, but the chances for the liberal-democratic, secular and scientific view to succeed is contingent upon similar tendencies in other religious communities joining together to combat separatism of all colours.

References

1. Paul R. Brass, *Language, Religion and Politics in North India* London, Cambridge University 1974 p. 280.
2. Khushwant Singh *My Bleeding Punjab, New Delhi UPBSD* 1992. p. 29.
3. Lord Dalhousie, who annexed the Sikh Kingdom in a note observed. Their great Guru Gobind sought to abolish caste and in a great degree succeeded. They are, however, gradually relapsing into Hinduism and even when they continue as Sikhs they are yearly Hindoofied more and more, so much so, that Sir George Clerk (Governor of Bombay 1847-48) has said that in 50 years, the seat of Sikhs would have disappeared". It was Dalhousie who laid down that the privileges meant for the Sikhs, should only go to the Khalsa. Khushwant Singh *'My Bleeding Punjab'* New Delhi, UPBSD 1992: pp 93. Also see Richard G Ford's *Icons of Punjab Culture in making;* Berkeley Univ. Press 1989: pp. 48, 87 & 141.
4. This has reference to Master Tara Singh's proposal in 1946 to carve out a province of Central Punjab, where the population would be equally divided between Muslism, Hindus and Sikhs, and the reactions to India's partition by asking "Muslims got Pakistan, Hindus got Hindustan, and what did the Sikh get?"
5. Kushwant Singh, p. 40.
6. Kapoor Singh: *Sachi Sakhi* (in Punjabi) Raj Rup Prakashan, Jalandhar 1972.

7. Harinder Singh Mehboob, *Sahje Rachiya Khalsa* (in Punjabi) Ashok Book Depot, Gardiwala, Hoshiarpur 1988. The author was the controversial winner of Sahitya Academy Award for his poetic collection which included an abusive poem on Indira Gandhi.
8. Depankar Gupta 'Sikh Militancy Today' *Seminar* 387, Nov. 1991.
9. Gurbhagat Singh: Punjab problem of Raj Promise (in Punjabi) *Punjabi Kaumi Masla* (ed), Malinder Singh Mali, Lok Getet Prakashan, Sirhind, 1989.
   Punjabi da Vikas: Sabhyacharate Darshani Prasang, *Tribune*, 8.2.86.
   Bharati Rajtantar cha Punjabi de Kaumi ate Bhasai Vikas di Sambhavana, *Tribune* 25.12.87.
   Quest for heterological model, *Tribune* 26.7.89.
   Punjabi ate Anterashtri bhaichara, *Tribune*, 3.9.89.
   Kendra di Punjab niti, Rashtri atamghat, *Tribune* 23.6.90.
10. Gurdarshan Singh Dillon. 'Perspective on Sikh Identity' *Indian Express*, May 21 & 23, 1991.
11. Gurdeepak Prakashan, Patiala, 1986.
12. Prof. Kishan Singh *Gurwan da Sach*, Sodh Prakashan, New Delhi 1970. Jagjit Singh: *"Sikh Inqlab"*, Lok Geet Prakashan, Sirhind 1987 Jasbir Singh Ahluwalia, *Sikhism Today; The crises within and without*, Guru Gobind Singh Foundation, Chandigarh 1987.
13. Introduction in Ahluwala's: *Sikhism Today*.
14. My Bleeding Punjab.
15. K.S. Duggal: Sikhs and the Secular Traditions' in Indian Unity and Security: Challenges, *Patriot*, New Delhi, 1985.
16. Presented in Indian Institute of Advanced Studies, Shimla, 1991.

SIKH REVIVALISM IN INDIA

PREM SINGH

The turmoil in Punjab starting with the Nirankari-Bhindrenwale clash in Amritsar on April 13, 1978, is an example of how religious revivalism can serve as a crucial factor in promoting regional instability. For more than a decade this border State has remained disturbed. Thousands of innocent lives have been lost, and business and economic development suffered. Aided and abetted by imperialists, and with logistics support and weapons given by the I.S.I. of Pakistan, the terrorists were able to use the Gurdwaras as sanctuaries and proclaim Khalistan as the aim of the Sikh Panth. The danger to India's integrity became very real because of the deep feeling of alienation among the Sikh masses, and also because the separatists at one time were able to establish a near-complete sway over the Sikh religious and political bodies. In some of the Western countries, notably the USA, U.K. and Canada where Sikhs live in sizeable numbers, organisations came up which proclaimed that in Punjab the 'Sikh nation' was fighting a 'war of liberation' which would not stop till a "sovereign Khalistan" was carved out of India. Some politicians of these countries also openly associated themselves with the separatist platforms, providing moral and material support to those engaged in splitting the country apart.

The bloody conflict has left the Punjabi society deeply fractured. But the elimination of the terrorist groups by the security forces has restored a semblance of peace, and the people once again are able to assert their commitment to secularism and patriotism. However, the scars of this unfortunate period shall take a long time to heal. One hopes that the lessons of this dark chapter in Punjab's history shall seep down in the minds of all concerned. It is worth considering why and how Sikh religious revivalism could be an input into the complex Punjab scenario.

Bhindrenwale Factor

The Punjab conflict was the consequence essentially of certain socio-economic developments leading to the assertion of new forces in the political arena, and the aggravation of contradictions over the control of resources and administration of the State. The crisis reached a climax with the induction of terrorism organised under the inspiration and guidance of Sant Jarnail Singh Bhindrenwale. Bhindrenwale, to begin with, was an obscure religious preacher of a lesser known seminary, the Damdami Taksal. But significantly, without the Bhindrenwale factor the Punjab crisis would have remained within manageable limits, and the need for the drastic measures, which had to be taken ultimately to eliminate the threat to regional stability, would not have arisen.

Though accentuated through violence, the Punjab conflict had its roots in the specific nature of the growth of its economy since the 1960's. This fact is vital as although terrorism has been contained, the political tussle remaines acute and the separatist voices continue to be heard. The new economic clout of the upper strata of the rich peasantry, whose leading representatives were in the process of becoming industrialists, found inadequate reflection in the State's political structure; and this cleavage formed the crux of the succeeding complex developments. This conflict could be seen in many other parts of the country where comparable economic processes had been made. But what gave the developments the unusual turn in Punjab was the particular demography of the contending forces. On the one side were the entrenched forces of bourgeois development of a mixed Hindu-Sikh complexion sailing under the banner of secularism, unity and integrity of the country, and on the other the upper strata of the beneficiaries of the 'Green Revolution', of exclusive Sikh complexion, relying on a communal identity and believing in the theory of inseparability of politics from religion, harbouring dreams of separatism and patronising terrorism, due at times to the fear of the gun.

Of special attention was the fact that this phase of religious revival among the Sikhs did not start with Bhindrenwale, but was already latently manifest. Among the many forms this revival wave found expression in were the construction of new Gurdwaras and extension and renovation of the old and historical ones, holding of *'Kirtans'* by 'Sants' wherein thousands of devotees flocked and campaigns of *'Amrit Parchar'*. Most of these activities were spontaneous, or at best due to local initiatives. Among the notable dates of Sikh religious resurgence of the times was the inauguration of the Guru Gobind Singh Marg, wherein the procession was led by the then Chief Minister of Punjab, Giani Zail Singh.

Resurgence was particularly visible in connection with the traditional religious festivals and other commemoration days associated with the Sikh history—*Gurpurbs*' i.e. the birthdays of the first and the tenth Guru, days of martyrdom of the fifth and the ninth Guru, of martyrdom of the Sahibzadas, the younger sons of the tenth Guru, and *Baisakhi*, the day of the birth of the *Khalsa* and so on.

Prosperity in Punjab and elsewhere was accompanied by definite turn towards religion, more in its form than content. This was true of the entire Punjabi society with the number of '*Jagratas*' and "*Akhand Paths*" on the increase. Even two or three decades back, these and other forms of worship were undertaken or organised by a relatively smaller number of people. Another kind of development of an apparently opposite nature was also taking place simultaneously. Except for a brief period when a certain code of conduct was thrust upon the people on the point of gun by Bhindrenwale's men, the Punjabi scene was marked by a big shift towards ostentatious life styles: large marriage parties, huge dowries, excessive drinking etc. All such negation of social refrom, became the hallmark of Punajb. Even as '*Amrit Parchar*', wearing of unshorn hair, flowing beards and yellow turbans, were on the rise, cutting of hair and trimming of beards also were on the increase among the younger generation Sikhs, even of the traditional and orthodox families.

Bhindrenwale's crusade initially was in response to these contradictory developments. The *nouveau riche* among the Sikhs praised him because in the name of justice he appeared demanding political power for his community. On the other hand, the rural Sikh youth who had been thrown out of the pail of the agrarian economy and were rendered aimless, flocked to him because he offered them hope, and later weapons, money and the intoxication of power, all in the name of the glory of the *Sikh Panth*.

The Shiromani Gurdwara Prabandhak Committee (SGPC), the Sikh body duly constituted under the law, over the years had become the embodiment of the Akali Dal's theory of inseparability of politics from religion. In the wake of the Sikh revivalist wave, the SGPC's relationship with the Damdami Taksal, the new powerful claimant to Sikh religious leadership, had become uneasy. Nevertheless, the SGPC did play a significant role in supplementing the political campaigns both of the Akali Dal and that of the Khalistanis. Through its well-established organisational structure of *'Parcharaks'* and local Gurdwara Committees and with vast financial resources at its command, the SGPC served to further enhance the destabilising role of Sikh revivalism in its later manifestation. It established a Relief Fund for the victims of the November, 1984 riots and a 'Shaheedi Fund' for the families of those who fell 'martyr in the Sikh struggle', giving Rs. 10,000 to each family of the 'martyr'. It engaged defence lawyers to fight the court cases of terrorists and of those Sikh soldiers who had deserted their regiments following Operation Blue Star. On every occasion during the Akali agitations, the SGPC used its authority to summon religious congregations, hold *Akhand Paths* and other forms of religious activity to extend full religious backing to purely political demands of the Akali Dal, including, in particular, the Anandpur Sahib Resolution. Simultaneously, the SGPC continued with its traditional activities like instituting public schools for Sikh children, financing its, higher educational institutions arranging to impart martial training to Sikh youth and organising *'Amrit Parchar'* and *Kirtan Darbar'* congregations to propagate the Sikh faith. Twice a weak *'Amrit parchar'* is held at the Akal Takht, besides special campaigns for the purpose.

Revival Conditions

Every phase of revival within a religious community bears the stamp of its times, and in fact, it arises as a reaction to specific social and historical conditions. But what distinguished the latest phase of Sikh revivalism is that in this case the compelling circusmstances like the threat of conversion to antoher religion or the danger of what the British historians had called "replapse into Hinduism", did not exist. And further, the revivalist sentiment could be used without any effective opposition either from any section of the Sikh masses or of the Sikh intelligentsia to subserve the political aims of the Akali Dal, as also of the separatists to varying degrees. Here, a comparison with the earlier movements of Sikh revivalism may not be out of place. If we take the period after the British annexation of Punjab in 1849, we find that the Nirankari movement started with the rejection of idol worship and its leader Baba Dayal asking the Sikhs to repose faith in the only God, the Nirankar, the formless, rejecting such of the religious practices as forbidden by the Sikh Gurus but still then prevalent due to the dominant influence of Brahmin priesthood among the Punjabis. The Namdhari, or the Kuka movement, advocated abolition of the caste system and opposed practices like Sati, child-marriage, infanticide, meat-eating and drinking. This movement, while seeking to revive the best traditions of Sikhism, was also profoundly socio-reformist in its aims at the same time. It was too much for the British when Guru Ram Singh even called upon his followers to boycott the postal, railway and educational services as well as the law courts and foreign cloth. The brutal supression of the movement by the colonial authorities is history now. However, its reformist potential more than one and a quarter century later, has not yet been completely exhausted.

The *Singh Sabhas* proliferated from 1873 onwards and continued to be a dominant factor in Sikh theology and in the socio-religious life of the community till the Akali movement came to occupy the centre stage in Sikh affairs in the early 1920's. Despite British patronage and their communal approach, at least partly these '*Sabhas*' were a factor in spreading literacy, English education, and Sikh literary and journalistic activities. The Akali movement arose with the banner of reform in the running of the Gurudwaras. The British opposition to the same made it an integral part of the country's freedom movement. Later, however, the Akali Dal drifted towards communalism. The pertinent issue is that in the past, Sikh religious revivalism was a reaction to certain acutely felt social, religious or spiritual needs and was articulated by dedicated reformers with vision about the uplift of their community. The latest phase, however, can at best be called service of the community, building of Gurdwaras and the '*Amrit Parchar*'. In the earlier revivalist movements, the then Sikh intelligentsia, though small in number was deeply involved and played an important role. In the case of the *Singh Sabha* movement, which was controlled by the loyalists, the educated were in the forefront. Again, during the Akali movement which was anti-imperialist, the leadership was in the hands of the intelligentsia. But the leadership of the latest movement was in the hands of those whose calim to the knowledge of Sikh theology and tradition was not acceptable to a large body of the Sikh intelligentsia. Moreover, because of its narrow base and limited objectives, the movement was easily hijacked for political purposes. It was no surprise, therefore, that those who managed to grab its banner had no qualms of conscience in using the strategy of planned murders and in propagating hatred and violence something unheard of in the annals of Sikh revivalism.

The Sikh masses were attracted to Bhindrenwale not because they thought him to be better exponent of *Gurbani* or that he had perfromed any notable service for the community, but because he, with his band of armed rustics, personified a defiance of the State, and because some well-known dignitaries in authority paid obeisance to him. In his discourses he gave a distorted version of Sikh tradition and history. But he was able to get away with it all because he was able to build an atmosphere of terror to stiffle all debate. In order to defend wearing of weapons, he recalled during his lectures that the 10th Guru loved weapons and he, as his "true son", would not be acceptable to him without the weapons on! Of course, he never told his audience that the same Guru had ordained that the sword could be used only as a "last resort".

In the context of revivalism it will be relevant to briefly examine a few theories and concepts which have gained currency in the recent past, and which have been put to use, apparently, quite effectively by separatists of various hue to reinforce their respective political claims. The central idea of these concepts was sharply expressed by Paul R. Brass, Professor of Political and South Asian Studies at the University of Washington. According to him:

> "During the past century, the Sikhs of Punjab have developed from a distinctive sect, a dispersed minority intermixed among the much larger Hindu and Muslim communities, into a subjectively self-conscious nationability, occupying a position of political dominance into a compact territorial unit created by their political efforts,"[1]

Variations of this concept are to be found in the writings of Sikh scholars, political commentators and others. This issue was raised at the International Seminar in New Delhi in January 1992 on Sikhism and Inter-Religious dialogue organised by the Guru Gobind Singh Foundation of Chandigarh.

> "Sikhism has, in the recent years become self-conscious for the first time in its history after the Guru period.... Contemporary Sikhism is becoming intensely aware of its ethno-religious, enthno-social, ethno-cultural and ethno-political identity and corporate personality".[2]

"Subjectively self-conscious nationality and awareness about "ethno-political identity" are the two sides of the same coin. It needs to be noted that the concept of a "Sikh nation" emodied in all the three versions of the Anandpur Sahib Resolution is the starting point of Sikh separatism. though the Sikh leaders have been using the term '*Qaum*' for their community, its translation into 'nation' leads to ambiguity, and quite expectedly is interpreted to mean the basis for a nation-state of Sikhs which also is the meaning attached to it by the separatically inclined Akali leaders. How the British colonial authorities prdmoted the concept of "Sikh nation" for their own purposes is well-known. The 1911 Memorandum of David Petrie, the Director of British Intelligence, has often been quoted in this regard. Those scholars who see in the recent developments the assertion of the idea of a Sikh nationalily are in a way carrying on the legacy of our former rulers.

Destabilishing the newly-developing countries form an integral part of the policy of U.S. imperialism. During the cold war, ethnic and religious identities were encouraged as part of this grand strategy, and all means, including research institutes, were deployed for the purpose. The end of the cold war has not signified the end of civil strife in the developing countries. On the other hand, more and more countries are falling prey to the forces of disintegration. There is no reason to believe that with the Soviet Union out of its way, the American imperialism's drive to completely dominate the world shall be any the less vigorous.

SIKH RELIGIOUS REVIVALISM AND ITS PHASES

V.D. CHOPRA

Sikh religious revivalism is a recent phenomenon, and in a way can be traced to the British policy of divide and rule. By the end of the last century, long after Punjab had been annexed by the British rulers, two significant developments had taken place which had a direct bearing on the Sikhs, particularly on the Sikh peasantry. After the fall of the Sikh Kingdom, the perceived peaceful spell which followed produced among Sikh minds an attitude of wariness and of superstitious rituals, which, forbidden by the gurus had earlier been reduced as adjuncts of the regal pomp and ceremony during the days of the Sikh power. The true teachings of the gurus which had supplied Sikhism its potent principle of reform and regeneration, were obscured by this rising tide of conservatism. The Sikh religion began to lose its characterisitic vigour, and its votaries were fast relapsing into beliefs and dogmas from which the gurus' teachings had extricated them to begin with. Absorption into ceremonial Hinduism seemed the course inevitably set for them.

After the 1857 uprising, however, a marked change took place in the British policy and the character of the British rule. The British policy shifted its centre to increasingly winning the support of reaction in India against the masses, and the system of annexation of the native Indian states into British India was abruptly given up. The then remaining princes were zealously preserved and installed as puppet rulers, but declared as "allied sovereign rulers". And the Sikh princely rulers of Punjab became the favourite of the British masters.

British Inject Animosity

The growing impoverishment and desperation of the peasantry as a result of the cumulative process of British capitalist penetration were beginning to assume serious dimensions by the second half of the 19th century. The peasantry of Punjab, particularly the Sikh peasantry, too was hit hard in this cruel process. Thus, by the last quarter of the 19the century, conditions had started growing ripe for the beginning of the Indian national movement and the Sikh masses were naturally drawn into it. However, in the midst of these changes, two distinct and opposing trends began to develop among the Sikhs—the pro-imperialist and the anti-imperialist. These diverse trends came again and again into conflict with each other, giving Sikh politics and its institutions a new dimension.

Prior to the British rule, there was no trace of any Hindu-Sikh conflict. Communal strife was, thus, a special product of the British rule, in particular of the last phase of its rule, or of the declining period of imperialism. It has nothing to do with the teachings of the Sikh gurus; although certain social forces and some individuals do even today play the game of their British mentors.

Punjab, especially the central districts of the erstwhile united Punjab, is the sacred ground for the Sikhs because every inch of this land is associated with some important event or another in the lives of their gurus or other martyrs of the community. The entire Sikhism movement turns round what may be called the "Gurdwara-cum-Sacred Book axle. To the devotees of the Sikh religion, the 'Gurdwara' is more than a mere place of worship and the '*Granth Sahib*' much more than a book of spiritual guidance. Both are interwoven with the social and spiritual life of the people and the growth of Sikh religion over the centuries. To the Sikhs, *Guru Granth Sahib* represents the body and soul of the lives and teachings of the gurus, while the gurdwaras are not only the embodiment of the struggles of the Sikhs but they are totally integrated with the day-to-day social and religious lives of the entire community.

Control Over Gurdwaras

After the death of Maharaja Ranjit Singh, the *mahants* of the gurdwaras had become negligent in their duties. After the annexation of Punjab by the British rulers, these *mahants* and *sadhus*, incharge of various gurdwaras, began to flout the guidance of the Sikh *sangat* and became hereditary masters of the sacred shrines. Gradually, even the essence of Sikhism stood diluted and the wearing of the beard and the turban remained the only distinctive marks of the keepers of the religious seats. The gurdwaras became dens of corruption and vice which follow in the wake of unaccounted for and unearned wealth.[1] The *mahants* assumed an arrogant attitude towards the disorganised and powerless *sangats* and began to look upon the shrines as their personal property. Idol worship was not only tolerated but encouraged in some of these shrines to turn them into additional sources of income from the orthodox Hindus. Even the most important gurdwaras were not free from corruption and debauchery in direct defiance of the principles preached by the Sikh Gospel.[2]

Two other significant developments took place during this period.

When canal irrigation was introduced in Punjab, the incomes of the gurdwaras from land increased enormously. The office of the priest became one of great prestige and power. Some of the priests openly revolted against Guru Gobind Singh's tradition of democratic control; they denied Sikhism and asserted that the gurdwaras were '*Udasi*' places of worship. Hindu idols were placed in several gurdwaras alongwith the *Granth Sahib*, even as anger mounted among the devotees of the Sikh religion. The British, on the ruse that 'peace was threatened', assumed control of the four most important Sikh shrines at Amritsar, Anandpur, Patna and Nanded (in Hyderabad). In the others, numbering 260, the *mahants* were allowed to be in power.

At many places, members of the *sangats* tried to gain control of the gurdwaras, filing suits against the *mahants* who, being rich and resourceful, were able to delay justice through prolonged legal proceedings and confound those who dared question their rights. In 1914, the agitation for the control of the gurdwaras took the shape of an anti-government movement. The government, busy in extending its new capital, had acquired portions of the land of Rakabganj Gurdwara in New Delhi. When it started pulling down the walls of the gurdwara itself, there was great commotion among the Sikhs. But for the outbreak of World War I the agitation would certainly have turned violent and unmanageable.

After the war, the agitation was resumed all over Punjab: a body called the Sikhs League was formed in 1920, and a Gurmukhi paper called the *Akali* was started.

The Congress lent full support to this movement. At a meeting in October 1920, which was attended by Mahatma Gandhi, a resolution was passed by the Sikh League to non-cooperate with the government. Though the Rakabgunj dispute was settled peacefully, the Sikhs all over India began occupying gurdwaras on their own. Some of the *mahants* agreed to democratic control and the Shiromani Gurdwara Prabandhak Committee (SGPC) was formed to administer these shrines. But in 1921, the government, sensing that these important institutions were passing under the control of the nationalists, encouraged the *mahants* to resist the forcible occupation of the gurdwaras. In Tarn Taran, a group of Sikh leaders who had gone to dicuss the handing over of the gurdwara to the SGPC was assaulted. Two of them were killed and 17 others were injured. Immediately following this, 130 worshippers were massacred at the hands of the *mahant* of Nankana Sahib, the birth-place of Guru Nanak. The government tried to protect the *mahant*, but public opinion became militant. Gandhiji visited the shrine and the government retreated by handing over the gurdwara to a committee of seven. In 1921, the British authorities tried to gain control of the Golden Temple by seizing the keys. This again was foiled by ddetermined public resistance. During the agitation to prevent the nominee of the government from entering the Golden Temple, Master Tara Singh came into prominence for the first time. He was one of the three leaders who were subsequently arrested.

From the end of the last century, the British had tried to manage the affairs of the Sikh shrines directly by appointing managers of the gurdwaras and arbitrating in disputes by fixing the share of the *mahants*. Even while the control of the chief shrines of the Sikhs such as the Golden Temple, the Akal Takht, Tarn Taran Sahib, Baba Atal etc. continued to remain in the hands of the government, most other Sikh sacred places with incomes of lakhs of rupees remained in the possession of the *mahants*, who always acted as stooges of the British authorities. Some *mahants* had even been made honorary magistrates, *darbaris*, title-holders, nominated members of municipalities and notified areas, etc. Most of them being unmarried and having large revenues at their disposal without any accountability, naturally squandered the wealth in unworthy pursuits and activities.

The Akali Movements

In keeping with the teachings of the Sikh gurus, people from the lower castes and Harijans were freely allowed entry into the Sikh religious shrines, including the Golden Temple, and offer prayers. Later, however, this privilege was gradually withdrawn or curtailed. The *mahants* had fixed certain hours when the poorest strata of the population could go to the Sikh shrines: even during these hours, the *Karah Parshad* offered to the *Guru Granth Sahib* was not accepted if it had been touched by them. These low caste men, therefore, had to engage the services of a man of a higher caste to carry it into the temple.

The Akalis were determined to ensure that the sanctity of the Sikh shrines was restored and its affairs conducted by the *sangat*—the congregation—in line with the original teachings of Guru Gobind singh. With this began the struggle for the liberation of the gurdwaras.

The year 1919 saw a wave of mass unrest throughout India, and Punjab was no exception. The movement assumed the undeniable character of an organised revolt against the British Raj.[3] What shocked the British rulers most was the extraordinary fraternisation among the Hindus, Muslims and the Sikhs. It was in this situation that the Congress at Nagpur in December, 1920 declared that the attainment of *Swaraj* was its new objective. This decision gave a new direction to the national movement and had a tremendous impact on the masses in Punjab, particularly the Sikh masses. However, the growing national consciousness among the Sikhs found its immediate expression in their peaceful struggle for the democratisation of the management of the gurdwaras. "Just as the rising sun awakens the people from sleep, in a like manner preparations for *Swaraj* have raised the Sikhs from their slumber. That is why they have demanded religious freedom as the first step towards the attainment of their objective", declared Jathedar Bhai Karter Singh at Nankana Sahib when Gandhiji, Maulana Shaukat Ali and Dr. S.D. Kitchlew visited that shrine consequent upon the mass killing of the Sikhs by the *mahant* and his goons. The struggle for the liberation of gurdwaras from the clutches of the stooges of British imperialism now merged with the struggle for "libe-ration of the bigger Gurdwara, that is India"!

There was hardly any significant Congress leader who did not visit Punjab in those days to give moral and material support to the Akalis in their peaceful struggle for democratic control of the gurdwaras.

The Akali movement of the early twenties was essentially anti-imperialist in character, though its form was obviously religious. That the Akali movement evoked keen interest in Gandhiji further confirms this conclusion, because he too was trying to build a national wave by bringing about some sort of a synthesis among the various religions. However, an important matter to note in this connection was that next to the Sikh feudal aristocracy, the closest allies of the British rulers were the Sikh religious preachers and the *mahants* of the gurdwaras. As mentioned earlier, the British rulers gave *Jagirs* to Sikh landlords, while allowing priests of some of the historical gurdwaras at Amritsar, Anandpur and Tarn Taran to retain a large portion of their endowments.[4]

Any sociological survey of the Gurdwara Reform Movement would reveal that it was confined mainly among the middle and lower strata of the rural Sikh peasantry and the Sikh intelligentsia.[5] It is also noteworthy that Jat landowners were most active throughout the agitation.

In the midst of this Akali movement, a terrorist group emerged, particularly after the Sikh killings in Nankana Sahib. This group was called the Babbar Akalis. The Gurdwara Act of 1925 was the achievement of this broadbased movement.

Within the Akali ranks, three distinct trends emerged. Some elements constituted the core of the orthodox Akalis: others joined the Congress and some came over to the communist movement. However, it was the Akali Dal in the main which started projecting itself as the spokesman of the Sikhs as a religious minority.

Between 1925 and 1939, the main areas of Akali activities concerned the struggle to control the SGPC and voice the political demands of the Sikhs for a share in political power as a religious minority. Later, as a party it did not launch any movement to articulate the demands of the Sikh peasantry, though its followers did join the national freedom struggle and participated in agitations for some specific demands of the peasantry, such as reduction in land revenue and '*abiana*' water rates.

The struggle for the control of the SGPC is undoubtedly the dynamic part of Akali politics, influencing Sikh politics as the most decisive matter in Punjab. Neither the Congress nor the left—both the CPI and the CPI(M)—has ever successfully challenged the Akali Dal in Punjab on the political or ideological plane. In this sense the Akali Dal has always held a key position in Punjab politics, though its mass influence has always been out of proportion to its real strength.

In the first few years after the formaton of the SGPC, which is an elected body on the basis of adult franchise of the Sikh population in Punjab, its control was exercised by Baba Kharak Singh's group. Later, it passed into the hands of Master Tara Singh. His group started calling itself the Akali Party, while the Kharak Singh group assumed the name of the Central Akali Dal. That the Akali Party had the strongest political influence amongst the Sikhs has to be acknowledged from the fact that in 1947 four out of the five Sikh members returned to the Constituent Assembly were Akalis. However, the popularity of the Akalis did not mean then—as it also does not mean even now—that it was a united organisation. Within the Akali party, groups existed round Master Tara Singh, Giani Kartar Singh and Isher Singh Majhali. Master Tara Singh was acknowledged as the "undisputed leader" till he maintained neutrality between the other two groups. These groups, in their turn accepted his leadership only as long as the Master enjoyed the support of the rich individuals like Sardar Baldev Singh (former Defence Minister) and Sardar Ujjal Singh.

Concept of 'Sikh State'

The heavy overtones of communalism that politics of all brands show in Punjab today is the result of three decades of narrow opportunism practised by many of its leaders. The Akali Dal did not begin as a communal organisation; it started as a movement for social reforms and gathered strength when the sturdy Sikh peasantry of Punjab attained political awareness and began to lend its full support to it. A second wave of nationalist awakening swept through Punjab, especially among the Sikhs, after World War I, even as the Indian national movement assumed a mass character. Like the Khilafat movement among the Muslims, the Akali movement spread among the Sikhs—religious in form but essentially anti-imperialist in content.

By 1925-26, two opposite developments emerged within the movement—a left nationalist trend consisting of nationalist Sikhs and communists and the other of pro-imperialist elements mainly centering around landlords and urban traders. In the late thirties, the opportunist group within the Akali party took a sharp turn away from nationalism. On the eve of the 1937 elections, the Akali leadership arrived at an understanding with the pro-imperialist Sunder Singh Majithia group, and in the post-election period, it made desperate efforts to join the Punjab ministry. When World War II broke out and the Congress decided not to cooperate in the war effort, Master Tara Singh chose a different course and called upon 10 lakh Sikhs to join the British India army. This opportunism led to the Shaukat Hyat Khan-Bladev Singh pact and the Akalis joined the Unionist ministry. In North-West Frontier Province (NWFP) the Akalis joined the Muslim League ministry. Within a decade of its formation, the Akali movement had thus shed most of its progressive and democratic character and had come to be dominated by separatism and communalism. The Muslim League slogan for the partition of the country made the Akalis sectarian and communal more than ever. When the Cripps Mission came to Indian in 1942, the Akalis demanded that an "Azad Punjab" state be created simultaneously with Pakistan and Hindustan. In this "Azad Punjab", the Akalis visualised that the population of Hindus would be 40 per cent, Muslims 40 percent and Sikhs the rest of 20 per cent. Subsequently, the concept of "Azad Punjab" was developed into a "Sikh State" in 1945 by Giani Kartar Singh, then Master Tara Singh's chief lieutenant in the Akali Dal. The Akalis fought the 1946 elections on the slogan of a "Sikh State" and won 23 seats. They joined both the central and the provincial governments as Panthic leaders.

Tara Singh *Vs.* Sant Fateh Singh

After Independence, the Akalis joined the Congress, but just before the first general elections, broke away under the leadership of Giani Kartar Singh. In the elections, out of the 57 seats they contested, having substantial proportion of Sikh votes, the Akalis could win only 12 seats. This defeat was a great setback to the Akali prestige, but soon after when the Akalis won 110 out of 132 seats in the SGPC election, it was like a shot in the arm. Basking under this morale-booster, the Akalis launched an agitation demanding Punjabi Suba. Even as a large number of Akalis were arrested, Master Tara Singh made use of the opportunity to bargain with the Congress from a position of strength. A Congress-Akali compromise was reached in 1956 on the eve of the second general elections: the Akalis agreed to give up the slogan of a "Punjabi Suba", and in return the Congress offered what has come to be known as the "Regional Formula". Master Tara Singh, hankering for recognition as the sole spokesman of the Sikhs, however, was never satisfied with the formula. He expressed his dissatisfaction over distribution of tickets, and went to the extent of opposing every Sikh candidate who was not his nominee but had been put up by the Congress.

During the next decade, between 1955 and 1965, an intense struggle ensued among the Akalis, both for the control of the SGPC and the Akali Dal. A series of agitations were organised in this period from within the precincts of the Golden Temple. In these manoeuvres Master Tara Singh took a hawkish stand, while Sant Fateh Singh maintained a relatively moderate posture. Sant Fateh Singh, who had risen to prominence from an obscure religious preacher in Ganganagar district of Rajasthan to a redoubtable Akali leader, managed to ease out Master Tara Singh from Akali politics. A desperate Master Tara Singh now started demanding a "Sikh homeland" with complete autonomy. Since this demand had isolated the Akali Dal from the people of the state, including a large section of the Sikhs. Sant Fateh Singh decided that a purely communal demand would not get him the support of the Punjabi people. He, therefore, decided to press the demand for reorganisation of Punjab on the linguistic basis.

Linguistic Reorganisation

Late one night in January 1961, the Master, enfeebled by 18 days of fast and seven months' detention in the Dharmashala jail told the Sant that it was "a terrible *Dharamyudh*". The Sant replied, "No Masterji, we have conducted it as a struggle for the language". This was the beginning of a clash between two powerful currents in Akali politics—a clash which became sharper and sharper in the subsequent years. It culminated in an open split in the Akali Dal and Sant Fateh Singh captured both the SGPC and the Akali Dal.

Thrice within five years between 1960 and 1965, the Sant had threatened self-immolation after shutting himself up within the precincts of the Golden Temple, the highest Sikh religious seat. On all the three occasions, the threat had something to do with the demand for the "Punjabi Suba". But it has to be admitted that in all these agitations, the Akali Dal and its followers had remained peaceful.

Another significant fact which needs to be mentioned here is that in 1965 Sant Fateh Singh had announced that he would undertake a fast-unto-death from September 10, and in case he survived the first 15 days, he would set himself on fire at the Akal Takht, inside the Golden Temple complex. But he put off his fast when Indo-Pak hostilities broke out. In fact, the Akali Dal under his leadership actively participated in the defence of the country and the Sikh peasantry in the border districts stood like a rock behind the Indian armed forces.

Soon after the hostilities were over, the then Union Home Minister G.L. Nanda appointed a parliamentary committee headed by the Speaker, Hukam Singh, to go into the question of linguistic reorganisation of the state. This committee broadly recommended that Punjab should be reorganised on a linguistic basis, and that the boundaries should be those of the "regions", mentioned in the scheme of 1956. The Congress working Committee then passed a resolution that a "Punjabi-speaking State be carved out of the existing Punjab State", and the Union government appointed a boundary commission to demarcate the boundaries of the State. The Union Government accepted in substance the recommendations of the boundary commission, with the modification that Kharar tehsil should be bifurcated, a part of it going to Punjab, and Chandigarh be made a Union Territory in which was to be located the Capital of both the new states of Punjab and Haryana.

Sant Fateh Singh did not accept the 1961 Census as the basis for demarcation of the boundaries of the two regions, but appeared to be satisfied with the reorganisation of the state, and went out of his way to press that the disputed points should be settled through negotiations. In an interview he said on July 26, 1966. "I am satisfied with its form". In reply to another question, he emphasised: "Peaceful negotiations are the only method to my mind" to settle all disputes, Later in London, according to an agency report, he said on September 18, that he was "satisfied with the decision of the Government of India on the creation of a Punjabi Suba and hoped (that) the minor boundary questions would be settled amicably."

During this period many of his lieutenants hinted that the Sant would enter into an electoral alliance with the Congress for the next general election. He himself whenever he spoke of the elections, mentioned alliances with "other parties, including the Congress."

The reorganisation of the State in 1966 on a linguistic basis was primarily the result of pressures from the Akali Dal. But in the given circumstances, historically and politically, communalism and language had got inextricably mixed. Even after the reorganisation, just as before it, the demand for the merger of additional Punjabi speaking areas continued unabated. The only difference was that earlier it was rooted in the communal notion of political deprivation, while later the main thrust was the communal notion of economic discrimination. The peculiar demographic composition of the newly carved state of Punjab, coupled with 'green revolution', gave a distinct tongue to the assertion of various communal groups in politics.

This peculiar demographic composition is evident from the 1971 Census, according to which Sikhs form 60.22 per cent of the total population of Punjab and Hindus 37.54 per cent; whereas according to the 1951 and 1961 Census in composite Punjab, the Hindus constituted 62.3 per cent and 63.7 per cent of the population, respectively.[6] The demographic composition indicates that Sikhs are largely concentrated in the rural areas, except in Hoshiarpur, and Hindus in the urban areas.

Experiments in Power Sharing

Nevertheless, after the trifurcation of Punjab and creation of a Punjabi-speaking state, a process of secularisation of Akali politics within the framework of anti-Congressism began, though it turned out to be only a brief phase. Between 1967 and 1971, the Akali Dal was able to form three coalition governments with the help of the Jana Sangh. Three main factors were responsible for this new 'secular orientation' of the Akali Dal.

Notwithstanding the fact that in the reorganised Punjab, the Sikh constituted the majority population, the Akali leadership through experience had come to the conclusion that it could not come to power on its won. Though the Akali leaders pretended—and continued to do so till the other day, in fact, they do so even today—they knew it more than anybody else that they did not enjoy the support of the entire Sikh community in the state. The social base of the Akali Dal despite expansion, was confined to a section of land-owning Jats and urban Sikh trading community. As a matter of fact, both the Congress and the two Communist parties continue to retain their influence among a large section of the Sikh peasantry.

According to a survey, the proportion of Jat Sikhs to the total Sikh population roughly varies between 35 per cent and 66 per cent in different districts. In Patiala, Sangrur, Kapurthala, Hoshiarpur, Faridkot and Amritsar, more than 50 per cent of the Sikhs are Jats. The other Sikh castes are Ramgarhias, Mazhabi and Khatri (Bhapa) Sikhs.[7] The total votes secured by the Akali Dal in 1977 was 31.43 per cent, the percentage of Sikh votes polled by the Akali Dal has usually varied between 30 and 43 per cent.

There were, thus, two options open for the Akali Dal to gain political power in the existing democratic set-up. They had to align themselves with the Congress or with the Jana Sangh, and later on with the Janata Party. So far they had chosen the second course, though there have always been influential persons in the party wanting to come to long-term understanding with the Congress. A section of Akali leadership has been striving to come to a political understanding with the Congress on the condition that the Akali Dal rules the State, and gets some share in power at the Centre.

When the Akali Dal was in power in the state in 1977, it shared power with the Janata Party at the Centre, and the inner conflicts in the Dal remained within manageable limits. The Akali Dal leadership was able to deal with many a serious internal challenges with dexterity and confidence. One such challenge was during the Akali-Nirankari clash in April 1978 which signalled emergence of a new fundamentalist force. Soon followed the formation in August of a militant Sikh youth organisation named Dal Khalsa which was committed to the achievement of an "Independent Sovereign Sikh Nation". Still, the rulling Akali leadership was able to withstand with assurance the pressures by this militant group led by Sant Jarnail Singh Bhindrenwale as is evident from the 1979 SGPC elections in which the 32 candidates supported by Sant Bhindrenwale lost.

Emerge Bhindrenwale

Nevertheless, between 1979 and 1984, particularly after the Akali agitation over sharing of river water which came to be known as the 'Nehar Roko Morcha", three power centres developed within the Akali movement—one led by Sant Bhindrenwale, the other by SGPC president Gurcharan Singh Tohra and the third by former Chief Minister Parkash Singh Badal. In this triangulav power-struggle Sant Bhindrenwale became the most decisive factor mainly because Jathedar Tohra who controlled the SGPC oscillated between the moderates and the fundamentalists, to the advantage of the latter. The potential for forcing the Akali Dal towards an extremist, fundamentalist direction was already there, irrespective of the fact whether or not a section of the Congress leadership provided a cushion to Dal Khalsa and Sant Bhindrenwale. The Akali Dal itself provided the ideological base for it and the internal struggle for power created conditions for this group to consolidate itself. The emergence of the breakaway groups of Jathedar Jagdev Singh Talwandi and Sukhjinder Singh further compounded the situation because they took to separate agitations on pronounced extremist lines. Against the backgrounds of Dal Khalsa's violent activities, including political murders, the mainline Akali Dal led by the moderate Sant Harchand Singh Longowal was pressurised to fall in line.

Domination by Extremists

In retrospect, it can be said after 10 years of experience that any negotiated settlement with the dominant section of the Akali leaders on issues like Chandigarh, sharing of river waters and territorial adjustments would have been impossible so long as the extremists and fundamentalists dominated the political scene and controlled the Golden Temple complex.

In the eighties, particularly after the moderate Akalis lost their political relevance and the leadership of even the fundamentalists passed into the hands of terrorists, the entire complexion of the Sikh revivalist movement changed. "Operation Blue Star", in the Golden Temple, assassination of Prime Minister Indira Gandhi, the rising trend of killings by the terrorists both in Punjab and, other parts of India and above all, overt and covert support to the terrorists by Pakistan, brought about a radical change in the consciousness of the common Sikh masses. While the injury to the Sikh psyche is still dominant, the cleavage between the Hindus and the Sikhs continues to persist, though there is evidence of a downward trend. The law and order situation in Punjab has begun to improve after the formation of the popular Congress government in 1993. But it will be naive to believe that the Sikh religious revivalism has lost its mass base.

An interesting question about all movements, particularly terrorist movements, is what type of deflections do these movements experience in their aims and objectives as they pass from the mobilisation stage to the phase of institutionalisation. It has been observed that most movements take off with a relatively popular and broadbased purpose, but suffer subsequent deviations in their aims in the interest of the elitist strata of the society. Thus, there is always a big gap between what was originally intended by a movement and what it subsequently obtained. The Sikh religious revivalist movement too is passing through such conflicting pressures, though the alienation of the Sikh massess from the national mainstream has begun to weaken through their own bitter experience. The outstanding feature of the current Sikh psyche is that its revulsion against violence, terrorism and interference of Pakistan have begun to assert; yet the process of its fusion with the Indian nation-state has yet to gain sufficient momentum.

References

1. Ruchi Ram Sahni: *Struggle for Reform in Sikh Shrines* (edited by Dr. Ganda Singh): "Sikh Ithas Research Board. p. 6.
2. Ibid, PP. 9-19.
3. Sir Valentine Chirol, *India*, 1926, p. 207.
4. Extracts from the Administration Report: Punjab 1851-52 G.W. Leitner as quoted by Joginder Singh in his article in *Punjab Journal of Politics*, July-December 1983, p. 3.
5. Gobinder Singh. "The Gurdwara Reform Movement", *Punjab Journal of Politics*, July-December 1963, P. 64.
6. Pramod Kumar and others, *Punjab Crisis Context and Trends*, Chandigarh, 1984, p. 49.
7. Parmod Kumar & others, *Punjab Crisis Context and Trends*, Chandigarh, 1984, p. 50.

PAK ELECTIONS 1993 AND ISLAMIC FUNDAMENTALISM

KALIM BAHADUR

The elections held on 6 and 9 October, 1993 have atleast set at rest one widespread belief that the people of Pakistan—as distinct from its leadership—are rooting for an Islamic State and Islamisation, as was being clained by the leading fundamentalist party, the Jamaat-i-Islami. During the 11 years of General Zia's rule, this propaganda had also received state support. In the very first speech after deposing Prime Minister Zulfikar Ali Bhutto in July 1977, Gen. Zia had said that Pakistan was created in the name of Islam and would survive for the sake of Islam. For the past 46 years, the fundamentalists had been demanding in chorus an Islamic state in Pakistan. But in the 1993 election, most of the fundamentalist parties were defeated, and the electorate voted for a liberal and progressive social system displaying no tilt towards any of the Ulama parties.

A brief analysis of the strategies and problems of the Islamic fundamentalist parties during the elections gives an insight into the implications of the rout of these parties. Basically, there are three major Islamic fundamentalist parties in Pakistan. They are the Jamaat-e-Islami of Pakistan (JI), the Jamiat-e-Ulama-e-Islam (JUI), and Jamaiat-e-Ulama-e-Pakistan (JUP). The Jamaat-e-Islami was the fundamentalist party founded by Maulana Abul Ala Maududi in the forties, and opposed both the Congress and the Muslim League in pre independence India. The JUP was part of Jamiat-e-Ulama-e-Hind which constituted itself in Pakistan as the Jamiat-e-Ulama-e-Pakistan. And the JUI was the breakway faction of Jamiat-e-Ulama-e-Hind formed by the pro-Muslim League Ulama in the mid-forties. In Pakistan, the JUI and the JUP broadly comprise the Deobandi and Barelvi Ulama. Both these parties are faction-ridden, and have split several time since 1947. During the 1993 elections, the three parties adopted a deliberate policy of distancing themselves from the mainstream political parties and contest the elections on their own. They could not form a united front of all the Islamic groups, and could only form three distinct alliances consisting of two or more of the Islamic groups. Because of sharp sectarian and ideological differences they, could not come together.

Three Islamic Fronts

The main Islamic front, called the Pakistan Islamic Front (PIF), comprised the Jamaat-e-Islami, some Jamaat sympathisers and some retired army officers. For all practical purposes, the PIF was the Jamaat-i-Islami under a new name with a very different style of politics as against its earlier puritanical image. The Jamaat had been influenced by the Algerian fundamentalist party and projected its Amir, Qazi Husain Ahmed, rather than its ideology and programme. Under the Qazi, the Jamaat had chosen a more pragmatic approach to politics with populist slogans and even music with songs rhyming with controversial Indian film songs. This turnaround in the Jamaat's posture was not liked by a section of the party's members and sympathisers, and led to gross dissidence within the organisation.

The other Islamic front comprised the JUI of Maulana Fazlur Rahman and JUP of Maulana Shah Ahmed Noorani and was called Islamic Jamhoori Ittihad (IJM). Both the parties are significant religio-political forces in their own right. The alliance also represented electoral cooperation between the two important groups of Ulama of the Deobandi and Barelvi schools. The JUI under the leadership of the late Mufti Mehmood had secured a number of seats in the NWFP and had formed the government in coalition with the Awami National Party of Khan Abdul Wali Khan in the early seventies. Later, the JUI under Mufti Mehmood's son, Maulana Fazlur Rahman, had taken a persistent anti-Zia stand. The JUI, therefore, had notable performance during the 1988 and 1990 elections. The JUP under Maulana Noorani had a very strong electoral base in Karachi in the seventies. Maulana Noorani had also taken an anti-Zia line and in the process his JUP had been split. The rise of the Muhajir Qawmi Movement (MQM) displaced the JUP in Karachi and urban Sindh and routed it during the 1988 and 1990 elections.

The third Islamic front, called the Muttahida Deeni Mahaz (MDM), comprised one faction of the JUI led by Samiul Haq and Sipah-e-Sahaba, a militant Sunni group. The latter group is mainly centred in Jhang where it is known for its anti-Shia activities.

The PIF which had put up 103 candidates for the National Assembly, could only win three seats. The chief of the party Qazi Husain Ahmed had contested two seats, but had lost in both. Other leaders of the Jamaat-e-

Islami also suffered humiliating defeats. The claim of the PIF to emerge as the "third force" thus remained unrealized. The other Islamic fronts did no better. The IJM got four seats in the National Assembly, whereas the MDM got only two. Thus, the total tally of the three Islamic fronts could not reach even double digits. The PIF had boasted to cut into the vote bank of the Pakistan Muslim League (Nawaz). This also did not happen; on the contrary it transpired that the Jamaat voters had shifted to the PML(N) and in most constituencies where the Jamaat candidate was pitted against the PML(N), the former got very low percentage of votes.

Attraction of Fundamentalism

But has the election resolved the problem of fundamentalism in Pakistan? The power of the ideas of fundamentalism should not be underestimated. But then what is fundamentalism? What are the factors that make it attractive to the general mass of people ?

Fundamentalism, in its recent phase, has caught the attention of the Western leaders after the famous Ramzan Arab-Israeli war in 1973 when many Arab countries imposed a ban on the supply of oil to pro-Israeli Western countries. However, fundamentalism in Islam is often dated to the earliest period of Islam. Many scholars also deny that there is anything like a fundamentalist trend in Islam: Islamic fundamentalism is not a clearly defined category of religio-political thought. It is more or less a general tendency among some religio-political parties and groups in modern Muslim societies. Social scientists hold it as a general response of Muslim societies to trends of Westernisation and secularisation.

During the last three centuries, ever since the industrial revolution when Muslims of Asia and Africa became part of the world capitalist system, the impact of science, reason, industrialization and urbanisation, have removed religion from some spheres of life and replaced it by science and scientific temper. Secularism is not necessarily anti-religion. Islamic fundamentalism in all its forms is opposed to modernistic interpretation of Islamic teachings which are being attempted by liberal minded Muslims.

Islamic fundamentalism, therefore, can be defined as a religio-political movement; it essentially means going back to the original sources and roots of Islam. It advocates adherence to the original beliefs of the religion in their literal interpretations as fundamental and basic principles, thus transcending all social, economic, political and cultural transformations which span a period of 14 centuries.

Features of Fundamentalism

Some of the characteristic features of Islamic fundamentalist movement may be noted. Its militant and aggressive violence is an essential aspect of this ideology. This arises out of the general conviction that the state, classes and bureaucratic elite of the Muslim societies are incapable of bringing any radical changes and reforms in the unequal social, economic and political systems of their underdeveloped economies and corrupt leaders. The Muslim Brotherhood of Egypt and the Jamaat-i-Islami have frequently used violence against their opponents. The former has even a separate military wing of the party.

This is also related to the fundamentalist opposition to pluralist politics. Since they believe that they are the true exponents of Islam and that any view different from that of theirs is un-Islamic, it should not be allowed to be expressed. Maulana Maududi, the founder of the Jamaat-i-Islami, had declared that democracy and secularism were un-Islamic. The argument has been that there were no political parties, opposition parties, etc., in Islam. Once something has been declared contrary to Islamic teachings, it is unthinkable to allow it later under any circumstances. This becomes serious if people like those of the Jamaat-i-Islami were to capture levers of powers in any country. The example of Khomeini's Iran is instructive in this regard.

The rejection of the fundamentalist parties in the Pakistani poll should not be read as a rejection of Islam, or even a dilution of the people's faith in religion. It was only that the people of Pakistan rejected the Islam as expounded by the fundamentalists of the conservative variety. Fundamentalism can be broadly categorised in two streams of Islamic thought. The fundamentalism we have discussed so far is of the conservative type, which is a supporter of *status quo* of semi-feudalism. It interprets Islam in legal ritualistic terms as a political instrument to suppress and exploit the masses. Fundamentalist parties of this type had supported Islamisation of Pakistan during the military dictatorship of General Zia. This

Islamisation could not have promoted basic restructuring of social, economic and political system of the Pakistani society.

Some scholars erroneously believe that fundamentalism as practised by the Khomeini's regime in Iran and Gaddafi's Libya is a type of radical fundamentalism which is anti-elitist and anti-imperialist and which has brought social and economic changes in those countries. The radical reforms in Iran or Libya have not abolished exploitation of man, nor have they helped in reducing class differentiation, much less strengthen democratisation of the society.

In fact, a radical Islamic fundamentalism is yet to be developed into a comprehensive ideology to socio-economically transform the society. Whether Islamic teachings can provide the groundwork for such a revolutionary ideology is still a moot point, though it will always remain an ideal for the Muslim masses, so beautiful yet so far—like a mirage.

The Case of Pakistan

The factors that moved the Muslim masses in pre-partition India to support the idea of Pakistan were not exactly to create an Islamic state. No wonder, the mainstream Ulama did not support the demand for Pakistan. The main argument of the Jamaat-i-Islami against the idea of Pakistan was that the Muslim League leaders were too Westernized, and were not known for their religiosity; therefore they were in all likelihood to turn Pakistan into a secular-democratic state.

The Muslim League leaders were far too shrewd politicians, and were always careful not to spell out the type of social system Pakistan would have. Once Pakistan came into being, the fundamentalists cornered the Pakistani leaders on their own ground. They had often claimed that Pakistan would be an Islamic state, and since it was now a reality they were asked to make it one. The fundamentalists led by the Jamaat-i-Islami were provided a fertile ground in Pakistan as the Muslim League, the ruling party, was unable to put forward a concrete socio-economic programme of national reconstruction to draw the common man and enthuse him in the task of nation-building.

One reason for this was that the demand for Pakistan mainly emanated from the Muslims of the Muslim minority provinces. The dominant classes of the areas that later formed a part of Pakistan did not support the demand for partition. Soon after independence and assumption of power by the Muslim League, the party lost whatever credibility it had in the new country. It was the collapse of the ruling party and the gradual emergence of bureaucracy and military in the power structure which created the fertile ground for the Islamic fundamentalists to entrench themselves in the political space.

As the ruling elite were unable to give the people any viable nation-building programme, the problems of the people, of poverty, illiteracy, social backwardness and exploitation, continued to aggravate with every successive regime. If one accepts this basic premise, it must however be said to the credit of the main fundamentalist parties that they made sustained intellectual effort to create a well-reasoned and logical outline of the Islamic political, social and economic system.

Over the years these Islamic groups carried on a relentless propaganda of their ideology, which played upon the common Pakistani's sincere belief that Islam can provide a social system to ensure justice, fair play and emancipation from exploitation. This created a popular media image of the Pakistani masses rooting for an Islamic state. The Iranian revolution, the Afghan civil war and General Zia-ul-Haq emerged on the scene almost at the same time. Gen. Zia, who had overthrown the first ever democratically elected government of Zulfikar Ali Bhutto, caught on to the Islamic bandwegon to legitimise his military regime. The spectre of an Islamic fundamentalist bloc of nations in South-west Asia comprising Iran, Afghanistan and Pakistan created a lot of concern in the Western capitals, and got much publicity in the media.

Gen. Zia was the first ruler of Pakistan to make Islamization of the society as the Pakistani state's official programme. He went on to denigrate Western democracy, political parties, opposition parties, elections, manifestoes etc. as unknown in Islam. His ideas on Islamization were somewhat closer to those of the Jamaat-i-Islami; and the Jamaat and the other fundamentalists never had it so good. Here was a ruler without any opposition, who wanted to Islamise the country which they could only dream of! The only fly in the ointment was that they could not accept the implications of Islamizaton by a military dictator. It was as if Pakistan could be Islamised only by a military dictator under the threat of the ruler's machine-gun.

General Zia-zul-Haq went on to experiment with a nominated assembly, a partyless assembly and a spurious referendum. The Islamic fundamentalists supported him in his attempts to build an alternative political system in the name of Islam. Gen. Zia's introduction of Islamic punishment of public flogging repelled the populace, but was applauded by the fundamentalists. He introduced laws reducing the status of women which also earned him their hostility. Interestless banking was a hoax inflicted upon the people in the name of Islam.

Islamic fundamentalism of Zia or the Jamaat-i-Islami variety divided the people and aggravated ethbic and sectarian tensions. The 11 years of Zia's military rule had fuelled the Shia-Sunni tensions and encouraged assaults on the rights of Ahmadis, Hindus and Christians. Sindhi-Mohajir, and Punjabi-Pathan relations also deteriorated during this period. It was clear for the people of Pakistan to see the damage done to Pakistan's national psyche in the clamour about Islamization. Given the differences of sects and schools of thought among its Muslim population, no consensus has ever been possible on various aspects of Islamization. Moreover, the people had seen the game behind the rumpus about Islamization indulged in by the military dictator and his collaborators, the Jamaat-e-Islami. This explains to some extent the reasons for the resounding blow the people delivered to the Jamaat in the elections by reducing its share in the total votes by half, i.e., below 3 per cent from the high of 6 per cent in 1990. The people of Pakistan in 1993 have voted for a liberal and progressive polity, rejecting Islamic orthodoxy and obscurantism.

NATIONAL QUESTION AND THE RIGHT OF SELF-DETERMINATION

INAYATULLAH BALOCH

Afro-Asian 'state-nations' have emerged on the political map of the world in the 20th century. In the fields of politics and history they are termed "non-Western nations"[1] arising out of traditional societies and in colonial settings. The map of South-West Asia consists of "state-nations" like Pakistan, Iran, and Afghanistan, with differences among their diverse linguisitc, ethnic and cultural groups. The majority of these new-born "state-nations", without any cohesive basis of nationalism, face the demand of the right of self-determination by their nationalities.

What is the future of these "state-nations?" The problem of survival of these states is linked to the concept of nationalism. Nationalism is the demand and struggle of a nationality or people aware of their national identity to form a state on the basis of a common culture, language, history, and geography. John Stuart Mill suggested that: " A portion of mankind may be said to constitute a nationality, if they are united amongst themselves by common sympathies, which do not exist between them and any other...which make them co-operate with each other more willingly than other people, desire to be under the same government, and desire that it should be governed by themselves".[2]

The feeling of oneness is very essential for the development of a nation and a state. Several South-West Asian states maintain non-ethnic boundaries. For instance, the Afghan and Iranian "state-nations" emerged during the 19th century due to the "Great Game" in which different nations were divided by British and Russians imperialism. In fact, very few "state-nations" have been successful in achieving national integration. Consequently, many political philosphers are sceptical about the viability of a multinational state. John Stuart Mill strongly advocated that "the boundaries of government should coincide in the main with those of nationalities".[3] Joseph R. Strayer has a similar view: "A state whose boundaries bear no relation to an earlier political unit, whose inhabitants are well aware that their state is only a splinter of an ancient political or cultural grouping, and whose institutions have no connection with the mores of the people , is a state which will certainly not become a nation and which will probably soon cease to be a state."[4]

Case of Baluchistan

The boundaries of Pakistan, Iran, and Afghanistan were drawn by the colonialists, without taking into account geographical, cultural or historical factors. The 'international' boundaries of these countries run through territories inhabited by individual peoples, dividing them into several parts.

Baluchistan's borders were demarcated during the middle of the 19th century without consulting the Baluch people, who objected and revolted against the colonial decisions. In the 1930's Baluch nationalists protested against the division of Baluchistan. In 1947, the Khanate of Baluchistan became independent and announced as its goal the unification of the Baluch area. But in 1948, Pakistan forced the Khanate to accede without consideration of the Baluch people's right to self-determination. The case of so-called British Baluchistan and the tribal areas of Baluchistan was "solved through an un-representative council of elders nominated by the British authorities.

Pakistani scholars and government authorities refer to the All-India Muslim League session at Lahore in 1940, where a resoultion for the creation of a separate Muslim state in the sub-continent was passed. It may be of interest to note that just at the time when the Muslim League adopted the "Pakistan" or the Lahore Resoultion in 1940, the President of the Muslim League, M.A. Jinnah, as a legal adviser to the Khan of Kalat, was fighting a constitutional battle for an independent, sovereign state of Baluchistan! Also of interest is the fact that Baluchistan was not represented in the historic Lahore conference. Despite this, in 1947, the Khanate of Baluchistan became an independent state, recognized by Pakistan, until 1948, when, with the collaboration of the British Government, Pakistan managed the "accession" of the Khanate without the popular consent of the Baluch people.

The forced merger of Baluchistan into Iran and Pakistan automatically raises the question of the right of self-determination. What is this right? Though it is difficult to give a precise, universally-accepted definition, the right of self-determination essentially means that each nationality has the right to decide for itself how it shall be governed and by whom. Cobban calls the principle of self-determination as the belief that 'each nation has a right to constitute an independent state and determine its own government."[5] Selassie writes that "the principle of self-determination was derived from a set of old doctrines, the most important of which was the proposition that government must rest on the consent of the governed".[6] Emerson says that since the 19th century there has been an assumption that "man is a national animal, the government which he will thus consent to is one representing his own nations".[7] The term "self-determination" has many meanings and explanations. It may be used in Europe with the connotation of "national self-determination", whereas in the third world the meaning is 'colonial self-determination'. In "state-nations", people refer to 'secessionist self-determination' or 'separatism'. Thus E.S. Lent regards self-determination as "a fine sounding but highly ambiguous term".[8] Sexena also has pointed out that definitions of self-determination are vague and unclear.[9]

Core or Self-Determination

Brownlie writes: It is true that it is not easy to give a precise definition of the principle of self-determination, but it appears to have a core of reasonable certainty. This core consists in the right of a community which has a distinct character to have this character reflected in the existence of the government under which it lives.[10] An international commission of jurists has agreed on the definition of a people as those who share certain common characteristics due to a common history, geography, culture (including language), religion or ideology, and economy.[11] As essential element ignored in their definition, however, is that "a people begins to exist". Hans Kohn regards this consciousness as "a state of mind in which the supreme loyalty of the individual is attached to his country or nation-state.[12] The consciousness of being differenct from other nations leads to the demand of the right of self-determination".[13]

Karl Deutsch considers communication as an important factor for the development of a nation-state. According to him, the people who cannot communicate with each other cannot form a nation.[14] The lack of communication among the different nationalities in a "state-nation" or in 'artificial' states leads to an increased sentiment towards the right of self-determination on the part of those peoples whose minority position in the artificial" state induces conditions of oppression. To achieve the goal of self-determination, peoples in history have passed through different stages. In the West, the history of self-determination is linked with the content of sovereignty derived from the American and French Revolutions in the 18th century, when there was great emphasis on the concept of equality and liberty.[15] In the 19th century, the concept of self-determination emerged in the writings of Marx and Engels, and was further worked out by Lenin in the 20th century. But Emerson, an American scholar, has given the "whole" credit of enunciating the right of self-determination to the American President Woodrow Wilson: "At first, at the close of World War I, Woodrow Wilson and others proclaimed the right of self-determination in universal terms, but for practical purposes with a concentration on the European territorial settlement following the war... In the second, follwing World War II, the focus of attention has been the disintegration of the overseas empires which had remained effectively untouched in the round of Wilsonian self-determination."[16]

To understand the right of self-determintion demanded by the oppressed and divided nations, one has to consider the Marxist-Leninist school of thought and briefly contrast this with the Wilsonian legacy.

Marxism-Leninism

Communism stands for a classless and stateless society and regards nationalism as directed against the interest of the working class. Therefore, Marx and Engels did not show their interest in the theory of national self-determination uncil 1850. Marx in his later life showed his interest in the national question of Ireland and supported "the right of the peoples to self-determination" in Poland against Tsarist Russia.[17]

In their study on Ireland and the Irish question, they developed general principles on the right of self-determination. Initially, Marx supported an autonomous Ireland within a British federation, but later in the sixties he was convinced that the independence of Ireland was one pre-requisite for the liberation of the English working class. Marx and Engels clearly emphasized that "no nation can be free if it oppresses other nations", opposing the forcibly imposed union of Great Britain and Ireland, while appealing to the English working class (the members of the dominant nation) to support the Irish liberation movement.[18]

In 1853, Engels came across the issue of the national question amongst the Balkan nations under the Ottoman Empire and favoured the disintegration of the Ottoman Expire so that the oppressed nations of the Balkans could achieve the right of self-determination.[19]

With his contribution to the discussion on the national question, Lenin "greatly developed the Marxist theory based on the fundamental slogan of national self-determination ".[20] Even before the Bolshevik revolution in Russia, Lenin had paid attention to the question, when in 1903 the programme of the Russian Marxists was announced, supporting the right of self-determination for all nations.

Supporting Norway's secession from Sweden, Lenin wrote: "The geographic, economic and language ties between Norway and Sweden are as intimate as those between the Great Russians and many other Slav nations. But the union between Norway and Sweden was not a voluntaruy one... Norway was ceded to Sweden by thr monarchs during the Napoleonic wars, against the will of the Norwegians, and the Swedes had to bring troops into Norway to subdue her".[21] Despite the very extensive autonomy which Norway enjoyed (she had her own parliament, etc.), there had been constant frictions between Norway and Sweden for many decades after the forced union and the Norwegians strove hard to throw off the yoke of the Swedish aristocracy. At last, in August 1905 the Norwegians succeeded in holding a referendum. The overwhelming majority about 200,000 as against a few hundred voted for complete separation from Sweden. After a short period of indecision, the Swedes resigned themselves to the fact of secession. After the case study of Norway's secession from Sweden, Lenin asserted to Marxists and revolutionaries that "this example virtually proves that it is the bounden duty of class-conscious workers to conduct systematic propaganda and prepare the ground for the settlement of conflicts that may arise over the secession of nations.... in the way they were settled in 1905 between Norway and Sweden. This is exactly what is menat by the demand in the programme (of the Bolshevik Party) for the recognition of the right of self-determination".[22]

In the case of Norway's secession from Sweden, Lenin discussed the duty and role of the Swedish Marxists and Socialists, stating that they "would have betrayed the cause of socialism and democracy if they had not fought with all their might to combat the dominant nation (Sweden) for Norway's right of self-determination.[23]

In March 1919, Lenin criticized the communist leader Bukharin, who opposed the right of nations to self-determination. Lenin told the party that denial of the right of self-determination to oppressed nations would lead to distrust among the oppressed nations and the rise of chauvinism among the dominant nations. Referring to the case of Finland, he stated: "The Finns have experienced the dictatorship of Germany; they are now experiencing the dictatorship of the Allied Powers. But thanks to the fact that we have recognized the right of nations to self-determination, the process of differentiation has been facilitated there".[24]

Since nations are at different stages on the road from medievalism to bourgeois democracy, and from bourgeois democracy to proletarian democracy, this thesis of out programme is absolutely correct. Every nation must obtain the right of self-determination, and that will make the self-determination of working people easier."[25] He further added, "We cannot say: 'down with the right of nations to self-determination. We grant the right of self-determination only to the working people'. This self-determination proceeds in a very complex and difficult way... It only exists nowhere but in Russia, and, while foreseeing every stage of development in other countries, we must decree nothing from Moscow. That is why this proposal is unacceptable in principle."[26]

On November 22, 1919, Lenin, addressing the second All-Russia Congress of Communist Organizations of the People of the East, emphasized the importance and need to support bourgeois nationalism in the East and impressed on the Communists the need to show their solidarity with the exploited peoples of the East.[27]

On June 5, 1920, Lenin prepared his draft thesis on the national and colonial questions for the Second Congress of the Communist International, in which he emphasized "the duty of the class-conscious communist proletariat of all countries to regard with particular caution and attention the survival of national sentiments in the countries and among nationalities which have been oppressed the longest."[28] In his last days, he continued writing on the national question and the right of self-determination He wrote: "A distinction must necessarily be made between the nationalism of an oppressor nation and that of an oppressed nation, the nationalism of a big nation and of a small nation.

"In respect of the second kind of nationalism, we nationals of a big nation, have nearly always been guilty in historic practice of an infinite number of cases of violence. Further more, we commit violence and insult an infinite number of times without noticing it. It is sufficient to recall my Volga reminiscences of how non-Russians are treated; how the Poles are not called by any other name than Polyachishka; how the Tatar is nicknamed prince; how the Ukrainians are always Khokhols and the Georgians and other Caucasian nationals always Kapkasians.

"That is why internationalism on the part of the oppressors, or 'great' nations as they are called (though they are great only in their violence, only great as bullies), must consist not only in the observance of the formal quality of nations but even in an inequality of the oppressor nation, the great nation, that must make up for the inequality which it obtains in actual practice. Anybody who does not understand this has not grasped the real proletarian attitude to the national question, he is still essentially *petit bourgeois* in his point of view and is, therefore, sure to descend to the bourgeois point of view."[29]

Lenin recognized Finland's right to self-determination and hailed the role of the Swedish socialists in the case of Norway's right to self-determination. He condemned all secret agreements by the Allied aiming to divide the Turks, the Persians, and the Arabs, and directed the communist parties as well as Soviet diplomats to help the oppressed nations' fight for their right of self-determination. For instance, in the credentials issued to Y.Z. Surits, the first Soviet Representative in Afghanistan, signed by Lenin in 1919, it was stated that the Council of People's Commissars appointed Y.Z. Surits the "Representative Extra-Ordinary and Plenipotentiary of the Soviet Federative Socialist Republic in Central Asia, empowering him to maintain diplomatic relations with the peoples of independent Afghanistan, independent (tribes of) Baluchistan, and the peoples of India fighting for their liberation".[30]

In September 1920, the first Congress of the Peoples of the East was held in Baku, aiming to support the right of self-determination for all nations and to call for international revolution. The conference was attended by 2,050 delegates, including delegations from Baluchistan, Kurdistan, Palestine, Iran, Afghanistan and British India. The Congress ended with an appeal "To the peoples of the East" that a holy war be waged for the liberation of the East, that the oppression of the peoples there be abolished, and that there should be complete and equal independence irrespective of language, colour and creed.[31]

In 1913, Lenin told Stalin to write a paper on the national question. Lenin's advice resulted in the famous essay by Stalin on "Marxism and the National Question". The paper was based on the ideas and policies of Lenin and the Bolshevik Party. Stalin wrote that common characteristics, language, territory, economic life, and psychic formation are the basis of "a nation" and supported the cause of the right of self-determination. "The right of self-determination means that a nation may arrange its life in the ways it wishes. It has the right to change its life on the basis of autonomy. It has the right to enter into federal relations with other nations. It has the right to complete secession. Nations are sovereign and all are equal".[32]

In a lecture given by Stalin at Sverdlov University on the "National Question", he divided the national liberation movements into two categories, "reactionary" and "progressive". He described all those movemenets as "reactionary" which are supported by "absolutism" and "imperialism", and regarded those nations fighting against imperialism and national oppression as "revolutionary". Thus, he considered the struggle of the Afghans against British imperialism to be revolutionary, though the leadership was in the hands of a monarch.[33]

Stalin's policies in South-West Asia, however, were not on the lines of Marxism-Leninism. Stalin and the Communist Party of India (pro-Stalin) supported the creation of Israel and Pakistan, states based on religion. Stalin also failed to help the Azri Turks and the Kurds in their democratic struggle against Persian oppression supported by British imperialism. Finally, his regime did not cooperate with the leaders of the Baluch resistance movement (1943) against the British-supported occupation of Baluchistan by Pakistan.

What has been the practice of the other socialist countries besides Stalinist Russia, with regard to the principle of self-determination? Socialist Yugoslavia has refused to grant the right of secession of Croatia. The constitution of Mao's China stands for autonomy and refuses to grant the right of self-determination to Mongolia, (former) Turkistan, and Tibet.[34] Several Marxist-Leninist states agree to autonomy, instead of the right to self-determination. But in the words of Davis: "Autonomy is like religious toleration; it can be terminated at any time."[35] For instance, in 1972 the socialist Iraq announced its support for the Baluchi demand for the right of self-determination. Five years later, when Iraq and Iran patched up their differences and Iran promised not to give help to the Kurds in Iraq, Iraq agreed not to help the Baluch of Iran and Pakistan. The Baluch national leaders were forced to take refuge abroad.

If the teachings of Karl Marx, Engels and Lenin are still valid in respect to the right to self-determination by the Baluch people, then it becomes the duty of the Punjabi working class and the progressive forces in Pakistan as well as the responsibility of the progressive forces of Iran belonging to the dominant nations to support the right of the Baluch to self-determination. Certain "socialists" oppose this right for the Baluch, denouncing it as "separatism", but they ignore the fact that the right of self-determination for the Baluch would lead to the unification of the two parts of Baluchistan, occupied by Iran and Pakistan, thus bringing about the unity of the Baluch people. Lenin declared: "A socialist who is a member of a dominant nation and does not further the right of oppressed nations to separation during peace or during war is neither a socialist, nor an internationalist, but a chauvinist."[36]

Western School

In 1862 Lord Acton, in an essay on "nationality", wrote that before the French Revolution, the right of self-determination and autonomy of nationalities were not recognized; the interest of the ruling classes determining the frontiers of states instead of the nationalities or nations. "In the old European system, the rights of nationalities were neither recognized by Governments nor asserted by the people. The interest of reigning families, not those of the nations, regulated the frontiers."[37]

The modern problem of nationality began with the division of Poland in the 18th century. The partition of Poland gave birth to the theory of nationality based on the principle of the right to self-determination. Acton wrote: Thence forward, there was a nation demanding to be united in a state; a soul, as it were, wandering in search or a body in which to begin life over again." Acton's theory of nationality was supported by the liberals of Europe. The theory was usually confined to "civilized" nationalities of Europe, such as the Poles, the Finns, and the Serbs, etc., the nations of Afro-Asia being outside of its scope. It is worth noting that the socialists of Europe were confined to the problem of "civilized" nationalites of Europe until the end of the 19th century.

American President Woodrow Wilson was the first leader in the capitalist bloc who favoured the theory of self-determination for the rest of the world by incorporating it in his 14 points: "A free, open-minded and absolutely impartial adjustment of all colonial claims, based upon a strict observance of the principle that in determining all such questions of sovereignty, the interests of the population concerned must have equal weight with equitable claims of the government whose title is to be determined."[38] In February 1918, President Wilson in his message to the Congress stressed that "national aspirations must be respected, peoples may now be dominated and governed only by their own consent." He supported a clause of self-determination in the covenant of the League of Nations, which was finally dropped because of the British opposition to it.[39]

The Western countries agreed to the principle, and it has been accepted by international jurists as well as by the United Nations. But the principle remains only valid for colonies and not for the nationalities of "state-nations". The U.N. declaration does not support the right of self-determination for divided nations, ruled by the "state-nations". In 1971, when the Punjabi ruling classes of Pakistan invaded the then East Pakistan and refused to recognize its democratic rights, the issue of East Pakistan and its demand of the reight to self-determination was discussed in the U.N. The majority of the member countries of the U.N. favoured a peaceful settlement of the crisis of East Pakistan, with the aim of supporting the territorial integrity of Pakistan, a member country of the U.N.[40]

It is hard to predict the attitude of the member-states of the U.N. in the case of the Baluch for the right of self-determination. The case of Baluchistan has very little similarity with that of former East Pakistan. The historical background for such a case for Baluch self-determination would include the following points:

— Baluchistan was never been a part of the Indian sub-continent. On the contrary, she had her own independent, sovereign state recognized by Ottoman Turkey, Persia, the Sultanate of Muskat-Oman, and Durrani's Afghanistan.

— The British government recognized the Khanate of Baluchistan as an independent state under the Treaties of 1854 and 1876, In 1947, Pakistan recognized the Khanate of Baluchistan as a sovereign state.
— The Baluch were not represented in the famous "Lahore Resolution" adopted by the All-India Muslim League aiming to from an independent state of Muslims of India in 1940.
— Baluch people did not participate in the movement of Pakistan, as the Muslim Bengalis did.
— Baluchistan's accession to Pakistan was the result of the military action of the armed forced of Pakistan and British intrigues. The Baluch were not given any right to determine their destiny.

In the light of the above, we can make the following conclusions: that international peace and security cannot be achieved unless the principle of the right of self-determination is recognized and practised by "state-nations."

That the acceptance of the principle of the right of self-determination provides hope to the oppressed and divided nations for their future, as well as a sound basis of international peace.

References

1. Myron Weiner, "Political Integration and Political Development,"*The annals,*" Vol. 38 March 1965, pp. 52-64.
2. John S. Mill, *Considerations on Representative Government*, p. 287.
3. Ibid., pp. 291-292.
4. Joseph R. Strayer, "The Historical Experience of Nation-Building in Europe", in karl W. Deutsch and W.J. Foltz (eds.) *Nation-Building*, p. 25.
5. A Cobban, *National Self-Determination*, p. 4.
6. Berekct II, Selassier, "Evolution of the Principle of Self-Determination", *Horn of Africa*, Oct-Dec., 1978, p. 4.
7. Rupert Emerson, *Empire and Nation*, p. 197.
8. E.S. Lent, *American Foreign Policy and the principle of Self-Determination*. p. 133.
9. J. Saxena, *Right of Self-Determination*, p. 2.
10. Ibid., p.2
11. Ibid., p.2
12. Ibid., p.3
13. Hans Kohn, *Nationalism*, p. 1.
14. K.W. Deutch, *Nationalism and Social Communication*, p. 98.
15. The American Declaration of Independence (1776) stands for the right of self-determination in the following words: "When in the course of human event it becomes

necessary for one people to dissolve the political bands which have connected them with another, and to assume among the powers of the earth, the separate and equal station to which the Laws of Nature and of Nature's God entitle them, a decent respect to the opinions of mankind requires that they should declare the causes which impel them to the separation." *The Declaration of Independence, the Constitution of the United States of America,* (N.D.), p.1.

16. Saxena, op, cit., p. 3.
17. *Karl Marx, The First International and After, Political Writings,* Vol. 3 p.93 E.A. Carr, *A History of Soviet Russia, The Bolshevik Revolution,* p. 416. Jullius Braumnthal, *Geschichte der Internationale,* Band 1, p. 336.
18. Marx and Engels *Selected Works,* Vol. 1, p. 336. See also Marx and Engels, *Ireland and the Irish Question* and Marx and Engels, *On Colonialism.*
19. Michael Lowy. "Marxism and the National Question", in Robin Blackburn (ed.), *Revolution and Class Struggle,* pp. 139-140.
20. Ibid. p. 152.
21. V.I. Lenin, *Critical Remarks on the National Question, The Right of Nations to Self-Determination,* p. 70.
22. Ibid.
23. Ibid. p. 72.
24. V.I. Lenin, The National Liberation Movement in the East, p. 233.
25. Ibid., p. 236.
26. Ibid., p. 237.
27. Ibid., for detail, see pp. 242-253.
28. Xenia Joukoff Eudin and Robert C. North (ed.), *Soviet Russia and the East,* pp. 64-65.
29. V.I. Lenin, op. cit., pp. 323-324.
30. G. Nondarevski, "Bolsdhevik Policy and the Peoples of the East", *Mainstream,* December 3, 1977, p. 34.
31. Brain Pearce (Translated and Annotated), *Baku, Congress of the Peoples of the East,* pp. 174-180.
32. J.V. Stalin, "Marxism and the National Question," *Collected* Works Vol. 2, pp. 300-381.
33. J.V. Stalin, The Foundations of Leninism, pp. 77-78.
34. Chang Chi-hui, *Chin meen Qaumi Sawal,* pp. 134-135. See also Fei Hsiao-tung, *Towards People's Anthropology,* and H.B. Davis (ed.), The *National Question.*
35. H.B. Davis (ed.), *The National Question,* p.38.
36. V.I. Lenin, *The National Liberation Movement in the East,* p. 109. The author has also benefited from A.R. Ghassemlou, *Kurdistan and the Kurds,* chapter XII.
37. John B.E.D. Action, *Essary on Freedom and power,* pp. 144-146, and G.E. Rasnacht, *Action's Political Philosophy,* pp. 126-139.
38. J.N. Saxena, op. cit., p. 3.
39. Ibid., p. 4.
40. For detail see, the Secretariat of International Commission of Jurists, *The Events in East Pakistan, 1971,* part V: *Right of Self-Determination in International law.*

SURGE OF FUNDAMENTALISM IN BANGLADESH

S.R. CHAKRAVARTY

Bangladesh could not have escaped the recent surge of communalism the world over. Communalism, the use of religion for political gain, dates back in Bengal to the foundation of the Sen rule in 12th century A.D., which replaced the four-century-old Pal-rule. The Buddhist intellectuals and the masses were persecuted during the Brahmin-dominated Sen rule. Many of these intellectuals had fled to neighbouring Nepal and other places. Later, a big section of the masses adopted Islam preached and propagated by the Sufi Saints. The Sufis fought against the orthodox Muslims and did not allow the latter to take over the Muslim masses. The Sufis also encouraged the development of the Bengali language, literature and culture.

The Muslim society, however, was engulfed in communalism in the wake of the imposition of the British rule. In the last decades of the 18th century, puritanist Islamic movements developed in Bengal in the form of Wahabi and then Faraiji movements which sought to restore the pristine glory of Islam deeply influencing the then contemporary Muslim society. A conscious effort was made to evolve a mixed language consisting of Arabic, Persian, Urdu and a little of Bengali expressions instead of pure Bengali, with the elite sections using Persian and Urdu in their literary, cultural and societal affairs. The Muslim also kept themselves away form modern English education and the emerging renaissance in Bengal. The influence of puritanist efforts were also there in the reform movement launched by Nawab Abdul Lateef and others. Lateef advocated the introduction of Urdu as the medium of instruction for "High Class Muslims" and the mixed language (or Islamic Bengali) for the "Lower Class Muslims". The apathy towards Bengali language was so deep that the traditional educated class considered it substandard for their literary pursuits.

A strong non-Bengali section—those who did not consider Bengali as their mother tongue—provided leadership to the Muslim society in Bengal till a middle-class of intellectuals and professionals emerged from among the Bengali-speaking Muslim community in the last decades of the

19th century. In course of time this new class assumed the leadership of the community. New cultural, literary and socio-political movements emerged. 'Bongya Muslim Shahitya Samaj' was founded in Calcutta in 1913 to provide opportunities to the young people to cultivate the Bengali language and literature. A socio-economic programme-based peasant movement started from 1914. In the mid 1920s another socio-cultural movement was founded in Dhaka called 'Shikha Group'. Both the 'Samaj' and 'Shikha' sought to popularise the Bengali culture, language and literature among the people. The 'Shikha movement' campaigned for the "emancipation of the intellect", which came to be known as the "Buddhi Muktir Andolan" seeking to liberate the Muslim masses from the age-old social backwardness and illiteracy. The 'Nikhil Banga Praja Samity' was founded in 1929: It was renamed the 'Krishak Praja Party' in 1936. The KPP had a progressive socio-economic programme, and in the 1937 elections, the party defeated the Muslim Legue (ML) candidates in most of the areas which now form Bangladesh. Although the elections were held under the communal electorate system, even the communal Muslim League failed to win an absolute majority. This shows that till the late 1930s, communalism was kept under check by the emerging middle class.

Communalism, however, took over the Muslim masses again when the movement for Pakistan—the communal deamnd for a homeland of the Indian Muslims—was launched. The movement culminated in the partition of Bengal on communal lines. Alongwith the movement for Pakistan, a cultural movement was also launched to provide the ideological and cultural background to the Muslim homeland movement. Two organizations—the East Pakistan Renaissance Society (Calcutta 1942) and the Purbo Pakistan Shahitya Samaj (Dhaka, 1943)—were founded. As in the political field (secular politics was sidelined with the KPP completely losing the 1946 elections), the communal cultural movement also sidelined the secular cultural movements founded by the Bongya Muslim Shahitya Samaj and the Shika group. One of the basic reasons for communalism getting ascendency was the glaring socio-economic disparities between the Hindus and the Muslims. Most of the 'Zamindars' were Hindus, and a section of the Muslim leaders interpreted the socio-economic disparity from the communal angle.

Saga of Secularism

The language movements of 1948-1952, which were launched to protest against the language policy of Pakistan, changed the entire ideological outlook of the society, and gave birth to an amalgamated nationalist movement. This was, in fact, a successor of the 'Bengal Renaissance'. The Bengal Renaissance had first attracted the notice of the Bengali Muslims in the late 19th century when Meer Mosharaf adopted modern Bengali, a product of the Renaissance, as the medium of his literary creations. Meer was the first modern Bengali Muslim author. The Renaissance also found full expression in the works of Kazi Nazrul Islam who added a new dimension in the Tagorian era of Bengali literature. In his conception "Hindu and Muslim are the two flowers in one branch" (*Eki Brinte Duti Phool*). He sung the songs of revolution, patriotism, and anti-imperialism.

The post-1948-52 language movements revived the old trends of Bengali culture, rekindling the movements which had been sidelined by the growing communal movements of the 1940s, and gave birth to a new band of poets, authors, novelists, artists, dramatists, singers, cinematographers etc., and helped push new socio-cultural and political consciousness. The Awami League was the political successor of this renaissance, and the cultural movements found organized shape in annual literary and cultural conferences, fairs, etc. The famous Kagmari Cultural Conference of 1957 was organized by Moulana A.H.K. Bhashani, and organizations like "Chaya Note" etc., came up in its wake. As the movement spread to the remotest corners of the country, every village, town and city felt the impact of the renaissance. The political impact of the language movement can be gauged by the rapid decline of the Muslim League and other communal parties, The mainstream of the League broke away and the Awami League was founded in 1949. The Muslim League was completely wiped out in the 1954 elections.

After the seizure of power by President Gen. Ayub Khan's military regime in 1958 attempts were made to stall the progress of the Bengali cultural and national movements. Ayub Khan barred the established political leaders from contesting elections, encouraged obscurantist communal forces to re-emerge, and founded the Convention Muslim League, splitting the orginal Muslim League. Although his economic policy did help to develop certain industries it at the same time created a heavy service sector which was not committed to the society. As the rich-poor gap increased, the unemployment problem became more acute and transfer of wealth from East Pakistan (now Bangladesh) to West Pakistan (now Pakistan) increased. The Ayub regime formulated education and cultural policies to strengthen the obscurantist forces and culture. Higher education was made costly, while educational institutions lost their autonomy. Even as students and teachers were barred from taking part in politics, the democratic atmosphere in educational institutions was vitiated by encouraging the unsocial and communal elements to form pro-regime students' units and fake student movements. A Text-Book Board was formed to publish books for the students to mould their career on Islamic requirements. Associations like the Lekhok Sangha, the National Reconstruction Board and the Pakistan Council were established with official blessings to attract young authors and writers. Strict press censorship was imposed; study of Rabindranath and broadcasting of Tagore songs were discouraged, while Nazrul Islam was attempted to be 'Islamised'. Disparagement of the Bengali language continued, meanwhile.

However, all these regressive measures failed to check the onward tide of the Bengali national movement. Ayub's every move faced angry protest and stiff resistance, and the national movement went on gathering momentum. In the 1970, decisions the Awami League, in the vanguard of the national movement, won almost the unanimous verdict of the people. The communal parties faced a shattering defeat, and in the wake of independence in 1971, communal politics itself was banned.

Revival of Communalism

Although the forces of communalism were relegated during the liberation struggle, the mass-scale killing of intellectuals and activists of the socio-cultural movements by the defeated Pakistan army in the fag end of the war, in collusion with communal forces led by the Jamaat-e-Islam and its front organizations like Al-Badres, Al-Shams, etc. (collectively known as the Razakars), decimated the leadership of the secular-democratic cultural movements. The elimination of this leadership weakened the progressive, cultural and the democratic movements, and the vacuum provided new opportunities for the dying communal forces to regroup. Yet, till the Awami League was in power these elements could not raise their heads. But the coup of 1975 again emboldened these dark forces. General Ziaur Rahman established the military rule, and restricted free functioning of the political parties in general, and the secular forces in particular. Generating splits in various parties, he founded a praetorian party—the Bangladesh Nationalist Party (BNP) with the help of the splinter groups, simultaneously lifting the ban on communal parties and politics. He allowed anti-liberation forces, including the Jamaat-e-Islam, to function openly and contest elections. Jamaat leader Golam Azam who had fled to Pakistan was allowed to return in 1978 despite mass protests. Ziaur Rahman also initiated the process of Islamising the Bangladesh constitution. The clause on 'secularism' was replaced by a clause reposing full trust in Islam. He even proposed to revive the hated 'separate electorate system' which had been abolished in 1956 by the then East Pakistani Provincial Legislative Assembly. Zia reintroduced the two-nation theory-based nationalism, known as Bangladeshi Nationalism to counter the influence of Bengali nationalism. He thus infused fresh life into a dying monster and rehabilitated the disgraced socio-cultural and political forces. The process of Islamisation was further intensified by General H.M. Ershad (1982-90). He promulgated the 8th amendment to the constitution to accord formal status to Islam as the State religion.

The economic and cultural policies of the successive Military regimes also strengthened the fundamentalist forces. Ziauer Rahman liberalized the economy by initiating the process of disinvestment of the nationalised enterprises and opened the country to foreign investments as prescribed by the World Bank and the International Monetary Fund. Ershad further liberalised the economy, landing the country in a more chaotic situation. The whole development strategy totally failed as new industries did not develop. On the contrary old industries declined, a heavy service sector developed and the country almost sunk in foreign debt. In this situation, a new rich class emerged who pocketed the public money but did not invest in industrial development. The rich transferred their money to safe financial havens in foreign countries, and established monopoly in the export-import business. These classes are much interested to ensure that the established order continues. Therefore, they are friendly towards the communalist forces who are also the votaries of the existing order. Therefore, even after the restoration of democracy in Bangaldesh, encouragement to communal politics and the use of religion for political gains have not been discontinued. In the elections held in 1991, the BNP won 140 seats and the Jamaat-e-Islam got 18 in the 300-member Jatiya Parishad. The BNP with the support from the Jamaat formed the government. The Jamaat had opposed the freedom struggle, killed hundreds of intellectuals in 1971 and is a party of fanatics. Yet the BNP felt no qualms of conscience while seeking support from the Jamaat. The BNP's role in the communal flare-up following the Ayodhya incident has not been commendable, the general opinion being that the government failed to protect the minority community from the wrath of the communalists. The religious places of the Hindus were dishonoured and demolished, their properties were looted, thousands were rendered homeless, women were dishonoured and many Hindus were even killed or forced to leave the country. Yet the BNP stated that nothing so serious happened! Even the Ahmadis and the Kadianis complain that the BNP government observes strict neutrality when their mosques and religious places are attacked by Islamic fanatics. By way of protest the Hindu community did not celebrate the Durga Puja festival in 1993 with traditional gaiety and grandeur.

Communal Parties and Politics

Bangladesh (or former East Bengal/Pakistan) inherited only one religion-based political party, the Muslim League, in 1947. The ML however soon lost its support base; the main stream Muslims leaving the League to establish the Awami League in 1949. Two new Islam-based parties were formed in 1953—the Nezam-i--Islam (NI) and the Khilafat-i-Rabbani (KR). During the Pak military rule in the 1960's, Jamaat-i-Islam (JI) and Jamiat-al-Ulema-i-Islam (JUI) founded their Eastern Pakistan wings. Two new parties were also formed during that period—Imrat Party and the Pakistan Demorcratic party. The Muslim League later split into several groups and one of them supported Gen. Ayub to form the Convention Muslim League (CML). These parties opposed the liberation struggle and cooperated with the Pakistan Army. But Bangladesh was born, nontheless. and all religion-based parties were banned.

Following the 1975 coup, Ziaur Rahman lifted the ban. At once, all the old religion-based parties became active while a few new ones were also formed. There were some attempts to unite all the pro-Islam parties, and as a result two fronts, the Islamic Democratic League and the Muslim Democratic Front, were founded. But neither the IDL nor the MDF could continue in their orginal form for long. During the first spell of militaty rule (1975-1982) nearly 10 political parties, committed to Islam, functioned. Zia's own party, the BNP, though not openly declaring its adherence to Islam, accommodated a large number of pro-Islamic froces and used religion for political gain. During the second spell of military rule (1982-1990), four new religion-based parties were formed. Ershad founded his party—the Jatiya Patry. Akin to the BNP, it also accommodated many pro-Islamic forces and used religion for political gain.

Currently the active parties with total commitment towards Islam are: 1. Khilafat Andolan: 2. National United Front: 3. Freedom Party; 4. Zaker Party; 5. Islamic Democratic League and 6. Jamaat-e-Islam.

The *'Islam Pasand'* parties have gained ground during the successive military regimes. As their numbers have increased, so have their representation in the legislature. In 1970, all the parties taken together had secured only four seats in the provincial legislature and one in the National Assembly. In the 1973 elections not allowed to contest openly, they fought from different platforms, but failed to win a single seat. But in the 1979 elections the *'Islam Pasand'* parties contesting directly won 20 seats; and quite a few won as BNP candidates. According to an estimate there were about 80 members with 'absolute commitment' towards Islam in the Jatiya Parishad in 1979. In the recent election the Jamaat won 18 seats, but many pro-Islamic elements won either as BNP or as JP candidates. If one scans the bio-data of the present members of Parliament, at least 100 members would be found having full commitment towards Islam in the House. It is widely claimed that more than half of the BNP ministers are known Razakars (members of the Jamaat-led Al-Badres, Al-Shams who killed intellectuals towards the fag end ot the liberation war in 1971). The President of Bangladesh himself is a committed Muslim Leaguer belonging to pro-Ayub faction of the Muslim League. That is the first time after 1954 that such a big contingent of communal forces is represented in the legislature.

Golam Azam Issue

Golam Azam is the top leader, "Amir" of the Jamaat-e-Islami Bangladesh. His party had opposed the liberation war, and Azam, with the help of the Pakistani army and his own killer groups, had masterminded the 1971 genocide. With the defeat of Pakistan in the 1971 war, Azan and many of his cohorts fled Bangladesh and stayed in Pakistan as Pakistani citizens. In the wake ot the liberation, his Bangladeshi citizenship was cancelled by an executive order in 1973, and he was declared as 'enemy of the nation.' But in 1978, Gen. Ziaur Rahman, the then Bangladesh dictator permitted him to come back to Bangladesh on a Pakistani passport, and he stayed on. He reorganised his party, supported the BNP to form the government and also helped the BNP women nominees win from the 30 reserved women seats in the Jatiya Sansad. In late 1991, he was formally elected the 'Amir' of the Jamaat.

This raised a controversy. How could a foreign national become the leader of a Bangladeshi Party? A non-political committee with a long name, the "National Coordination Committee for the Implementation of the Spirit of the Liberation War and Elimination of the Killers and Collaborators of 1971", popularly known as the "Nrimul Committee", was formed. It launched a social movement with a passionate appeal to fight out the Golam Azam issue in all its remifications. The movement is gaining mementum. The Jamaat and its allied forces, Chhatra shiber, etc., are coming into frequent clashes with the "Nirmul Committee" in different parts of the country. The government, maintaining a sort of 'administrative neutrality' has failed to maintain peace. The Committee, which is appealing to the government to take its side as a force of independence and liberation, is getting increasingly disenchanted as it finds the government soft toward the Jamaat.

The government has merely charged Golam Azam with a technical case of non-citizenship, whereas the sponsors of the Gana Adalat have charged him with sedition. In early 1992, a peoples court (Gana Adalat) was formed to try Golam Azam for sedition. The court, consisting of prominent citizens, heard the case for days in the presence of thousands of people and them passed a sentence of death against Golam. As the "Nirmul Committee" wanted the government to execute the 'peoples court' verdict, the government came out with the citizenship case. A three-member bench of the Bangladesh High Court gave its verdict on the case in April 1993, declaring by majority decision that Azam was a 'citizen of Bangladesh', rejecting the executive order of 1973. It is alleged by many that the government's decision to institute the citizenship case with the court was a diversionary tactics, and at the same time to restore citizenship to Azam. The "Nirmul Committee" staged a sit-in demonstration around the Bangladesh Secretariat against the verdict in defiance of a government ban, but the judicial decision emboldened the Jamaat and its allies. Recently, the students wing of Jamaat, the Chhatra Shibir has made functioning of the universities and colleges impossible by ransacking hostels where democratic-minded students stay and misbehaving with teachers. Jamaat members have attacked the followers of minority Muslim sects such as

Ahmadis, Kadiamis, etc., and their religious complexes and demanded that they be declared non-Muslims. The Jamaat has also been spearheading movements against progressive writers and films made on liberation war themes.

Attacks on Taslima Nasreen

Since the beginning of 1993, religious fundamentalist forces have been attacking an young woman author-cum-social activist Taslima Nasreen. They have even passed a 'death sentence' against her and declared Tk 50,000 as prize money for her head. The Jamaat has issued a 'fatwa' to eliminate Nasreen for her alleged defiance of 'Islamic laws'. Taslima, in her book, *"LAJJA"* (shame), has made a trenchant criticism against the communal fundamentalist froces and the nonchalant government which is aiding and abetting these elements. The communalist forces have dubbed Taslima as an 'Indian agent', a common label against any progressive force, and declared her a heretic. She was even manhandled at a book fair held on the occasion of Martyr Day on February 21. The government did not intervene, on the contrary the regime has transferred her to an unprotected remote village. Taslima by profession is a government medical practitioner. Yet, she is neither being given any protection nor allowed to leave the country. Recently the fundamentalists ransacked Sylhet town on the pretext of a strike called by them in support of their demand for severe punishment to Taslima.

Not only Taslima, most of the objective social activists and writers in Bangladesh are now on the 'hit list' of the Jamaat. Poet Shamsur Rahman, Begum Sufia Kamal, Faiz Ahmed, Jahanara Imam and many others have already been 'warned'; it appears that those who had 'escaped' in 1971, are now under threat of being eliminated. In Bangladesh today, whosoever talks of secularism, democraccy or tries to uphold the value of the liberation war, invites the wrath of the fundamentalists.

Such incidents are not new to Bangladesh. Since the days of Ayub's military rule, such types of attacks on writers had been engineered on several occasions. First 'victims' were Rabindranath Tagore and Kazi Nazrul Islam, though posthumously. Tagore was accused of being anti-Islam and pro-Hindu. The Kazi could not be declared a heretic, but before "accepting" him, he was thoroughly "Islamised" by replacing so-called

"Hinduised" words and expressions in his works by so-called Islamic Urdu terminologies. The situation reached a climax when Badruddin Umar, then a professor of political science, in Rajshahi University, wrote and published a book entitles, *"Samprodaikata"* (Communalism), exposing the communal character of the state of Pakistan and how in the name of religion people were being exploited. The book also highlighted the impact of communalism on the society, and the fundamentalists expectedly rose in arms. Ayub issued a 'Fatwas' against the book, which was then setting like hot cake. The government ordered Umar either to wirthdraw the book or face dismissal, Umar preferred the second option and retaliated by writing a few more books. Since those were the high days of national movement, the dark forces could not stop Umar from writing against communalism and fundamentalism. Such an issue once again vitiated the atmosphere in 1974 when a young poet Daud Hyder wrote a poem condemning the divisive role of religion. The forces of fundamentalism raised cudgles against him and he was "gheraoed" (encircled). Then the Awami League was in power, and the government immediately swung into action and he was given protection and was allowed to migrate to Calcutta.

The Taslima Nasreen issue has been raised not only because she wrote the book exposing the atrocities on the Hindus, she also highlighted the status of women in the conservative Muslim society. Through her book she has expressed strong indignation and disdain against the growing communal and faundamentalist forces in her country. Also expressed was her dissatisfaction against the political forces which for the sake of vote politics were not taking a principled stand against the growing menace of communalism and fundamentalism. She is a crusader for human rights, which is virtually unacceptable in any orthodox society. She has been fighting since long for the cause of emancipation of women, exposing through her writings the pathetic condition of the women in orthodox, religion-based society of her country. The attack on Taslima requires to be studied in the context of the growing social movement demanding emancipation of and equal status for women in Bangladesh. The country has been suffering from the alarming rise of polygamy, desertion of wives and dowry deaths, and a social movement is on to check these growing social evils. Recently, a woman member of the Jatiya Parishad moved a Bill which seeks to make permission of the court mandatory for a husband seeking divorce or a second wife without giving up his first wife. The Bill is likely to be passed by Parliament, which may come as a hard blow to orthodoxy.

Simultaneous with the Taslima controversy a few films have also recently reocked the country. These films concerned events connected with the liberation war of 1971. The films which failed to get official sanction are *"Nadir Nam Madhumati"*, *"Dhusar Jalra"* and *"Ekattorer Jishu"* (Jesus of '71'. These films depict the heroic struggles of the Muktibahini (the liberation force) for the liberation of Bangladesh and the atrocities committed by the Pakistani troops. The Censor Board banned the films from public showing, succumbing to the pressures from the Jamaat men and the official machinery. However, the Supreme Court has since allowed these films for public viewing.

Causes of the Surge of Communalism

The rise of communalism in Bangladesh is not an isolated phenomenon. It is part of an international campaign. The surge of communalism in the world primarily owes its origin to the US policy of combating communism and democratic nationalism. The forces of fundamentalism get direct encouragement form the USA and are used by the latter to fight communism and dislodge democratic governments from power. In 1958, the USA supported the military coup in Pakistan. In the 1960's, the USA encouraged extremist movements in different countries to dislodge the democratic forces from power. In the 1970's this policy was further sharpened. In 1975, the religious forces led by Khondkar Mustaq Ahmad were encouraged and supported in Bangladesh to stage a coup. In the late 1970's the religious extremists were armed in Afghanistan to fight the pro-communist government there. All this US support emboldened the religious extremist forces everywhere to spread their activities. The recent surge may also be attributed to the setbacks in the international communist movements. First the split, and then the decline of the communist movement created a vacuum which the religious extremists filled up forthwith. the communists in various countries had worked and mobilized the people against the divisive forces of communalism. Now in the absence of such a movement, the ideological struggle against fundamentalism has become weak.

While the US policy and the setbacks to the communist movement strengthened religious fundamentalism in the world, the sucessive military regimes in different countries also provided ground for religious extremist forces to flourish. In the erstwhile East Pakistan Ayub encouraged these dark forces to raise a support base for his regime. In Bangladesh, Gen. Ziaur Rahman and Gen. Ershad rehabilitated these forces and Islamised the constitution and the society. They raised parties with the help of the communal forces, which subsequently went on to aid and abet revivalist forces. The economic development strategies prescribed by the World Bank and the International Monetary Fund and adopted by the successive governments in Bangladesh, have so far failed to usher in any viable economic system. Instead, the accentuating econiomic crisis has given birth to social tensions. Economic backwardness is a Bangladesh reality where the unemployment problem is acute. The rich-poor gap has since widened, with absolute landlordism and landlessness among peasants, increasing. The new rich class in order to maintain the existing order uses the communal forces (who are ideologically supporters of the established order) as their (rich class) support base. Extreme poverty and unemployment create frustrations among the youth. These furstrations instil an unwanted faith in the religious rituals and obscurantist forces, which help the fundamentalist forces to exploit the youth in their favour. The situation has been further aggravated owing to the decline of the progressive ideology-based socio-economic movements in the country. Popular movements are now organized mainly in the urban areas. The MRD is by and large, an urban phenomenon and does not have any programme for the rural poor. Foreign NGOs which are active in remote areas also at times encourage the communal forces. The recent rise of communalism should also be attributed to the participation of the Jamaat-e-Islam in the movement for restoration of democracy.

The movement for the restoration of democracy (MRD) began with the establishment of the Military rule in 1975. For a long time the MRD had been exclusively an affair of the Awami League and its allies. The BNP joined the MRD after the seizure of powers by General Ershad in 1982. The third force which joined the MRD was the Jamaat-e-Islam during the finale phase of the movement. The Jamaat neither had any ideological quarrel with the Military rule, nor any commitment to democracy. The Jamaat by its opposition to the war of liberation in 1971, had lost its face among the people, but found that its participation in the MRD could improve its image and widen its support base. Although there was no formal alliance between the AL, the BNP and the Jamaat-led MRDs, there were also no differences in the MRDs with regard to their form and content. To the people all the MRDs appeared to be the same. Neither the AL-led MRD nor the BNP-led MRD did clarify its stands *vis-a-vis* the

Jamaat-e-Islam. They also did not expose what the Jamaat wanted to gain by joining the MRD. On the contrary, Jamaat's participation was supported. It is claimed by many that the BNP had maintained a secret alliance with the Jamaat and used it to counter the AL's influence. However, Jamaat's participation in the MRD helped restablish it as a political force to be reckoned with.

Possible Impact

What can be the impact of the growing communalism upon the society? Restoration of real democracy would not only be delayed, but may be finally stalled. Democracy cannot be restored without demolishing the authoritarian structures, including the fundamentalist forces, which have been raised over the years of miliatary rule. Democracy does not merely mean the holding of periodical elections and alteration of one set of people in power by another.

Democracy establishes a set of norms for the running of the society; it guarantees fundamental rights, it liberates the people from obsolete ideas and prejudices, it protects people from arbitrary actions of the strong, and, above all, it establishes a society based on the rule of law. Bangladesh, during the two and half years since the fall of the Ershad regime, has not registered sufficient progress in that direction. Communalism, which is totally an undemocratic ideology, still has the upper hand. If it is not checked, the condition of the minorities, including the Ahmadis and the Kadianis, may further worsen. Their stay in Bangladesh may be made impossible. The worsening communal situation, alongwith economic crisis, would surely force the common people irrespective of caste and creed to leave the country. And their first attempt shall be to migrate to India. The unwanted migration would increase the problem in the border states of India as also exacerbate the communal tension. It is, therefore, necessary for India to be cautious.

The tide of communalism in Bangladesh can be checked if the country embarks upon an economic development capable of providing the bare necessaries of life to the common people. The government can benefit if it sincerely goes through the documents collected by the Task Force during the interim government of Justice Shahbuddin. Political forces which claim to be democratic shall have to leave slogans likely to hurt the sentiment of others; they shall have to call "a spade a spade". There cannot be any compromise on ideological issues. They have already been harmed by not exposing the real intention with which the Jamaat-i-Islam had participated in the MRD.

Despite Bangladesh being predominantly an agricultural country, unfortunately, the peasant movements have so far remained very weak. The anti-communal movement should start with the launching of peasant movements against absentee landlordism, uncertain sharecropping system and such other legacies of the feudal order. Bangladesh has a tradition of progressive socio-cultural movements. That tradition needs to be restored. Bangladesh had also a very strong tradition of Sufism. A number of top class Sufi saints who were born and flourished in the country, have left behind legacies of religious tolerance and universal humanism. The progressive forces should formulate plans to launch cultural movements to spread the Sufi ideals among the people. In the education system, Sufism should be made part of the academic curriculum.

The Power of Religious Rituals: A Case Study of Iran

CYRUS VAKILI-ZAD

With the exception of a few simple societies whose members are more or less equal, almost the entire human population now lives in stratified groups. They stratefied in regard to sharing of such social rewards as property, power, and prestige. Often access to these social rewards translates into political power and cultural domination. As a result a large segment of the population suffers political and economic deprivation and cultural alienation at the hands of the ruling elite, and the system. These conditions do exist in many societies under oppressive regimes, without any hope of freedom and without creating revolutions. Cultural or economic grievances are alone not enough to bring about a successful revolution; revolutions above all require organization, leadership and an ideology with a potential, not only to legitimize the uprising, but also to delegitimize the ruling regime.

Revolutionary organizations have often used armed struggle to bring down the system, as in the French Revolution of 1789, the Russian Revolution of 1917, or the Cuban Revolution of 1959. Very few were able to restrain the population and follow non-violent confrontation to succeed. Prime examples of the latter case are India and Iran. During the 1978-79 Revolution in Iran, in spite of scattered guerilla activities by some small groups, the major forces involved in the struggle has used street demonstrations and mass strikes to paralyse and bring down the system. In spite of brutal violence by the security forces against unarmed demonstrators, Imam Khomeini insisted on non-violent actions and refrained from calling on the Iranians to an armed confrontation, or a holy war '(Jihad'), with the Shah's regime.

During the process of the Iranian Revolution, the selective aspect of this Shi'ite culture of annual mourning ceremonies, was effectively, used, not only to mourn a dead comrade, but also to mobilise the masses. Mass mobilization was carried out by relying on the traditional rituals of the third, the seventh, and, especially, the fortieth day commemoration of the dead. These rituals were also used as a conscious mechanism to generate resources. It is important to understand that it was not the funeral ceremony by itself which created the momentum for the revolution, but the ideology supporting its existence and the cultural images ingrained among the participants. Political funerals in the Russian Revolution of 1905, in the Irish struggle against British domination and in the Prague uprising of 1968-1969, had not created similar revolutionary situations as in Iran in 1978-79.

Chronological Survey

On January 7, 1978, an article published in *Ettela'at*, a semi-official newspaper in Tehran, attackes Imam Khomeini directly for the first time. The article was entitled, "Iran and the Red and Black Reactionaries", and was signed with a pseudonym "Ahmad Rashidi Mothq". The article called the religious movement a "black reaction" and Imam Khomeini, "an adventurer without faith, a man with a dubious past, tied to the more superficial and reactionary colonialists." The article claimed that Imam Khomeini was the one who instigated the June, 1963 riot, and the reactionaries of the Red and Black had chosen him to fight the Iranian Revolution. This unprecedented direct attack by the authorities on the religious movement, especially the slandering of Imam Khomeini with malicious accusations, caused an uproar among the religiously oriented population of Iran. There were spontaneous, angry demonstrations in many major cities. The bazaar closed down, and religious leaders refused to hold Friday prayer (a symbolic sign of withdrawing of public allegiance) and demanded a public apology.

On the next two days, January 8 and 9, the last days of Moharram, the month of mourning, people took to the streets, defying the government and calling the Shah "Yazia" (the Caliph responsible for the murder of Hussain, the Prophet Mohammad's grandson) and demanding the return of Imam Khomeini.

In Qum, thousands of theology students staged a sit-in and later organized a massive demonstration, which later claimed at least 70 lives. The next day, Imam Khomeini issued a declaration congratulating the Qum students and the *Ulama* for their firm stand against the government, and asking for a broad coalition of students, bazaar workers, pesants and others for more demonstrations and united resistance. Eighty-eight prominent religious and opposition leaders, called upon the countrymen to observe the 40th day of the Qum massacre by staying away from work and peacefully attending mosque services.

February 18, 1978 was the '40th day' which was observed all over Iran, but more dramatically in large urban areas where the mosques were more active and mobilization was easier. Declarations were pasted on the walls and the doors of all major mosques, and the flyers called for mass participation in the mourning ceremonies to be held in the major mosques.

In Tabriz, a major city with strong religious orientation, the 40th day at Qom, bacame another massacre day setting off a chain reaction of massacres and mournings which mobilized the entire country and, finally brought down a monarchy believed by the people to be the throne of Yazid and manifestation of everything evil, corrupt and alien to the Islamic culture and society.

People had gathered at the Mosque of Haj Mirza Yousof Aga Mujtahid in Tabriz on the fateful day to find out about the plans for the day's ceremony. But the security forces were already alert to the occasion. Police blocked the entrance to the mosque, a violation of the cardinal Islamic tenet which states that the doors of a mosque must always remain open. When a police officer ripped down the pasted flyer, a young man attacked the officer, who, drawing his pistol shot the man dead.

The dead man became an instant martyr, and in a few minutes thousands gathered to carry his body through the streets. The planned peaceful mourning ceremony to commemorate the Qom massacre soon turned into a violent demonstration, with angry denunciation of the Shah and his American supporters. The riotess took to the streets of Tabriz, burning banks, movie houses, and hotels. The security forces, which at the beginning were hesitant to interfere, finally confronted the crowd and started shooting. The death toll reached over 100; thousands more were injured (*Davani*, 1983, VII:-73-78). March 30 was the next 40th day, of the Tabriz massacre of February 18. Scattered anti-government riots and strikes erupted throughout the country, leading to more deaths and injuries.

On March 29, Imam Khomeini still in exile glorified the Tabriz uprising and for the first time forecast the revolution, calling for a day of mourning for those who had died, declaring:

> "The ruthless massacre of Qom has shaken the Iranian people. The people of Tabriz rose in a mass revolt against the tyranny. The massacre of Tabriz has sent a trembling shock across the country and pushed it toward an ultimate explosion, an explosion which, with the help of God, will cut all the foreign hands for ever. An explosion which will avenge the blood of the oppressed from the Shah and erase the disgraceful Shah's bloody dynasty from the pages of the Iranian history". (*Davani*, 1983, Vol. VII 106-111, translation author's).

All the high *Ulama* joined Imam Khomeini in glorifying the Tabriz uprising as "heroic" and called for more action and resistance. Riots in Yazd on March 30 resulted in the death of as many as 25 people after police opened fire on demonstrators. On May 6, Imam Khomeini was interviewed by a *Le Monde* reporter in Najaf. He was asked about the riots in Iran. Ayatollah Khomeini replied:

> "The oppression by the Shah and his father has deprived our people of freedom and independence, social and economic progress. People are also fed up with government lies, especially in the last 15 years. These are the real roots of the riots today. The cultural, social and economic deterioration and the unbearable supression were also part of the problem. These riots are only the prelude to great explosion with incalculable consequences. Every massacre will set the stage for another massacre in the next 40 days. (Bid: 161, translation author's).

May 9-10 was the third '40th day' for all those who died in Qom, Tabriz, Yazd and other cities. In Qum, dissidents leaving funeral services in a mosque took to the streets, setting fire to buildings and cars, and destroying government property. On May 9, the mourning ceremony at the house of a cleric was interrupted by security forces, and a theology student was killed. On May 11, a large crowd of demonstrators calling for the overthrow of the Shah clashed with security forces in Tehran.

On June 5, a general strike was called by the coalition of anti-government forces to commemorate the 15th anniversary ot the June, 1963 uprising. On June 17, thousands of people in Qom staged a peaceful anti-government demonstration which occasioned the end of the '4oth' mourning for the death of the theology student in Qom.

On July 23-24, riots erupted in the holy city of Mashad after the funeral services for the Shi'ite leader Ayatollah Ahmad Kafi. Police and troops intervened, resulting in the deaths of about 40 people. On August 20, two movie houses in Rezai eh and Shiraz were set ablaze. On August 21, the Rex cinema in Abadan was set on fire (allegedly by the government) and 430 people were burned alive.

On August 21-22, anti-Shah riots broke out in Abadan during the burial ceremonies for the victims of the theatre fire. Crowds shouting, "Death to the Shah", attacked government buildings and clashed with security forces. From that day onward, neither the government's many reconciliatory measures (changing the Prime Minister, abolishing the newly adopted imperial calendar closing down of all gambling houses and casinos) nor its coercive methods (such as declaration of martial law) made any change in the direction, spread or the speed of the movement.

September 8, 1978, marked the last turning point for the revolution with an event which came to be known as "Black Friday". On this day between 2,000 and 3,000 demonstrators were killed in Tehran alone. After the "Black Friday" massacre, there was no room left for the government to compromise with opposition that was willing to walk into firing machine-guns for its ideals. The government faced an opposition that did not hesitate to die. For the Shah, the "Black Friday" marked the end of any hope to halt the revolution.

The Shah was finally forced to leave Iran on January 16, 1979. On February 1, Ayatollah Khomeini returned home where more than 3,00,000 people welcomed him. The welcoming committee had organized 75,000 youngmen who marshalled a human line that stretched more than 10 miles, from the Tehran airport to the Behesht Zahra cemetery, where he delivered his first speech.

This chronology—from January,7, 1978 when that anti-Khomeini article was published in the Iranian paper, to the fall of the Shah and the return of Ayatollah Khomeini on February 1, 1979, presents a vital case study in the evaluation of political funeral ceremonies as menas of mobilization of the masses, and potential for a revolution.

SHADES OF ISLAMIC MILITANCY IN WEST ASIA

M.S. AGWANI

The growing cult of Islamic militancy in parts of West Asia owes much more to socio-political than to religious factors. The major causes of Islam being articulated as answer to the prevailing ills of the West Asian polities are basically two: the failure of the West Asian political elites to evolve responsive political systems to take the place of traditional ones which no longer exist; and the humiliating defeat of the Arabs in the Arab-Israel war of June 1967 which caused reverberations not only in the West Asian region but also in the wider Muslim world.

In traditional Islamic political theory the State rested on three pillars: the *Ummah*,the Caliphate and the *Shari'ah*. Except perhaps in the early decades of Islam, this theory, however, did not always conform to what obtained in real life.

The *ummah*, meaning the community of believers, embodies an ideal which could not be realized in full even in the early period of Islam. As long as Islam was confined to Arabia, the *ummah* was a homogeneous community held together by the bonds of Islam. But once Islam spread into the non-Arab territories to the north, the dichotomy between the Arab and non-Arab Muslim arose. The Arabs found it difficult to accept the non-Arabs as full members of the *ummah* and gave them the unflattering title of *mawla* or client. The Persians accepted Islam but refused to be reconciled to Arab supermacy and led the revolt against the first Arab-Islamic Empire headed by the Umayyids. The Abbasids, who succeeded the Umayyids, were accommodative to non-Arab Muslims. From the 10th century onward, regional pressures reinforced by ethnic self-assertation splintered the Empire and it was progressively displaced by feuding kingdoms across the massive arc stretching from the plains of Central Asia to the Atlantic coast of Africa. In the 16th century, the Ottomans did succeed in bringing large chunks of the Arab world under the umbrella of a Turkish Empire but remained at loggerheads with the Shia rulers of Iran, called the Safavids. Towards the end of the 19th century, the Arabs were stirred by sentiments of modern nationalism and took full advantage of the opportunities offered by World War I to break loose from the Ottoman hegemony. The 20th century has witnessed Iran and Turkey emerge as independent states, and a fragmented Arab world into 20 old nation-states. The *ummah* had thus ceased to be a fact of political life long before the advant of the present day nation-states.

The institution of Caliphate emerged out of a practical necessity in the aftermath of Prophet Muhammad's death. His closest companion, Abu Bakr was chosen to head the *ummah*, and he assumed the modest title of '*khalifah*' ('caliph' being its Western corruption) or deputy. But within the span of a few decades, the Caliphate degenerated into an absolute hereditary monarchy. Islamic political theorists supplied the necessary religious underpinnings for the institution to suit its changing requirements. It was generally hald that the Caliph must be from the Quraish (the Prophat's clan), he was the defender of the faith and the political head of the *ummah*, and all Muslims were obliged to owe allegiance to him. The principle of hereditary sucession also found general acceptance. In later centuries, power slipped from the hands of the Caliphs but the Caliphate lingered on as a notional institution. Kings and Sultans of the Muslm world found it expedient to seek the Caliph's formal recognition in return for offerings of saluations and gifts. The Shias, of course, did not recognize the Caliphs and looked to their own *imams* for political leadership and spiritual guidance. Emperor Akbar, who was no Shia, designated himself as the Caliph. The late Ottomans staked their claim to Caliphate, if only to beef up their bargaining power *vis-a-vis* the European states. But when the empire disintegrated after World War I, the new Turkish leaders, aspiring to build a modern republican state, abolished the Caliphate in 1924. Since then, there has been no serious proposal from any quarter to revive this supra-national, politico-religious institution. Even the Islamic Conference Organisation (ICO) which pays lip service to Islamic solidarity, takes ground realities into account to exclude political unification of the Muslim world from its proclaimed agends.

Long Way From Orginal Shari'ah

In the field of *Shari'ah* or Islamic law too, the West Asian societies have traversed a long way from the early beginnings when the divine law, derived mainly from the Quran and the sayings of the Prophet *(Sunnah)*, governed all departments of life. In classical argument, the institution of Caliphate itself was justified in terms of the need for a central authority to enforce the *Shari'ah*. Ironically enough, it was under the late Ottoman Caliphate that the application of *Shari'ah* was progressively circumscribed. Beginning in the mid-nineteenth century, the Ottomans launched legal reforms, supplanting the *Shari'ah* from the penal and commercial fields, under the grand project of *Tanzimat*, or "putting things in order". The project also stipulated creation of secular courts *Nizamiah)* to adjudicate the man-made penal and commercial laws. The 1917 Ottoman law of Family Rights made inroads into the hitherto forbidden territory of Muslim personal law by introducing administrative regulations governing divorce and relief to deserted wives. Violation of these regulations was punishable under the secular criminal law. Most of the successor-states of the Ottoman Empire, stretching from Iraq to North Africa, effected further reforms in the Muslim personal law, besides endorsing the general principle of sovereignty of legislatures to enact laws for all departments of life.

It can thus be said that in most of the West Asian countries today, the *Shari'ah* applies only to limited segments of life involving marriage, divorce and inheritance. There are, however, two sets of exceptions to this rule. At one end of the spectrum stands Saudi Arabia and the smaller states of the Arabian Peninsula which enforce, with varying intensity, the Islamic penal and civil codes. Iran, too, falls into this category. At the other extreme is Turkey which, in the wake of the Kemalist revolution of the early 1920s, adopted a militant secularist stance. It proclaimed modern secular laws for all areas of life, including marriage and divorce. It is seldom realized that outside the Communist fold, Turkey is the only Asian state to opt for fullscale secularisation of social and political life in an strictly modern sense of the term. And it has stayed that way since the days of Kemal Ataturk, notwithstanding recurrent clamour by the Islamists for a return to the *Shari'ah*.

It follows from the above that the concept of *ummah* and the institution of Caliphate had either become dysfunctional or changed beyond recognition long before the advent of Western influence in the region. It was only in the field of *Shari'ah* that increasing contacts with Europe and modernization of social and economic life contributed to its shrinking influence.

Some Efforts At Alternatives

While West Asia's modernized political elites can justly claim credit for managing the transition in certain areas with reasonable efficacy, they cannot escape blame for their failure to provide a credible alternative to the traditional system of governance. This is not to say that no effort was made in that direction. On the intellectual plane, a whole generation of thinkers, from Kawakibi to Lutfi al-Sayyid, Ali Abd al Raziq and Taha Hussain joined the quest, in the late nineteenth and the early part of this century, for an alternative order based on reason and rule of law. The Syrian-born Abd al-Rahman al-Kawakibi argued that despotism had been the bane of Muslim politics through the ages; that the just State, in which men could find fulfilment, was one in which individual was free, and freely served the community; and that the government should be controlled by the peopole and act as watchdog to ensure that freedom. Lutfi al-Sayyid, for his part, made the case that good Government is one that springs from the will of the people. All other forms end up in tyranny. The case for an out and out secular order was, however, made by Ali Abd al-Raziq in his *Islam va'l Usul al-hukm* (Islam and the Bases of Political Authority, 1925). A product of Al-Azhar and Oxford, Raziq used his theological scholarship and analytical skill to advance the thesis that the entire theory of Caliphate—the kingpin of Islamic political thought—has no basis in the *Quran* and the *Sunnah* and that the practice of the Caliphate was often at variance with its theory.

Rasiq's book aroused a storm of protest. But the works of Taha Hussain—also an alumnus of Ali-Azhar—were greeted with much less hostility. For Taha Hussain approached his subject from a pragmatic rather than theological angle. In his *Future of Culture in Egypt*, he argued that the dichotomy between religious dogma and everyday secular practice is an inescapable part of life. Early Arabs, he reasoned, had no inhibitions about borrowing extensively from Greek and Persian civilizations and they gained a great deal in the bargain. Hence contemporary Arabs need not be averse to borrowing from the Western civilization.

On a practical footing, the quest for alternative bases of polity found expression in an eclectic approach. It favoured liberal borrowings from Western constitutional forces adapting them to local need and circumstances. In quick sucession, Iran, Iraq, Syria, Lebanon and Egypt adopted constitutions patterned after the British, French or Belgian models. This stupendous experiment in constitutionalism, however, did not carry much creditability as it was generally devoid of democratic content. In the1950s, most of these edifices collapsed like houses of cards. A succession of *coups d'etat* and civil disorders made the whole region reverberate with the sound of crashing thrones. Monarchial Egypt and Iraq turned into republics, and the soaring spirit of republicanism rattled the remaining monarchies in the region.

Birth of Islamic Militancy

Then came the era of charismatic leaders espousing heady ideologies of pan-Arabism, socialism and redressal of the unequal relationship with the West. Even the Shah of Iran donned the mantle of a modernizing monarch heralding his 'White Revoltion'. In most cases where some form of constitutional structures existed the single-party system of political mobilizations was introduced. But this was mostly used as a facade behind which dictatorial rule thrived. The press and other media were firmly controlled. The system allowed no possibility of free debate on public priorities or policies. Even the Shah of Iran felt tempted to emulate the undemocratic devices designed by the radical republics in the region which he otherwise abhorred.

As for the paternalistic kingdoms and emirates of the Arabian Peninsula, the rate of their social and economic transformation in the wake of the oil boom of the 1970s has been mind-boggling. Literacy advanced in rapid strides and the benefits for housing, health and general economic welfare were extended to all sections of these sparesely populated oil states. But there was no corresponding change in the political arena. Political power still vests in kings and emirs amidst growing popular clamour for accountability and rule of law.

If the absence of creditable political systems responsive to popular expectations has driven the people to protest under the banner of Islam, the failure of the ruling elites to hold their own against an expansionist Israel or to contain Great Power pressures on the region gave a militant edge to the call for *jihad* against the internal and external foes of Islam.

The Islamic militants, commonly called 'fundamentalists' because of their strident call for a return to the fundamental tenets of Islam, view the defeat of Arab arms at the hands of the Zionists in a series of wars beginning in 1947, and the loss of entire Palestine to Israel in the process, as catastrophe for the Arab and Islamic peoples. The fundamentalists no doubt blame the Zionists and their Western backers, in particular the Americans, for this calamity; but they blame their own rulers even more. They asacribe the Arab-Islamic defeat to the alienation of the ruling class from Islam, its worship of the false idols of nationalism—local as well as pan-Arab—and its addiction to foreign ideologies such as socialism, communism or capitalism. The same malaise, they argue, accounts for the apathy and inaction of the present rulers in face of the ongoing crises in Bosnia and Somalia.

Exacerbating the grievous injury to the Arab sense of dignity and honour caused by defeat is the relentless pressure and manipulation of the industralized West on the region which not only accounts for close to two-thirds of the world's proven oil reserves but also serves as a lucractive market, thanks to the oil boom of the 1970's, for their consumer products and weapons. The Islamists see in this a replay of the medieval crusades.

It is, however, necessary to point out that the fundamentalists in West Asia are not a monolithic entity nor their upsurge is irreversible. The fundamentalist camp, though clamouring for Islamic solidarity, suffers from inner divisions and disjunctions. Saudi Arabia, for example, has long been the home of what might be calles "controlled fundamentalism". The Saudi Royalty took shelter behind Islam to deny its people a constitution. And to gain respectability for their archaic domestic set-up the Saudi rulers created the *Rabita al-Alam al-Islami* (World Islamic League) to mobilise goodwill of Muslim *ulama* from all over the world through an elaborate system of patronage. With a substantial spurt in oil royalties in the 1970's, Saudi Arabia sponsored the Islamic Conference Organization as a handy platform to demonstrate its Islamic credentials. It is hardly suprising that the United States found Saudi Arabia's championship of Islam as a convenient weapon to beat the Arab radicals with, and looked benignly on it. In the wake of the Suez War which spelled disaster for Britain as a custodian of Western interests in the region, President Eisenhower seriously toyed with the idea of promoting King Saud as the 'Pope' of Islam. But the project failed to take off.

Iran and Saudi Arabia

For some time now, Saudi Arabia is having second thoughts about the efficacy of its own brand of Islam as an instrument of its foreign policy. It all started with the Iranian clergy mounting a rebellion against the Shah and eventually seizing political power. In 1979, the Pahlavi monarchy of Iran was replaced by an Islamic Republic with Ayatollah Khomeini as its Supreme guide. The cause of Saudi Arabia's discomfiture lay in the fact that whereas Riyadh has always invoked Islam to uphold political *status quo,* Iran's new rulers presented Islam in a revolutionary attire seeking to topple despotic kings, ushering in an egalitarian social and economic order, and fighting foreign dominace in the region. The Saudis were indeed scared when, in 1979, a bunch of home-grown fundamentalists occupied the Holy Mosque of Mecca in an undisguised attempt to overthorw the monarchy, ironically, in the name of Islam.

In Iran, too, in the past 15 years since Ayatollah Khomeini returned to Iran from his long exile, public zeal for the Islamic revolution has steadily diminished. Khomeini strongly believed in the unquestioned power and efficacy of Islam to establish and sustain a just social and political order. He encouraged export of the Iranian revolution to other parts of the Muslim world and envisaged eventual trimpuh of Islam the world over. He came to be identified with what may be called "messianic fundamentalism".

Khomeini, however, glossed over one basic fact about the Islamic revolution: it was made possible by the active support and sacrifices of a good section of the educated youth and the merchant class who would loathe to see Iran converted into an obscurantist theocracy. As it happened, the clergy squeezed their non-clerical partners out of the newly created governing institutions and eventually suppressed them. The eight-year-long Iran-Iraq war, which was patently senseless for both sides, scotched all hopes of a just and humane order taking shape in Iran. In the end, Khomeini was compelled by his closed advisers to swallow his pride and call for a cease-fire. The post-Khomeini Iran is surely, though haltingly, moving towards a rational and pragmatic approach to the moulding of Iran's domesitc and foreign policies. Quassam Sholeh-Saadi, an outspoken member of the Iranian Parliament representing the famed city of Shiraz, recently observed: "We must decide whether we want a parliamentary system or an Islamic government—the two are incompatible: Predictably, he was shouted down by the Islamists but not before he made it clear that there were many more who shared his views but would not utter them publicly. President Ali Akbar Rafsanjani, for his part, knows that he cannot bring the fruits of revolution to the restive people of Iran without the inputs of science, technology and modern managerial skills. He is, therefore, keen to loosen the stranglehold of the clergy on the system so that Iranian technocrafts who fled the country in the wake of the revolution can return and a new generation of technocrats could be trained at home. Rafsanjani admittedly sees no contradiction between modernity and Islam and he speaks of the need for close cooperation between Iran, India and China so that they can have a say in post-Cold War world politics. All this is a far cry from the heady days of early 1979 when Khomeini had unfurled the flag of "Islamic revolution".

Ikhwan Al-Muslimeen

Hence the real breeding grounds of militant Islam and Islamic fundamentalism today are not in Iran or Saudi Arabia or the mini states of the Gulf. On the contrary, these states are either apprehensive of Islamic militancy, or, as in the case of Iran, having second thoughts about its efficacy as an instrument of public policy. Islamic militancy is, however, rampant in the more populous Arab states of Egypt, Algeria and Sudan. (These three countries are outside the geographical West Asia. But their cultural and political interactions with West Asia necessitate discussion on Islamic militancy in this wider context.) All the three have certain features in common: population explosion, soaring unemployment and varying degrees of supression of political dissent. And this has given rise to Islamic protest movements which can be generally designated as "retributive fundamentalism".

The political stalemate in Egypt during the 1940s, resulting from the triangular conflict between the British, the King and the mass-based Wafd Party, and public disenchantment with the politicians in the wake of Egyptian defeat in the first Arab-Israeli war of 1947-48, swelled the ranks of the *Ikhwan al-Muslimeen* (Muslim Brethren), founded by Hasan al-Banna in 1929. The *Ikhwan* preached that the redemption of Egypt and of the Arab and Islamic world—lay neither in reform nor in reinterpretation of the Islamic doctrine but in its full-scale resurrection. It declared that the real issue was not Islam's inadequacy to meet the challeges of modern times but that it was never given a chance to prove its efficacy, and that the *Quran* and the *Sunnah* provide essentials of a just political order and a universal brotherhood of men. Above all, the *Ikhwan* claimed that the fault lay not in Islam but in its internal and external foes: the West strangled it politically and economically from outside and the Westernized Muslims undermined it from within.

On the eve of the military revolution of July 1952, which toppled the monarchy and put Naguib and Nasser into power, the *Ikhwan* claimed a million followers in Egypt alone. Two years later the *Ikhwan* forced a showdown with the military regime and lost. For a while, Nasser's Egypt offered a future of hope to its teeming millions. Pursuit of the ideals of socialism, unification of the Arab world into a single polity, and an independent role in world affairs enthused the whole Arab world from one and to the other. But the defeat of Nasser's Egypt in the 1967 Arab-Israeli war turned that dream into a nightmare. Nasser's image as savior of the Arabs was shattered and he died soon after. That was the time when the Islamists regrouped and mounted a frontal assault taking advantage of Egypt's mounting economic problems, the occupation of Egypt's Sinai Peninsula by Israel, and the vacillations and waywardness of Anwar Sadaat, who succeeded Nassar. Sadaat's compromise agreement with Israel over Sinai was seen by the Islamists as a "betrayal of Egypt and Islam" and as a justification to take up arms against the regime. The turmoil gave birth to several militant groups, collectively known as *Jama'at al-Islamiya* (Islamic Groups). Currently, the intensity of their violence and the virulence of their propaganda make the old *Ikhwan* look like a moderate outfit. One such group, called *Jihad* plotted the assassination of President Sadat in October 1981. Amongst their principal targets were top members of the ruling group, Coptic Christians who make up over ten per cent of Egypt's population, and foreign tourists. The most visible protagonist of the movement is 55-year old sightless Shaykh Umar Abd al-Rahman, now under detention in America for his alleged involvement in the car-bomb attack on the World Trade Centre at New York, in February 1993, that killed six people and injured many more.

In Algeria, the monopoly on power enjoyed by the National Liberation Front and its failure to find credible solutions to the nation's economic problems, notwithstanding its substantial oil and gas reserves, has thrown up an Islamic backlash. Opponents of the FLN rallied under the banner of Islam not because Islam had ready-made answers to Algeria's political and economic woes but because the ruling group permitted no secular platforms to exist outside its own regimented ranks. In the early 1990's, the Government launched an austerity programme to grapple with rising unemployment. But the crisis aggravated and, in October 1988, widespread anti-Government riots occurred. The Government then belatedly revised the constitution to permit a multi-party system. Restrictions on the press were relaxed. Among the various political parties that emerged, the most articulate was Islamic Salvation Front (FIS), headed by Abbas Madani. It benefitted greatly from Madani's previous record of opposing the FLN and gained further popularity through impressive relief operations organised in the wake of the 1989 earthquake. Not surprisingly, therefore, the FIS won 67 per cent of the provincial and 55 per cent of the municipal seats in the regional and local elections held in June 1990. And in the postponed parliamentary elections, eventually held in December 1991, when the FIS won 188 of the 231 seats (in the 430 member parliament) decided in the first round, President Bendjedid stepped down to make way for Mohammed Boudiaf. The new president cancelled the elections. In March 1992, The FIS was outlawed. Boudiaf was assassianted on 29 June 1992. Thus, Algeria's cautions advance towards democracy came to a grinding halt.

In Sadan, Col. Jaafar Muhammad Nimeri seized power in a bloodless *coup d'etat,* in 1969, and followed in the footsteps of Egypt's Nasser, adopting a set of socialist policies and mobilizing mass support under the banner of the Sudanese Socialist Union, within the framework of a single-party system. In the Southern Sudan, assertively Christian and African in contrast to the more populous Arab-Islamic North, Nimeri followed a policy of accommodation by conceding autonomy and allocating resources for development. Nimeri's 16 year-long stint in power, however, left the economy tottering under the weight of rampant corruption at home and influx of refugees from Ethiopia, Uganda and Chad; the South suspicious and resentful of Khartoum's manipulations and the disgruntled conservative groups in the North breathing down the regime's neck. A few years before his fall in April 1985, Nimeri enlisted the support of the *Ikhwan* and Dr. Hasan Turabi's National Islamic Front by promising to turn Sudan into a full-blooded Islamic state. This desperate act alienated the Christian South to the point of insurrection. Nimeris exit has not made much difference to Sudan's political and economic woes.

It is noteworthy that a few months before his ouster, Nimeri's crusade for Islamization of Sudan had resulted in the hanging of Muhammad Mahmud Taha—the 76-year-old protagonist of a secular approach to politics. Taha's "crime" was that he and his associates belonging to the Republican Brothers has distributed a leaflet saying that the Islamic laws promulgated by Nimeri ran counter to Sudan's constitution and were indeed detrimental to integration of the Muslim North and the Christian South into one nation on the basis of equal rights for all citizens. Taha thus became the first martyr to the cause of secularism in the Arab world. The intrepid secularist refused to defend himself in the court, declaring that his prosecution was unconstitutional and the judges were unqualified and technically incompetent.

Finally, a word about the reversibility or otherwise of the fundamentalist wave in West Asia. As already noted, the challege posed by Khomeini's Iran has dampened the enthusiasm of Saudi and other peninsular rulers for politicization of Islam. In Iran itself, time and internal pressure for political openness and economic progress do not favour the clergy and their grandiose notions of Islamic resurgence. As for the predicament of Algeria, Egypt and Sudan, a major cause of the people turning to Islam and the Islamists for resolving their economic and political problems is the denial of opportunities to bring about political change through the democratic process. Arguably, the victory of Islamic Salvation Front in the Algerian election of 1991-92, which at any rate appeared certain, might well have defused rather than aggravated the political crisis in Algeria. In Egypt and Sudan, too, a liberal dose of democracy could bring a semblance of purpose and poise to the institutions of governance. As Walid Khalidi, a noted Arab political scientist, observes, the answer to the crisis of Arab polities lies in "genuine power-sharing or accountability in government". Finally, the recent accord between the Palestine Liberation Organisation and Israel on the framework of a political settlement, if carried to its logical conclusion, can blunt the edge of Islamic militancy in the whole region in a significant way. After all, the hurt and humiliation caused to the Arab psyche by the loss of Palestine, has been a vital contributing factor to Islamic extremism.

'Green Peril' or Islamic Radicalism in Arab-Islamic World

JAGDISH P. SHARMA

Religious revivalism is an international phenomenon. In recent years virtually all parts of the world witnessed religious resurgence. In the case of West Asia and North Africa, the religious revivalism has been termed as "Islamic fundamentalism". It is the movement to return to the fundamental scriptures of faith—the *Quran* and the practices of Prophet Muhammad as recorded in the *Hadiths*, which together form the *Sharia*, the Divine law of Muslims. But the Americans and the West consider this revival as a fanatic anti-American and anti-West movement. For them, Islamic radicalism is synonymous with political terrorism, hostage ordeals, suicide bombings. This part of the world has experimented with all kinds of ideologies like Nasserism, Ba'ath Socialism, Capitalism and Marxism between the forties and the sixties. The inadequacies of these ideologies have given birth to a new kind of Islamic radicalism. To a Western world pre-occupied with growing economic problems and security concerns, inflation, energy, environmental degradation, natural disasters, disintegration of the Soviet Union, the West Asian crisis, particularly the resistance movement in the Israeli-occupied Arab-Palestinian territories, the regional conflicts in the Gulf, the Afghan question and the Bosnian crisis—the new challenges of Islam appear disconcerting and even ominous. Few in the Western and Eastern worlds were able to anticipate an Islamic reaffirmation in the recent context. Contemporary West Asian and North African region, particularly Egypt, Algeria, Lebanon, and Israeli occupied Arab Palestinian territories can be viewed as a microcosm of the "Islamic radicalism" presently manifesting in that area.

During the later part of the 1970's, activist Islam became synonymous with political militancy and extremism. In the recent times voices have begun to counsel the Clinton administration that with Communism's death, America must prepare for a new global threat, that is, "radical Islam". Like the "Red menace" of the Cold War era, the "Green Peril" (green being the colour of Islam) is described by the Americans as a cancer spreading around the globe undermining the legitimacy of Western values and threatening the national security of the West and the United States.[1]

In the Middle East Islam has become the ideology of political opposition against the existing socio-political orders. In the early part of this decade (of the 90's) the Islamic resurgence began a new phase—Islamic movements began to participate in the political system instead of opposing it. Increasingly, the Iranian model has been shunned, and the radicalist's bullets have been forsaken for the ballot box. Yet, pockets of virulent militancy still remain strong, notably in Egypt, Algeria, Lebanon and the Israeli occupied Arab-Palestinian territories.

Symbols of Radicalism

The radical Islamic spectre seems to have been symbolised in the following events, viz: the fall of the Shah of Iran and the subsequent Islamic Revolution there, the US hostage crisis in Teheran, the takeover of Saudi Arabia's Grand Mosque in 1979, the assassination of Egyptian President Anwar Sadat in 1981, the bombing of the World Trade Centre in New York City, the civil war between the Islamic government in Khartoum and the Christians and Animists in Southern Sudan, terrorist attacks and the coup attempts to overthrow President Hosni Mubarak by radical Islamists in Egypt, the popularity of Islamic parties in Egypt, Algeria Jordan, Tunisia, Turkey and the Israeli occupied Arab-Palestinian territories, Arab-Islamic support for Bosnian Muslims, the Lebanese and Afghan struggle for political power and Islamic Iran's pursuit of military, economic and political influence in the Persian Gulf and Central Asia.[2] These examples have heightened the interest and confirmed the stereotype of millitant Islam.

Islamic radicalism also known as "Islamic resurgence", "Islamic awakening", "Islamic revival", "Militant Islam", "the Green Peril or "Islamic Fundamentalism" implies a strong attachment to the past. The term "radicalism" or "resurgence" (for the Arabic term *"Ihya"* appears to be appropirate than such commonly used terms like "Islamic fundamentalism", or "Islamic Conspiracy" to describe the Islamic political movement of the comtemporary period. It is not new to the Middle East. The causes for its latest resurgence could be outlined in numerous categories—chiefly, historical, religious, spiritual, moral, social, political, economic and psychological.[3] Viewed in its metaphysical dimensions, Islam represented an endeavour to rectify the false scriptures of Judaism and Christianity. It unfolded in time and space, denoting the continuation and culmination of other unitarian religions. Its Arabian nucleus expanded within a short period to encompass a far-flung empire, extending from India to Spain. (At present, the Muslim world extends from North Africa to South-East Asia. In addition to some 50 Muslim majority countries, Muslims constitute a significant minority in another 25 countries. The more than 850 million Muslims comprise almost a fifth of the world's population.)

Resurgence, reform or revival are recurring phenomena in Islamic history. They manifest themselves differently in different circumstances. Closely related to the above is the movement to return to the fundamental scriptures of faith, the *Quran* and the practices of Prophet Muhammad as recorded in the *Hadiths*. This means returning to the *Sharia* creative interpretation of Divine law.[4] The Divine law provided the blueprint for the Muslim society i.e. a comprehensive code of life which included laws that regulate socio-religious life and alms-giving as well as family, criminal, commercial, legal, economic and international law. This belief in the divinely ordained nature and mission of the Muslim community was validated and reinforced by their success and power throughout Islamic history. Within a hundred years of Prophet Muhammad's death, the original Islamic community, through expansion and conquest, became an empire more extensive than any the world had known.

Challenge of Western Colonialism

A major crisis in Islamic history and in Muslim identity was precipitated by the advent of Western colonialism. During the 19th century, the Islamic world succumbed to Western Christiandom militarily, economically, politically and, finally, socially. As a result, the very meaning and understanding of Muslim history was challenged. The disintegration of traditional Islamic political order and struggle aganist Western colonalist intervention and rule provided both an indentity crisis and a political purpose for Muslims in the twentieth century. Muslim countries followed a path of Westernisation and politicalisation as they increasingly adopted Western models in politics. law, economy and education. The Caliphs and Sultans were gone. Most of the Islamic laws were replaced by Western legal codes and modern politico-techonological, economic and educational systems were established under colonial tutelage.[5]

It was against this background that Islamic radical movements began to sprout in order to reinstate Islam in its pure and original state. During the twentieth century, Islamic relgion re-emerged in the politics of the Middle East, inspiring anti-colonial, anti-Western, national movements and their struggle for independence. The credit for conceiving Islam's global predicament and offering solutions must rest with Jamal al-Din al Afghani, the father of the modern Islamic reformist movement.[6] Having lived in all the important countries of the Middle East, as well as Britain, France, Russia and India, he called upon Muslims to resist Western Imperialism, seek political liberation and undertake an intellectual reawakening rooted in a return to Islam. Under Afghani's disciples the Egyptian Muhammad Abduh (1849-1905) and the Syrian Rashid Rida (1865-1935), the *Saafiyyah* movement through its reformist journal *al-Manar* sought to restate classical doctrines in order to bring about Islamic political, legal and intellectual reform.[7]

Hassan al-Banna (Egypt), for instance, went beyond pamphleteering and soliciting the support of the elites in Muslim countries, the techniques used by Afghani and Abduh. In tune with times of mass participation in political movements, he engaged the attention and energies of ordinary Muslims and created in the late 1920s *the Islamic Brotherhood* i.e. *Ikhwan al-Muslimeen* in Ismaillia in Egypt, a popular party with a slogan which included the *Quran*, Prophet Muhammad, God, constitutional government and martyrdom.[8] During the 1960's the re-emergence of Islam was rather a limited phenomenon, both geographically and politically. However, During the latter half of the 1970's, Islam dramatically re-emerged in Muslim politics in Middle East, attracting both geographic expanse and geopolitical implications.

Three basic attributes

Islamic radicalism in its current form is offered as a system, an ideology, and a comprehensive worldview. To some of its adherents it means a third alternative to Euro-American liberal capitalist or Marxist or socialist ideologies. It is proposed as a genuine and authentic "home grown" worldview, grounded in the teachings of the *Quran*. It provides its adherents a claim to parity with West and East.[9] Three basic attributes are said to be responsible for the revival of Islam. To start with, one of the most significant attributes of contemporary Islamic radicalism is its pervasiveness.[10] The movement of "return to Islamic roots" is a transnational phenomenon. It has been taking place virtually in every Islamic society or community regardless of size or political, economic and cultural environment. Indeed, the quest for a new Islamic identity is discernible not only in West Asia, but also in North Africa, Nigeria, Turkey, Malaysia, Afghanistan, Pakistan and Indonesia. It is manifest not only in countries where Muslims are numerically dominant, but also in Islamic minorities in India, the Philippines, the erstwhile Soviet Union and the Western countries.

The second unique characteristic of the Islamic resurgence movement is its polycentrism. The three potential centres which could provide leadership to the nascent movement are Saudi Arabia, Egypt and Islamic Iran. The attack on the Grand Mosque at Mecca by a splinter group of *Ikhwan* (Muslim Brotherhood) in November 1979 is a pointer in this direction. Besides, the expanding activities of the *mutawaeen* (religious police) who ensure that shops close for prayers and people behave in a seemly manner, atleast to the growing power of the religious establishment. There are calls for the young to limit their contacts with the West and for the young Saudis not to take foreign brides. In the case of Egypt, there has been a marked revival of religious activism since the 1970's.

Besides, Islam is a revealed religion. Like Judaism and Christianity. Islam requires the acceptance of certain articles of faith that have been realised by divine wisdom to gifted interlocutors.

The fourth most striking aspect of the phenomenon of Islamic resurgence is its persistence. The tendency toward Islamic regeneration persisted in the last century. During the early part of the 20th century, the Egyptian society went through a period of ideological tension, quite unprecedented in scope and force, which erupted as a result of the encounter between the world of tradition and the values of the modern, secular world of the West.

Factors for Resurgence

The contradictions between Western Imperialism and the Arab-Islamic world have manifested the recent trends. The West's refusal to accept realities based on justice for the Arabs has aggravated the situation. There is duality in the US policy towards this region. While the West encouraged Zionism, which is a kind of racism based on aggression, colonisation and expansion, it turns a blind eye to the sufferings of the Arab-Palestinian people. It encourages its enemies, and is viewed by the Islamic radicals as a kind of perpetuation of Western hegemony over the Arabs. US Imperialism used the *Ikhwan al-Muslimeen*, Islamic fundamentalist organisation in some of the Arab-Islamic countries to counter communalism. The case of Afghanistan is an example from the forties to the recent times. All of a sudden the US began to highlight all the evils of Islamic radicalism: after the collapse of the Soviet Union. The US views Islamic fundamentalism as a new enemy.

The basic issue which impinges directly on the Arab-Israeli dispute concerns Arab Palestinian rights. Were the Israelis to return the West Bank and Gaza Strip and let it be constituted as a secular independent Palestinian state the radical leftist and Islamists would then press for a legitimate struggle to recover the rest of the pre-1948 Palestine from the Israelis.

Islam has become the ideology of political opposition against the existing socio-politico-economic orders in the Middle East.[11] Among the political factors leading to the Islamic resurgence, the following were prominent, writes Dr. A.H.H. Abidi: absolute despotism; denial of basic human rights; loss of credibility by the existing governments; separation of religion form politics and bid to create rifts between religious elements and masses; reviving and glorifying the pre-Islamic past at the cost of the Islamic traditions and heritage; creating and sustaining a class system and domination of Muslims by non-Muslims.

The socio-economic causes of the resurgence of Islam are many. The negative fall out from the effects of modernisation, the demographic imbalance, migration from the villages and rapid urbanisation of overcrowded cities with insufficient socio-economic support systems; the rapid population growth, the breakdown of traditional family, religious and moral values were of equal concern. At the same time, the general economy of Arab-Islamic states had faltered. It was manifest in the grip of a vicious circle of increased money supply, rising expectations of the popu-lation, general inflation, corruption, economic hardship, inequalities of income leading to the gap between the rich and poor, price rise, common frustration and other socio-psychogical tension. Besides, to Dr. K.R. Singh (JNU), Islamic radicalism to some extent is rooted in the exploitation of Arab-Islamic oil of the South by the North i.e. the West and the U.S.[12]

Moreover, the current trend of Islamic radicalism is largely due to the disillusionment in the Arab-Islamic world with other ideologies such as Marxism, Zionism, Capitalism and Socialism, none of which appeared to meet their day-to-day difficulties, or find solution to the ongoing socio-politico, military, psychological conflicts or solve their economic problems On the contrary, the economic crisis and socio-politic problems that have resulted from these ideologies and conflicts have only deepened and become more complex.[13]

The leaders of the contemporary radical Islamic movements, in the Middle East try to rally the alienated and the under-privileged on the basis of Islam. They present Islam as a religion of justice and equity and decry the current ruling elite as unjust, un-Islamic and corrupt, which deserves to be overthrown, or at the very least, replaced non-violently by true believers. Many of the Sunni activists cite the 14th century political theorist Ibn Taymiyya to justify their revolt against established "illegitimate rule". The tactics used to achieve this objective vary: from setting up secret cells to addressing large congregations inside a mosque or outside. Also, from bloody confrontations with the security forces to peaceful participation in elections, from carrying out terroristic actions to holding non-violent demonstrations; and from subverting official institutions through infiltration to total withdrawal from society. The popularity of the Islamic ideology can be ascribed to a general acceptance of the fact that the present condition is intolerable. Evil has reached its limit and thus change must take place.[14]

To some of its advocates this transformation of individuals and societies does not necessarily mean a change to something new. It is seen primarily as a kind of check against backsliding, and is thus a remoulding: not into new forms, but into the perfect form. Revolutionary activity is essential in the light of human tendency to deviate, to innovate and to veer from the strainght path. Radicalism in this case acts as a dynamic, never ceasing impetus to stay the course.[15]

Case Studies: Egypt

What happens in present-day Egypt, Algeria, Sudan, Jordan, Israeli-occupied Arab-Palestinian territories, and Lebanon are curcial to the shape of things to come in the heartland of Middle East. Within the Arab-Islamic world, Egypt has often seemed a land apart—a nation of gentle and good humoured people who would rather break up a fight than join one. But Egypt deos not seem so peaceful these days. Recent terrorist incidents, media reports and reasoned articles convery the impression that Egypt is on the brink of a terrible upheaval.[16]

In the past two years, gunmen have sprayed a Nile tour boat with bullets and warned foreign visitors to stay away from the Pyramids and other historic landmarks. Islamic militants have planted deadly nail-bombs in crowded Cairo streets. Islamic radicals have fought bloody battles against Egyptian security forces and have attacked Coptic Christians, government officials, and secular intellectuals like Faraq Foda.[17]

The struggle has been most obvious in Cairo, where the radicals have claimed responsibility for months of high-profile attacks, including bomb explosion to assassinate Prime Minister Atef Sedki. But the main battleground is in the provinces of Upper Egypt, and other villages such as Beni Smei, 15 miles south of the provincial capital of Assiut. In the villages around Assiut, the atmosphere is charged with menace for any one suspected of collaborating with the authorities. By the early 1980's, the region's anarchic violence began to take on the outlines of organised rebellion. When President Anwar Sadat was assassinated in Cairo in 1981, Assiut was primed for explosion. Today the armed wing of the *Gamaa al-Islamiyya,* is the most radical Islamic group associated with the current waye of militant attacks. It is largely composed of southern Egyptians.[18]

Distinction: Moderates and Militants

A distinction should be made between the moderate Muslim Brothers and the militant groups. The former has been an element of the Egyptian political scene since its foundation in 1928, whereas the latter, while claiming spiritual and inspirational inheritance from the early days of Islam, emerged in Egypt in violent form in the 1970's. They both take a hostile view toward Israel and equate Islam with pan-Arabism.[19] The Muslim Brothers are at present non-violent and believe in active proselytisation. In contrast, the militants are aggressive and do not shy away from violence in thier total rejection of the existing political system in Egypt.

Islamic movement like the Islamic Brotherhood derive legitimacy for violence from the fact that they see themselves to be at war with anti-Islamic forces. Violence is also justified in reference to certain aspects of Figh (jurisprudence) literature, which argue that innocent Muslims may be sacrificed if an anti-Muslim enemy attempts to *shelter* behind them.

Because of the size of its population, Egypt seems to be vulnerable to this new Islamic radicalism. Besides, the manifestation of this Islamic revivalist trend in the public life of Egypt seems to be extensive: the overflowing mosques, the proliferation of the traditional garb, the flood of religious publications, the prevalence of Islamic norms, etc.

The quest for a return to the Islamic ethos in Egypt appears to be a natural response to the successive experiences like the disorienting political, economic, demographic and social impact of the Western oriented policies in Egypt, population explosion, social dislocation and alienation, skewed income distribution and acute sense of relative deprivation.[20] A series of diplomatic setbacks reflected in the stalemated peace process with Israel, dependence on the United States, increased proportion of imported food, the decline of national resources, the gap between the rising aspirations and realities, especially of the younger generation,[21] lack of economic opportunities, breakdown of the family support base due to materialistic interests, rapid urbanisation, etc. Capitalist oriented free market economic policies have also contributed to the recent violence.

Egypt under Nasser was on the whole a positive movement from the point of view of social and economic development. In contrast, during the succeeding periods, there has been a drastic decline in the socio-economic and demographic progress. The conspicuous characteristics of this decline are a major increase in dependency on external power, particularly the United States[22], decreasing capacity for vital self-sustaining capability accompanied by social, political and economic instability, and disintergration, as a result of growing sense of insecurity and helplessness among large segments of the populace.

When President Nasser came to power, he attempted to work with the existing ruling class, enjoining it to invest in Egypt's economy. Soon, however, he realised that state takeover of the country's resources, a planned economy, and the empowerment of the have-nots of the Egyptian society, (such as the landless peasants, the lower and the middle classes) was the essence of his concept of land reform, industrialisation and redistribution of wealth.[23]

In a country with a huge and ever-growing population, but meagre natural resources, the Nasser regime gave industrialisation a high priority. Capital was invested in heavy industry, one of those being steel. Between 1957 and 1970, industrialisation advanced at an average annual rate of 5.7%. Industry's share of the *GDP* increased from 15.3% to 23.2% between 1952-1970.[24]

The industrial progress provided employment and consumer goods at fixed prices, as well as social security for the workers. Advances were also made in education, expanding at an 8% annual rate and a drop in illiteracy, down form 75% to 65%. The advances which the Nasser regime made in agriculture were equally inpressive. The land reforms and the modernisation of agriculture achieved a degree of productivity and social justice as never before.

But an evaluation of the Egyptian society during the post-Nasser period shows an unmistakable reversal of the progressive trends due to causes indigenous to Egypt. Under President Sadat and President Mubarak, Egypt declined precipitously in the fields of agriculture, irrigation, industry, planning, supply and education. Egypt reverted to back to a dependent status, a status of subsistence on conditional Western aid, similar to its status prior to Nasser.

Post-Nasser Egypt became open for invasion by private interests and corruption. Sadat and his family took the lead in abusing their public positions for private gain. Sadat's Egypt fell into the hands of those who served the interest of a few, whereas in the Nasserist era the approach was to assure the progress of the society as a whole.[25]

The new regime's favour for the 'haves' at the expense of the public was evident in education, transportation policy, housing, medical care and almost every aspect of society. For example, little money was invested in public transporation, as a result, the sight of masses of humanity riding on the roofs of the buses or dangling from its sides was commonplace. Just as Nasser's policies of national pride and self-reliance articulated the aspiration of the lower, the lower-middle and the middle classes for a better life, Sadat's slavish reliance on the West articulated the old comprador bourgeoisie's longing for a return to the *ancien regime*, when the state was instrument in the hands of the Westernised elite.

Under Sadat, Egypt fell victim to a new class of opportunists who pushed it down the road of ruin. During this period President Sadat shifted to a more outward-looking "open door" development policy *Infitah* designed to encourage domestic and foreign private investment. New laws were enacted and incentives given to "improve" the investment climate and assure investors of the government's commitment to the private sector. Closer economic and political ties were developed with the West, with the United States in particular. But this policy proved unsuccessful. Industry continues to be burdened by excessive employment levels, insufficient capitalisation, price controls and an inappropriate wage structure.

The distributive effects of Sadat's *Infitah* policy were instrumental in promoting class divisions and tensions. The gap between Egypt's rich and poor widened. The shift in power from President Sadat to President Mubarak period continued the state of decline and degradation and erosion of the Nasserite model.[26] Sadat's *infitah* was based on a major flaw: that as a society of 50 million people, which had barely begun building its modern indentity, economy and institutions, should now look outside for the resources and inspiration for development.

The thrust of Nasserism was to build Egypt's productive base, to use its skilled but cheap labour to make it the industrial centre of the Arab world, and develop its hydraulic electric energy, agriculture, etc.

President Mubarak has adopted some alternative strategies to recoup the declining image of his country and to rehabilitate it not only in the Arab-Islamic world but in the world at large and thus is attempting to build a new Egypt. But this "new Egypt" in marked with a resurgence of Islamisation and radicalism. Increasing privatisation increased the opportunities for the "haves" in building up their economic wealth and power enabling them to increasingly exploit the large segment of the deprived and poor Egyptians. Lack of resources, education and other facilities which ought to have been provided by a welfare state have increased religious redicalism and bigotry. In Egypt today, Islam is seen as an alternatives to inadequate or inefficient government services and high-priced private institutions. Various Islamic societies at local levels have established hundreds of clinics and schools with first rate services at marginal or no cost.

The inherent danger in such a situation, with the entire country turning into an Islamic regime, will spell disaster not only for Egypt but for the entire Middle East. If President Mubarak can see the danger and muster enough courage to steer the country away from Islamic radicalism, then alone can Egypt hope for the fruits of adopting a Western model. Solution, therefore, lies in increasing economic justice to the vast majority of the under-privileged Egyptians although Islamic radicals are certain they will win power eventually.

The Algerian case

In Algeria, Islamic victories have not happened is a vacuum. In June, 1990, the Islamic Salvation Front (FIS) won an upset victory in Algeria's first multiparty election since independence from France 31 years earlier. This radical party captured 32 of the 48 of the regional assemblies and 55 per cent of the 1,541 municipal councils. The ruling National Liberation Front (FLN), which had dominated local and national politics since 1962, came in a poor second, winning 14 regional assemblies and 32 per cent of the municipal councils. Independents and a Berber party took the rest. In January 1992, the governing High State Council of Algeria cancelled the elections on the eve of the victory for the Islamic forces, saying that the radicalists would never allow another election if they won. Since then, fighting between the authorities and the Islamic Salvation Front (FIS) has taken more than 100 lives, including 127 deaths in August 1993 alone.[27]

Islam's appeal in Algeria has grown because of economic hardship, political failure, social turmoil and a combination of all the three. The Islamists' demand for a change are no different from the demands in East Europe. In a country with an unemployment rate of at least 30 per cent, people want jobs. In Algeria, where the legendary *casbah* is teeming with several times more people than it can hold, people also want housing. With a huge 26 billion dollar foreign debt, Algeria has limited funds to address the country's economic problems. This debt accounts for three quarters of the country's foreign earnings—money which should be spent on urgently needed raw materials for industry.[28] Almost 70 per cent of Algeria's oil revenues are spent paying off the deft instead of funding local development. In many of the municipalities where the FIS won, the local governments were effectively bankrupt. Algerians were voting as much against an inefficient system as for Islam. The day the election results were announced, the continuing discontent with the economic conditions was as visible as ever—gas station attendents were on strike causing long queues of angry motorists, a newspaper strike and a boycott by garbage collectors creating piles of garbage on streets throughout Algiers.[29]

The emergence of an Islamist current in Algerian politics was to be expected, since Islam remained the major source of cultural identity during the colonial period. For many of the nationalists who took up arms against France, nationalism was defined by thier Islamic heritage. Since 1962, Algeria's rulers had drawn their legitimacy from their role in the war between 1954 and 1962 for independence from France and the institutions forged during that period, notably the army and the National Liberation Front (FLN). During the 1980's that authority wore thin as the economy faltered and government corruption grew. As grievances accumulated in the 1980's. the Islamists' audience expanded. Many of their recruits were youngmen without jobs, others were shopkeepers resentful of the ruling party's socialist ideology. The latter were a source of funds for the movement as were some foreign governments such as Saudi Arabia, Islamic Iran and Pakistan in recent times, which permitted Islamist "brothers" to provide modest social services in poor, overcrowded Algerian neighbourhoods.[30]

The Islamic Salvation Front was an amalgam of several currents of Islamic thought. According to some sources it brought together four major groups; *Jamaat al Toblie* (the society of message); *Ahl Attalia* (the people of the vanguard); The holy war society; and *Dawa* (The call i.e. the propagation of the Faith). Since December 1991, when the Algerian military government unceremoniously annulled the results of elections which the radicals appeared to have won, Islamic radicals have waged a ruthless terror campaign against Algeria's secular establishment. Initially the militants targeted police officers, military men, political leaders and government officials. Recently. however, the attacks appear to have entered a new phase, with the singling out of French-trained intellectuals and other professionals. Boukhobza was the sixth prominent intellectual killed in the last six months. The dead include Laadi Flici, a doctor and writer, Tahar Djaut, an author and journalist; Mohfoud Boucebsi, a world renowed psychiatrist; wirter Ha-fidh Sendhri and Djiilali Lyabes, director of the National Institute of Global Strategic Studies.[31]

Algeria today remains under a state of emergency first imposed in February 1992. There is dusk to dawn curfew. Against this background, the government's plan for economic recovery appears to have little chance of sucess. And as long as the economic crisis persists, people will continue to turn to the Islamists as their only hope for the future.[32]

Islamic Experiment in Sudan

Since the introduction of the *Sharia* (Islamic law) by the former Sudanese President, Jafar al-Numayri in 1983, Islam has had considerable impact on Sudan's public life. Not only it is regarded as the source of legislation, but it also regulates social, political, economic and diplomatic activities. The imposition of *Sharia*, however, exacerbated long-established animosity between northern and southern Sudan. Catholic Bishops have accused the Sudanese government of waging a holy war against the State's Christians (almost ten per cent of the population) and those who follow African religions. *Sharia* has been reimposed with new vigour—lashings of women for inappropriate dress are now common; so are other corporal punishments, such as amputations for repeated theft, and stoning for adultery.[33]

The role of Islamic law in Sudan has been a bone of contention since independece in 1956. The *Sharia* was not adopted soon after independece, partly because of sharp divisions between the traditional political parties and partly because it was not perceived to be in harmony with Sudan's Islamic heritage, which is derived from the Sufi traditions.

Apart from the mid-1880's, when Muhammad Ahmad al-Mahdi spearheaded an Islamist revolution, Sudan's traditional religious sects *(Ansar and Khatmiyya)* have consistently sought to avoid revolutionary political activity. However, the major political parties are based on religious sects: the *Umma* party on *Ansar* the Democratic Unionist Party (DUP) on *Khatmiyya*, and the radical National Islamic Front (NIF) on the Muslim Bortherhood.

Since the Muslim Bortherhood was created in 1954, its primary objective has been to establish an Islamic order based on the *Sharia*. Under Hassan al-Turabi's leadership, who was elected the Movement's secretary in 1964, the Muslim Brotherhood has transformed itself into an effective political party, the NIF.

The present phase of Islamisation in Sudan can be traced back to 1977, when Numeiri, who has previously suppressed sectarian-based political parties, undertook reconciliation measures, which in turn gave the Muslim Brotherhood a valuable opportunity to influence government policy. Turabi made the best use of the opportunity provided by the process. He joined the then ruling Sudan Socialist Union (SSU) and subsequently occupied senior government posts, including that of the Attorney-General's. It was largely because of Turabi's manoeuvres and influence that Numeiri agreed to introduce the *Sharia* in September 1983. The NIF's fortunes improved further when General Abdulrahman Swareddahab, who overthrew Numeiri in 1985, liberalised the political system, thereby allowing opposition parties to operate. This enabled the *Umma* party, the DUP and the NIF to be re-established.

In the election of April 1986, the NIF won all the seats in Khartoum and controlled virtually all urban centres. Sadiq al-Mahdi's Umma Party obtained the highest number of seats in the National Assembly, but it did not have an outright majority and formed a coalition government with other parties which at various times included the DUP, the NIF and minor southern parties. Mahdi's three-year government (1986-89) proved ineffective and indecisive on many issues, especially on Islamic law and the civil war.[34]

In the eyes of militant Muslims, Sudan is a great success, with the introduction of *Sharia*, crime in the capital was reduced considerably. But the cost has been heavy—endless civil strife and unimaginable suffering. For a decade, Islamic soldiers of the Khartoum government and the Christian and animis rebels of the SPLA have fought a war that has killed over 600,000 people, displaced 3.5 million more and threatens another half a million with starvation. The fighting has grown more vicious since Lt. Gen. Omar Hassan al Bashir seized power in 1989 and turned Sudan into an Islamic radicalist state. Determined to defeat the SPLA and impose *Sharia* on the South, al-Bashir last year stepped up attacks on the rebels, bombing villages and massacring civilians.

Since the 1979 Islamic revolution in Iran, Sudanese Islamists have tried to associate Islamic resurgence with fighting injustice. However, in Sudan, the implementation of *Sharia* has been accompanied by the entrenchment of dictatorial rule, the erosion of civil liberties and a woresening economic malaise.[35] It has set secular and moderate Muslims against radicalists, exacerbated the civil war and virtually destroyed public institutions and the state in general.

In Israel Occupied Territories

Indeed, the most militant strains of Islam are in areas where Arab-Islamic liberation movements have been suppressed or where grievances have not been addressed to, notably in Israeli occupied Arab-Palestinian territories. Since the outbreak of the non-violent independence struggle of the young Arab-Palestinians i.e. the *Intifada* in 1987, Islamic activists have become increasingly important political forces. The two main Islamic activist groups in this part are the Islamic resistance movement i.e. *Hamas* and Islamic *Jihad*. Both these groups call for the restoration of Mandatory Palestine as a national homeland and reject international initiatives on exchanging land for peace. Both have their strongest support in the Gaza Strip, although *Hamas* has gained significant ground in the West Bank. Both are widely seen as new-comers to the Palestinian political scene.[36] Their emergence has brought about a state of imbalance in the political forces that had held sway for decades.[37] They claim that they are a part of the world Islamic movement. They feel it is the duty of every Muslim to liberate Palestine. The State of Israel is seen as an invasion of the Arab-Islamic world. At the moment, its struggle is within the framework of Arab nationalism whose primary task is the Liberation of Palestine. Although it declares war against the Jews, it does not exclude the other religious groups like Christians and the Jews in the Palestinian State. It accepts PLO as "father", brother, friend and a relative because the goal of both is the liberation of Palestine. It rejects partition of Palestine by United Nations in 1947 and the Madrid Peace talks join culminating in the PLO-Israel accord of September 1993.[38]

The *Hamas* movement started after the spontaneous outburst of the *Intifada* It is an offspring of Muslim Brotherhood which was not involved in politics since the proclamation of the State of Israel. Israeli government was somewhat lenient towards the Muslim Brotherhood as it did not join the liberation struggle of the Palestinians. But things changed radically in 1988 when it took up the *Intifada* leadership in Gaza Strip and parts of West Bank. It joined the *Intifada* under pressure from the masses. It is an Islamic answer to Zionism which is the worst kind of fundamentalist movement.[39]

Hamas enjoys popularity in Gaza and West Bank. It is opposed to Yasser Arafat's peace initiatives. After the signing of Sepetember 1993 accord it is spearheading the resistance against Israeli army in the occupied areas. The *Hamas* are the Palestinian hardliners who do not want any compromise or co-existence with Israel. Non-implementation of the peace accord on the scheduled date i.e. 13 December 1993 has led to the resurgence of *Hamas* militancy. If and when the accord is implemented, the *Hamas* would remain a threat to Arafat's self-government. It will work as the opposition party in the automonous independent Palestinian State. It's popularity is because of the sincerity, dedication and honesty of its cadres. The *Hamas* movement got an international dimension because of the deporation of 415 of its leaders and cadres by the Israeli government in December 1992.

The Islamist or *Ikhwan al-Muslimeen's* position has been further hardened as they were refused a chance to rule Algeria through their democratic victory. This was a grave mistake on the part of the regime. Had they been allowed, much of there militancy would have been diluted and they would have become a part of the democratic process. This would have set a precedent in the Arab-Islamic world and the Islamic radicals elsewhere would have been brought to the democratic process. In the case of Egypt, the revival of Islamists is because of the socio-economic and demographic problems that have plagued the Egyptian society after Sadat's "open-door" policy and compromise with Israel. In the case of Palestinians, the rise of *Hamas* is because the Palestinians are facing the worst kind of colonialism, racism and Zionist fundamentalism. In the case of Sudan, the rise of Islamic radicalism is due to under-development, extreme poverty and starvation. Above all, Islamic radicalism has replaced communism which has collapsed. In the Arab-Islamic world there cannot be a vacuum. Moreover, the humiliations, sufferings, exploitation, torture, genocide, enthno-cide inflicted on the Muslims of Palestine, Bosnia, and Lebanon by the West especially the US through Israel or others, is seen by the Islamic world in a different perspective. There is a sense of deprivation, alienation, anguish, Western imperialism, socio-economic, political and cultural led by the US is seen as the biggest enemy of Islam and Muslims of the world. The "Green Peril" as seen by the US cannot be contained unless the economically developed North addresses the major grievances of the Arab-Islamic world.

References

1. Leon T. Hadar, "What Green Peril", *Foreign Affairs,* Spring 1993, pp.27-29.
2. J.P. Sharma, "Islamic Resurgence in Egypt and Tunisia", *Ind-African* a (University of Delhi) Vol.I. No.2, October 1988, p. 67.
3. A.H.H. Abidi, "Islamic Revival in Iran" in Agwani, M.S. *The Gulf in Transition* (ed.) (Delhi, 1987) pp. 3-4.
4. Dilip Hero, *Paladin Movements and Idea: Islamic Fundamentalism.* (London, Glasgow, Toronto, Sydney, Auckland: Paladin Graftion Books, 1988, 1989, p. 270.
5. John L. Esposito, "Introduction: Islam and Muslim Politics" in his *Voices of Resurgent Islam* (ed.) (New York, Oxford: Oxford University Press, 1983) pp. 5-6.
6. J.P. Sharma, "Arab Nationalism and the Gulf Crisis" *World History: New Horizons* (Delhi: Low Price Publications, 1993) p. 370.
7. Ibid, p. 364.
8. For details see Ishak Musa Hussaini, *The Muslim Brethren: The Greatest of Modern Islamic Movements* (Beirut: Khayaat's college Book cooperative, 1956).
9. Yuonne Yazbock Haddad, "The Islamic Alternative", *Link* vol, XV, No.4, 1982, quoted in *The Muslim World* (Hartford) vol. LXXVI, nos.3-4, July-October 1986, p. 152.
10. EIU: *Regional Review: The Middle East and North Africa* (London: Economist Publications Ltd., 1986) pp. 41-46.
11. B. Tibi, "The Renewed Role of Islam in the Political Social Development of the Middle East" *The Middle East Journal* (Washington D.C.) vol.37. vol.1, Winter 1983, p. 5.
12. K.R. Singh, *The Persian Gulf: Arms and Arms Control* (Canberra: Heritage Publishers, 1983) and Dr. Singh's article "The Gulf on the brink of catastrophe", *Link* (Delhi) vol. 33, no. 3, 26 August 1990, pp. 4-8. Quoted in Sharma, J.P. "The Gulf Crisis: New Trends of Arab Nationalism" *Proceedings of the Indian History Congress* 51st Session, Calcutta University 1990. p.751. Also see K.M. Panikkar, *For a Few Barrels of Oil : Politics and Diplomacy in the Gulf* (Delhi: Patriot Publishers, 1991.)
13. J.P. Sharma, "West Asia today" *Link,* January 17; 1993 p.22. Also see Manosur Farhang, "The United States and the Question of democracy in the Middle East", *Current History* (Philadelphia) vol. 92, No. 570, January 1993, p. 4.
14. Sayyid Mujtaba Mustaba Musawi Lari, "Resurrection as a manifestation of Divine Wisdom and Justice" in *Al-Tawhid* (Teheran) Vol. IX, No. 2, November 1991-January 1992, p. 66.
15. *See* Youssef M. Choueiri, *Islamic Fundamentalism* (London: Pinter Publishers, 1990) Also J.P. Sharma, "Quest for Peace in West Asia" *Foreign Affairs Reports* (Delhi), vol. XXXVIII, No. 11, November 1989, pp. 139-156.
16. The struggle between Islamic radicals and the secular government of President Hosni Mubarak for control of Egypt is coming to the boil. *See* Guardian Weekly, December 5, 1993.
17. The killing of a state security officer and his six-year old son in mid-March in 1993 made headlines and earned nationwide revulsion. As security forces continued to search for the killers, police general Mohammad al Shaimi was assassinated on 11 April in the Upper Egyptian town of Abu Tig. For details see *The Middle East* (London) June 1993, pp. 9-10.
18. *Newsweek* (New York), August 2, 1993, p. 29.
19. Anthony McDermott, "*Mubarak's Egypt: The Challenges* of the Militant Tendency", *The World Today* (London), vol.42, No.10. October 1986, p. 171.

20. J.P. Sharma: "Political Sustainability of Changing Socio-economic profile in Egypt" Paper presented at a seminar on *Contemporary Political and Economic Changes in West Asia and Africa*, 17-18 March 1993 at the School of International Studies, JNU, Delhi.
21. K.R. Singh: "Political Ramifications of Socio-Economic Changes in North Aftrica" Paper presented at the Seminar on Demography, Democracy and Economic Reforms in West Asia, 17-18, March 1993, JNU. Delhi.
22. For details see Marvin G. Weinbaum, *Egypt and the Politics of US Economic Aid* Boulder; London: West View Press, 1987; George M. Guiss, *The Politics of United States Foreign Aid*, London and Sydney: Croom Helm, 1987, pp. 222-225. Also Tim Mitchell, "America's Egypt: Discourse of the Development Industry" *Middle East Report* March-April 1991, pp. 18-36.
23. Joel Gordon; *Nasser's Blessed Movement*, New York: Oxford University Press, 1992.
24. Robert Mabro, *The Egyptian Economy: 1952-72*, London, Oxford University Press, 1974, and John Waterbury, *The Egypt of Nasser and Sadat: the Political Economy of Two Regimes* (Princeton, Survey: Princeton University Press, 1983.)
25. Heykal, Muhammad Hassanayn: Kharif al-Ghadhab: *The Autumn of Fury* (Beirut: The printing company for Publication and Distribution, 1987) pp. 393-433.
26. J.P. Sharma, "Islamic Revivalism and Egypt" *Proceedings of the Forty-Eigth Session, Indian History Congress*, Goa University, 1987, pp. 667-674. Also see J.P. Sharma, *The Arab Mind: Egypt-Arab Unity and the World.*
27. *Newsweek*, September 13, 1993, p. 26.
28. *The Middle East*, April 1993, p. 17.
29. See Robert A, Mortimer, "Algeria: The clash between Islam, Democracy, and the Military", *Current History* (Philadelphia) vol. 92, No. 570, January 1993, pp. 37-41. Also see Dr. K.R. Singh's paper "political ramifications of socio-economic changes in North Africa".
30. *The Middle East*, February 1993, pp. 20-21.
31. *Newsweek*, July 19, 1993, p.11. Recently a total of 19 people were killed in the ambush (January 10, 1994 onwards) by an armed group that assassinated the first local governor since Islamic radicals took up their holy war against the military backed regime.
32. J.P. Sharma, "Crisis in Algeria: Emerging Trends", in *Democratic World* (Delhi), 6 November, 1988, pp. 13-14.
33. Judith Miller, "The Challenge of Radical Islam" *Foreign Affairs*, Spring 1993, pp. 48-49.
34. See John L. Esposito "Sudan's Islami Experiment" in *The Muslim World*, Vol. LXXVI, Nos. 3-4, July-October 1986, pp. 181-202.
35. See Ellen Gruenbaum. "The Islamist State and Sudanese Women", *Middle East Report* (Washington D.C.) November-December 1992, pp. 29-32.
36. "Hamas makes it to centrestage", *The Middle East*, February 1993, p. 9.
37. Ziad Abu-Amr, "Hamas: A Historical and Political Background", *Journal of Palestine Studies*, vol. XXII, No.4, Summer 1993, p.5.
38. For details on accord, see Mehmood Hussain, "Historic PLO-Israel Accord: The Territorial Question" and J.P. Sharma, "Yasser Arafat: The Master peace diplomat" in *Third World Impact* (Delhi) November 1993, pp. 10-14.
39. Mehmood Hussain, "Israel: Fountain head of Fundamentalism and Terrorism" in *Third Concept* (Delhi) April-May 1993, p.57.

Central Asian Republics and Islamic Revivalism

D. BANERJEE, AVSM

The Central Asian Republics (CAR) emerged on the international scene rather suddenly and perhaps somewhat reluctantly, at the end of 1991. In a rare juncture in Muslim history, alongwith Azerbaijan, five new Muslim states (Kazakhstan, Turkmenistan,Tajikistan, Uzbekistan and Kirghistan) appeared all of sudden on the global scene. This has occured in an area which was in the past an integral part of the Islamic world and where in more recent times the Turkish influence dominated. Many religious, social and cultural manifestations of Islam have not only flourished here for many centuries, but even originated in the splendorous cities of Tashkent, Bukhara and Samarkand.

For much of this century, however, since the October Revolution in Russia in 1917, this region remained detached from the mainstream Islamic world. But since 1991 the region has come to acquire considerable strategic importance. The area is contiguous to different versions of practising Islam. The Turkic, Iranian and Wahabi influences are all attempting to make their presence felt in the region. The region is situated at the underbelly of the former Soviet Union, with its separate geo-strategic remifications. The issues that arise, and which will concern the Asian continent in particular, is the nature of Islamic order that might emerge here and its larger influence in the region. Would Islamic revivalist tendencies prevail here as in the rest of the Islamic world? What form and order would emerge, now and in the near future? How will these Republics interact with each other and the world? Answers to these will evolve over time, but the process itself is of importance and needs to be analysed.

Recent History

It is imporant to turn back to recent history and examine how these five Republics were to find their political identity. Only after the October Revolution of 1917 the process of forming the new Republics began. This took place in three stages:

(a) A Turkestan Autonomous Soviet Socialist Republic existed as part of the Russian Federation in Central Asia. There were two Soviet People's Republics already, Bukhara and Khorasem, which were transformed in September 1924 and October 1923 respectively into Soviet Socialist Republics.

(b) In 1924-25, a special committee appointed from Moscow set the borders of two new Soviet Socialist Republics—Uzbekistan and Turkmenistan—as well as a Tajik Autonomous Repulic and two autonomous regions, Kara-Kirghiz and Kara-Kalpak. Simultaneously, the Kirghiz Autonomous Soviet Socialist Republic, which until that time was a part of the Russian Federation, was renamed Kazakh Autonomous Soviet Socialist Republic.

(c) In 1936, two more Republics became full-fledged Soviet Socialist Republic—Kazakhstan and Kirghizia.

By 1936, the five Soviet Socialist Republics of Kazakhstan, Uzbekistan, Kirghistan, Turkmenistan and Tajikistan came into being. The arbitrary drawing of borders created a number of problems. The rich Ferghana Valley was shared by three Republics (Uzbekistan, Turkmenistan and Tajikistan). The two prominent cities of Bukhara and Samarkand with their majority Tajik population were now in Uzbekistan. About one million Tajiks found themselves living in Uzbekistan and one million Uzbeks in Tajikistan. Subsequent developments resulted in a diaspora into and out of the region, creating a fascinating mosaic of ethnic peoples throughout the CAR. This is shown in two tables at the end of the chapter Table-1 shows the total population in the CAR, including the breakdown by major groups while Table-2 shows the ethnic composition of different groups by thier percentages.

There are other fascinating dimensions to the demographic question. First is the uneven growth of the Slav and Irano-Turkic Muslim populations. A study covering the period from 1959-1979 explains this well, and is shown at Table-3. While the growth has been 20 per cent for the Slav people over a 20 year period, it has been about 100 per cent for the Irano-Turkic Muslims. This is also shown in the national composition of the population in the CAR for the 30 year period from 1959-1989 (See Table-4).

Some other characteristics of recent demographic developments need to be noted:

— The Muslim population has shown a very rapid growth. At a rate of about 3 per cent per annum or more, it is nearly four times the growth of the Slav population. At this rate of increase they are likely to exceed 100 million by early next county.

— The decline in Russian population has been marked. It is on two counts: First, a low birth rate; and second, emigration. Though movement from the CAR has slowed down on account of the severe adverse conditions within Russia, any sudden outbreak of violence or change in policy such as the declaration of regional scripts as official languages, can rapidly alter the scene as has already happened in some of the Republics. The Russian exodus will adversely affect industry and economy of the CAR as they still form the bulk of the experienced managerial and bureaucratic work force. This in turn will also affect security, not the least beacuse of a genuine Russian importance with such developments.

— Next, is the question of preponderance of Uzbeks in the population of CAR. Today they number over 16 million, and constitute about 33 per cent of the overall population. They are present in all the Republics, but predominate in the Ferghana Valley and the rural areas of the CAR. They also extend into Afghanistan, where again they are a factor to contend with. This percentage is likely to rise as the Russian population, which comes next, continues to decline.

Islam in the Former Soviet Union

In spite of severe discouragement from the State, Islam prevailed in the country in various forms. The Communist Party realised fairly early that religion should not be suppressed altogether. Rather, it needed to be controlled and moulded to suit the State's purpose. Therefore, one had what can be called "Official Islam" supported by the Government. Next were the various forms of "Unofficial" Islam, and in particular the Sufi brotherhoods. Lastly, Islam was also preserved in the form of folklore and tradition. A brief examination of these forms of Islam is necessary.[1]

In an attempt at secularization of Islam, four Spiritual Boards or Directorates were set up in Tashkent, Baku, Makhachkale and Ufa in 1943.

In January 1990 another Board was set up at Alma Ata in Kazakhstan.[2] "Official" Islam sanctified the coexistence alongwith the atheist Marxist-Leninst state. The State in turn allowed minimal religious practices, including maintenance of mosques, some *madrassas* and printing of Qorans. In turn, the practitioners of "official" Islam moderated their Islamic practices. Yet, the overwhelming majority of people continued to follow Islamic marriage rites, circumcision of thier male children and buried their dead. In late 1980's, the Soviet State attempted to coopt "official" Islam in combating social crimes, such as corruption, alcoholism, and drug abuse. In turn, "official" Islam too got corrupted. The Muslim clergy became a hereditary office with substantial official perks and privilege.[3]

Simultaneously, "unofficial" Islam too flourished. In the absence of mosques and the general rejection of secularization, a non-establishment, non-orthodox Islam too flourished. A large element was the offspring of Sufi Islam. This Sufism had consistently opposed Russian conquest and played an important role in the Basmachi movement of the 1920's.[4] There have been reasons to believe that atleast some of these groups blended nationalism with religiosity.[5]

In Tajikistan, there had been a pronounced resurgence of Wahabism. This is one form of Sunni fundamentalism which seeks a "pure form" of Islam. Its spread was more noticeable in 1992 and early 1993, but seems to have suffered a certain set-back since then.

The final form of Islam that manifested itself in the pre-1991 period was the preponderance of *Folk Practices*. Bennigsen has put this in the category of "unofficial Islam", but Yaacov Roi would like to give it a distinct identity. In any case, the distinction between the two is quite blurred. It is more truly a blend of religious, quasi-religions, social and cultural activities falling broadly under the category of Islamic practices. This form of Islam particularly attracted the young in the pre-Independence period. In a way this had a very positive impact as Islam played the role of guarding ethical values such as prevention of alcoholism, drugs, crime and corruption.[6]

Islam and Politicization: The Perestroika Era

It was in the Gorbachev initiated Perestroika era that Islam asserted itself in the CAR. The larger Islamic identity, the *'Umma'* began to take shape. It was being generally asserted that without being a Muslim one could not become a true Kazakh, or Tajik or Kirghiz. However, this was by no means a predominant idea. Even though Islamic banners, green flags, and pictures of Khomeini began to appear, these were not as widespread as earlier assumed. Many prominent Soviet leaders of the era had accused the Islamic radicals of misleading the youth. The disturbances at Dushanbe on 12-14 February 1990, raised the possibility of the Islamic fundamentalists from Afghanistan and Iran of fomenting these ideas. However, they did not materialise, instead there was the rise of the *'Birlik'* movement.

Birlik, or Unity Party, emerged in Uzbekistan in November 1988. Led by Abdurrahman Pulatov, a member of the writers Union, then in his thirties, Birlik is neither fundamentalist nor Pan-Turkic, yet it is Islamic. Its branches are autonomous and can take to local coluring. Thus, it is very Islamic in the Fergana Valley, yet not so in Tashkent. It won its spurs by getting Uzbek adopted as the state language, championing the cause of the Arabic script, and having the Qoran translated. In February 1990, the *'Erk'* or Independence Party emerged as a splinter from this, perhaps to the satisfaction of the Communists.[7]

Kazakhstan has its *Alash Party*, with its orientation towards Kazakh nationalism. It enjoyed a certain prominence during the Revolution before being snuffed out by the Bolsheviks and then again emerged. It promotes Kazakh nationalism which excludes the majority Slavic population of Kazakhstan, but it regards Islam as the basis for the national regeneration of the Kazakhs. Owing to the traditional superficiality of Islam in Kazakhstan, this is not quite a potent force.

The process of Islamisation of CAR politics began from the late 1980's and received a fillip in the early 90's. The question remains regarding its current spread and furture possibilities. The disturbances that took place in the 1930's in the capitals and major provincial towns of CAR and their links with the spread of Islam is well established. However, the extent and depth remains in doubt. Almost all the provinces in Central Asia of the former Soviet Union witnessed some disturbances in 1989. Though their leaders played down the Islamic factor, the outside world remained deeply concerned. Gorbachev too highlighted these linkages in his sppeches in the West.[8]

In June 1991, the Islamic Revival Party was established in the then Soviet Union but its activities met with serious opposition from the authorities. Some regional Islamic Revival parties, however, as well as other Islamic organisations gained major support in Uzbekistan and Tajikistan, where they formed a formidable political force. But in other CAR states as well, Islamic influence among the population became quite substantial. Thus, for instance, according to latest polls, about 25 per cent of all Uzbeks living in the Osh region in Kirghizia favour Islam and Islamic values. In the same Republic, local Islamic leaders coined a slogan: Each village must have its own mosque, In spite of the terrible earthquake that inflicted multibillion rouble losses on the republican economy, mosques are now being constructed everywhere, even though there is a terrible shortage of money, labour and consturction materials to rebuild houses and schools.

These developments alarmed the West, and in 1991-92 much was made of the possible rise of Islamic fundamentalism in the region. The Greek Minister for National Defence, Loannis Varvisiotes, proclaimed that, "Greece will eventually become a Christian island surrounded by Muslims. I am concerned that the Mediterranean will be surrounded by Islamic fundamentalism."[9] He quoted the Turkish elections where 17 per cent voted for Islamic fundamentalists.

The Gulf War of 1990-91 drew particular interest of the West to the arc of predominantly Islamic countries of West Asia and Europe. These countries were very important Western allies in the Cold War against the Soviet Union. With its end, the perception also underwent a radical change. From Pakistan to Algeria, the entire region was seen as posing some sort of a threat. However, over the years this perception has undergone a change. Islam is seen as a nuisance, but no longer as a major threat.[10] There is a curious ambivalence in this posture, for there are other views that depict future conflicts based on civilizations. Here the boundry between Islam and the rest is seen as particularly prone to conflict. That "Islam has bloody borders" is being repeatedly articulated in the West.[11]

It will be useful to examine in particular the spread of Islamic fundamentalism in individual Republics, and its present and potential influence.

Islam in the Car

Uzbekistan: It is the most populous of the CAR and with its predominantly Uzbek population, constituting 33 per cent of the entire CAR population itself it has an important role and influence. The rich Ferghana Valley with its dense population is shared between three Republics. It is here that the spread of Islam would have the most important significance.

Islam has grown in Uzbekistan, but not at the same scale as in Tajikistan. But there is no manifestation of Islamic activism or anything approaching what may be understood as fundamentalism. "Official" Islam needs to shed its close association with the state if it is to gain popularity. Else "unofficial" Islam may spread.

Kirghistan: "Official" Islam in Kirghistan flourishes unlike in the other states of the CAR. It has established its own "Mufti", independent of Uzbekistan in the year 1992. The Islamic Renaissance Party continues to be banned in both Uzbekistan and Kirghistan. There is no doubt that funding from outside would normally go to "unofficial" Islam if it is from Iran or Sandi Arabia, it could have serious implications. However, there is little indication of that as yet.

The big question is whether "official" Islam will be able to meet this challenge. So long as it continues to enjoy the support of the state, such a likelihood is somewhat remote in this Republic.[12]

Kazakhstan: The situation in Kazakhstan is more complex. The Kazakh population is in a minority in the Republic. The cities have an even larger Russian population but the Kazakh language is being emphasised eventhrough Russian continues as a third language. There is greater Slav influence over the population. Basically a nomadic people, religion has never played a dominant role in the lives of the Kazakhs. Hence, one sees the least influence of Islam in the Republic. Its capital boasts of only one mosque. Attendance in its functions is thin. Kazakh nationalism is based on language, culture, its own unique way of life and characteristics, rather than an overt religious oreintation.[13]

Tajikistan: Tajikistan is the only Republic in the CAR whose language is almost the same as Persian, even though it is a Sunni State. Despite the latter characteristic, Iran has a dominant influence here. It was the first Republic where the Islamic Renaissance Party established itself in the CAR. It has shown the maximum susceptibility to political Islam.

The conflict in Tajikistan over the control of Dushanbe, its own peculiar character, proximity to Afganistan and hence influence from the fundamentalist elements there, have all contributed to making this an unique case. It is the influence of Afganistan and Iran that would most effect developments in this Republic. It is also the most vulnerable.[14] The spread of Islamic influence through the Ferghana Valley remains most critical for the CAR.

Turkmenistan: Turkmens, like the Kazakhs, have been nomadic and highly conservative. Ethnically too they are distinct from the others. Linguistically they are more closely associated with Azerbaijan and Turkey. These distinct cultural identities provide the Turkmens a great deal of diversity. Turkmenistan has a very long border with Iran and about a million Turkmens live there. The Sunni-Shia split, however, has kept the nations ideologically separate, even as economic cooperation is bringing them together. Islamic influence continues to remain strong at the local level.[15]

Discussion of Central Asia's political future inevitably turns to the subject of Islamic fundamentalism. Fundamentalism in any strict sense of the term has hardly emerged as a dominant force in the region. Power in the CAR states is held by secular leaders who have maintained their legitimacy by quickly shedding their roles as communist functionaries and donning the mantle of nationalism. More than 70 years of Soviet educational and cultural policies has created a secular intelligentsia that is still the most likely group from which future leaders are likely to emerge.

On the other hand, the history of independent Central Asia is much too short and domestic trends in individual states much too uncertain to rule out the growth of fundamentalism. With the end of Soviet restrictions on Islam, its influence in general has definitely grown; and may yer expand in ways that cannot be foreseen. The rise of the Islamic Salvation Front in Algeria whose attachment to power was stopped only by a military coup, demonstrates that the dominance of secular institutions and ideologies does not preclude the political triumph of fundamentalist religious movements.

The spectre of surging Islamic forces, however, persists in some discourse on Central Asia. This may well be a blend of the apocalyptic and the simplistic. But this scenario ignores the economic and political variations among the individual states of Central Asia. The relative stability of Kazakhstan and Kirghistan compares sharply with the chaos in Tajikistan. The challenge offered by Islamic organisations to secular regimes undoubtedly has transnational potential. Even allowing for its varied characteristic, Central Asia has a cultural unity that ultimately transcends national boundaries. The Islamic Revival Party, for example, operates in borth Tajikistan and Uzbekistan. Not surprisingly, Tajikistan's turmoil has created tension between the governments in Tashkent and Dushanbe.

The Muslim Face of China

An important question of the revivalism of Islam in Central Asia is its possible impact on China, and in particular on the Xinjiang Province. According to the 1990 census, the breakdown of Muslim population in China is as shown below:—

(a)	Total Chinese Population	-	1.04 billion
(b)	Total Muslims	-	17.6 million or 1.17 %.
	of which Hui	-	8.6 million
	Uighurs	-	7.2 million
	Kazakhs	-	1.1 million
	Rest	-	0.7 million

The Hui people mainly speak Chinese, live in the more central provinces and are largely assimilated within the Chinese nation even though they maintain their distinct identity. Many Muslim groups supported the earliest call of the Communists as they were expected to bring about a better way of life and equity. However, it was the Muslims who sufferend the most in the Cultural Revolution with large-scale massacres, mosque closings and indiscriminate persecution.[16]

There is no doubt that the independence movement in Xinjiang province has been encouraged by the developments in the CAR. China in its turn has become keenly aware that the Islamic world is observing its treatment of its own Muslims minorities. Therefore, China is handling this question with great care and circumspection. Economic cooperation with the CAR, mainly through barbar trade, is extremely widespread all over the region. China expects to be able to successfully deal with its minority population through greater attention to their development, by providing special attention to their needs and by ensuring that the conditions of the Chinese Muslims are better than they are in the CAR or in the Muslim nations further to the South.[17]

Possible Rise of Militant Islam

The rise of militant Islam in the CAR is still only a distant prospect. The overwhelming desire of the people in these Republics is, in order of priority, to achieve a higher standard of living, consolidate their respective nationalisms and evolve a higher socio-cultural ethos. Of course, a religious identity and belief meshes in with atleast some of these desires.

The situation could still change. There are usually three distinct steps through which Islam may move on its way to fundamentalism. These stages may be summarised as fellows:

(a) Once the people feel, with reasonable assurance, that their lives are morally, spiritually and materially unsatisfactory, a feeling develops that these issues could be addressed more effectively through an Islamic state.
(b) The next stage is that in this environment, should such a group function with relative autonomy and a free and fair election takes place, then such an Islamic group may well succeed in coming to power.
(c) Finally, of course, where it does come to power, it would be unable to fulfil the very same aspirations. Islam cannot be implemented in its true sense and after this it leads towards fundamentalism.[18]

Islam will surely grow in Central Asia in the future. Its long and foreceful suppression goes against the very basis of this religious belief. Yet it will find its own level in a new and emerging cultural and political ethos. Islamic fundamentalism will only emerge as a major force in the region, provided that either of the two following conditions are met:

(a) Relations between the native population and Russia (and this includes local Russian population), move sharply towards confrontation. In this "Islam versus Christian" context, Islamic fundamentalism will surely prove to be a rallying point.

(b) Second, is the rise of domestic opposition movements of a strong Islamic character in the face of disastrous economic and social conditions followed by the emergence of an authoritarian regime.[19]

Should events go badly, Islamic fundamentalism could emerge strongly in the CAR. This would then indeed have negative impacts on Russia, China and India, as well as affect the political dynamisms of the Islamic world.[19]

Among all the possible instabilities that may emerge in the CAR, and there are many, the rise of Islamic fundamentalism is surely not very high among the range of possibilities. Yet, many unexpected and surprising developments have been known to occur as recent developments in international relations have shown. It is imperative that an interactive set of relationships should be developed with the outside world, particularly with India, to forceclose such a possibility.

Table 1. Muslim Central Asian Republics Population 1990

Republics	Pop. (in mns)	Russians	Other Nationalities
Turkmenistan	3.6	10%	9% Uzbeks, 3% Kazaks & 1% Ukrainians
Uzbekistan	20.3	8%	5% Tajiks, 4% Kazaks.
Tajikistan	5.3	8%	24% Uzbeks, 1% Tatars, 1% Kirghiz, 1% Ukrainians.
Kirgistan	4.4	22%	13% Uzbeks, 3% Ukrainians, 2% Germans.
Kazakstan	16.7	38%	6% Germans, 5% Ukrainians.
Total	49.7		(9.6 mn Russians and 1.50 mn other Nationalities)

Source: Dervied from "The Soviet Union's Unequal Parts: Diverse and Restless, "The New York Time, Sep. 11, 1990; Time, Sep 9, 1991; Statesman's Yearbook, 1990.

Note: *The figs. for population etc. may vary in the charts depending on the year of data and source.*

Table 2. Ethnic Composition of Central Asian Republics (by Percentage)

Kazakhnstan	Uzbekistan	Kirghizia	Turkmenia	Tajikistan
Kazakhs-40	Uzbeks-71	Kirghizs-52	Turkmen-72	Tajiks-62
Russians-38	Russians-8	Russians-22	Russians-10	Uzbeks-24
Germans-6	Tajiks-5	Uzbeks-13	Uzbeks-9	Russians-8
Ukranians-5	Kazakhs-4	Ukranians-3	Kazakhs-3	Kirshizs-1
Others-11	Others-12	Germans-2	Ukranians-1	Ukranians-1
		Others-8	Others-5	Others-4

Table 3. Slav and Irano-Turkic Population Growth Rates

Ethnic Group	Millions of 1959	People 1979	Percentage Growth 1959-1979
Slavs			
Russians	114.11	137.40	20.4
Ukrainians	37.25	42.40	13.7
Belorussians	7.91	9.46	19.5
Irano-Turkic Muslims			
Uzbeks	6.02	12.46	107.3
Kazakhs	3.62	6.56	81.0
Tajiks	1.40	2.90	107.4
Turkmen	1.00	2.03	102.5
Kirghiz	0.97	1.91	96.8

Note : Rasma Karlins, Ethnic Relations in the USSR: The perspective from Below: (Allen & Unwin, Boston, Boston, 1986). p. 231.

Table 4. National Composition of Population in the CAR

Nation	1959	%	1989	%	An Annual % Change 1959-89
Uzbek	5,973,147	26.0	16,520,080	33.6	3.4
Kazakh	3,232,403	14.1	7,476,296	15.2	2.8
Tajik	1,385,835	6.0	4,162,524	8.5	3.7
Turkmen	985,643	4.3	2,672,174	5.4	3.3
Kirgiz	962,001	4.2	2,482,210	5.1	3.2
Russian	6,213,830	27.0	9,516,229	19.4	1.4
Ukrainian	1,034,965	4.5	1,234,556	2.5	0.6
Tatar	779,840	3.4	1,178,698	2.4	1.4
German	985,623	3.0	1,134,097	2.3	0.5
Korean	212,472	0.9	320,189	0.7	1.4
Belorussian	121,596	0.5	239,765	0.5	2.3
Uygur	92,974	0.4	258,952	0.5	3.4
Azerbaijan	102,169	0.4	187,273	0.4	2.0
Jewish	147,495	0.6	137,445	0.3	0.2
Armenian	47,066	0.2	111,064	0.2	2.9

Note : Robert J Kaiser, "Nations and Homelands in Soviet Central Asia", in Geographic perspective on Soviet Central Asia, ed. Robert.

References

1. Yaacob Roi, The Islamic Influence on Nationalism in Soviet Central Asia, Problems of Communism, July-August 1990.

2. Kazakhstanskaya Pravda, Alma Ate, 13 January, 1990.
3. Some Muslim dignitaries like Mamayusupov, the duftri of Central Asia in Uzbekistan, founds seat in the 'Congress of Peoples'Deputies in 1969.
4. For example Tajikistan, there were 1,000 illegal mosques, against 30 official ones.
5. E. Filimov: The Ideological and Social Essence of Religious extremism-Naukai Religia (Moscow), NO.8, 1984, p. 18.
6. Roi, No. 3, p. 55.
7. Gorbachev's Speech on 13 June, 1989, referred to the disturbances in the Fergane Valley, for example.
8. *Hindustan Times,* Ist July, 1992.
9. Susum Awahohara and Salamat Ali, "Fear of Islam" For Eastern Economic Review, 30 Jan, 1992, pp. 20-21.
10. Samuel p. Huntingston, Clash of Civilizations, Foreign Affairs Summer 1993, pp.22-49.
11. Graham E. Fuller, "Central Asia - the New Geo-Politics, Rana Publications, Santa Mumica USA, 1992, pp. 24-25.
12. Ibid, pp. 31-35.
13. Ibid, pp. 47-51.
14. Ibid, pp. 62-63.
15. Dru. C. already: "The Muslim Face of China", Current History, September 1993, pp. 276.
16. Ibid, pp. 277.
17. Ibid, pp. 277.
18. Ibid, pp. 278-280.
19. Godrej Samsen, Militant Islam: Strengths and Fatal Weakness, Middle East Intelligence, 7 Feb. 1992, p. 16.

Islamic Resurgence and Russia

DEVENDRA KAUSHIK

To be fair to the Russian policy in Central Asia, it has to be acknowledged that it was conducted in the spirit of civilized European liberalism. Russia did not interfere in the national life of the region, whatever it might have done in Ukraine or Latvia where it did follow a policy of oriental despotism. Unlike some West European colonial powers Russia made no efforts to proselytise the Muslim population of Central Asia. Despite certain similarties between the methods governing colonies and thier exploitation there was a difference in the position of the peoples of Central Asia under Tsarist colonial rule and those in British colonial possessions in India. The geographical contiguity of Russia with Central Asia enabled a large number of common Russians to migrate overland to that region. Their presence gave the Central Asian peoples an opportunity to come in contact not only with the Tsarist colonialists, Russian Kulaks and traders, but also Russian peasants and industrial workers, scientists, teachers, writers and revolutionaries.

This interaction with the progressive democratic representatives of relatively advanced Russian culture contributed to the development of democratic socio-political thought in Central Asia and had a positive influence in shaping the world outlook of many of their cultural and scientific leaders. Among such enlightened people mention may be made of Ahmad Donish (Tajik historian, writer and poet) and Sadriddin Aini (a leading Tajik writer), Uzbek poets Furgat, Mukimi, Zavki and Hamza Hakimzade Niyazi, Turkmen poets Seidi, Kemine, Zelill and Mollanepes, Kirgiz bard Toktogul Saltyganov, Abai Kunanbayev (Kazakh poet, educationalist and father of the new written language of Kazakh literature), Chokan Valikhanov and Ibrai Altinsarin, kazakh literateurs and educationists.

During the Stalinist period, new ethnic boundaries were drawn in line with the national principle, finally five Union Republics were constituted in three stages in 1924, 1929 and 1936. The economic and strategic aspects of the central authority were also given due consideration. Two language reforms—changing from Arabic script to Latin and subsequently from Latin to Cyrillic—were introduced to curb Pan-Islamism and Pan-Turkism. Stali-nist purges replaced the old national elites by a new local ruling class which strictly followed Moscow's directives in utter diregard to local nature, customs and traditions conducting itself as a true univeral *"Soviet man" "Homo Sovieticus"*. After Stalin's death, an idealist pursuit of "Homo Sovieticus re-emerged during the Khrushchev and Brezhnev era with its stress on "trinity model of flowering-rapprochement fusion".

According to French scholars on Central Asia and Islam in the Soviet Union—Halene d'Carrere Encausse and Alexander Benningsen—despite suppression of national customs and traditions during the Stalinist period, the *Homo Islamicus* emerged like. Phoenix from the ashes. The liberal atmosphere of the post-Stalin period also contributed to its rise. The Islamic revolution in Iran and the victory of the *mujahidin* in Afghanistan gave further impetus. Helene Carrere d'Encausse argued that the higher birth rate among the Central Asian Muslims, rising unemployment and the growing Muslim self-assertiveness posed a serious challenge to the Soviet power in that region. Benningsen forecast an inevitable "Showdown" between the Muslims of the Soviet Union and the Non-Muslims. He visualised independence for all the five Central Asian republics in a form ranging from revival of Sultan Galiev's national Communism" to conservative Islamic redicalism. Michael Rywkin in his work, *Moscow's Muslim Challenge (1982)* hinted at "the existence of growing racial antagonism between two non-integrated communities in Soviet Central Asia. However, Western scholars like Michael Zand, Gregory Massell and Nanoy Lubin did not share the pessimistic vision of d'Encausse, Benningsen and Rywkin. The latter believed that the Soviet rule had resulted in the establishment of various sub-types of "Russified Soviet subculture" and that the Soviets succeeded in co-opting the elite who stood alienated from their original ethno-cultural milieu. As the Western scholars debated the probable course of future developments in Soviet Central Asia and the region's likely new pattern of relations with Moscow, Mikhail Gorbachev's policy of *glasnost* and *perestroika* fanned the fire of nationalist separatism. Not pursuing any coherent policy he simply continued to muddle through, evading complex issues and problems. The failure of *perestroika* in the economic sphere resulted in the dwindling rise of the national cake, which only produced new strains and stresses in the centre's relations with the national republics over its distribution.

The pursuit of the policy of *glasnost*, or openness, further aggravated the problem. As American scholar Gail Lapidus observes, "Under the umbrella of *glasmost* what had been an Aesopian dialogue among intellectual elites, was increasingly transformed into publicly articulated demands by newly emerging cultural and socio-political movements devoted to national revival which adopted names like "Awakening", "Rebirth", "Revival" to convey their goals.

Gorbachev's Mistake

Gorbachev made his own direct contribution to the souring of Central Asian people's relations with Russia through his thoughtless action in initiating the so-called "Uzbek affair" after the death of the Uzbek Party Chief and (Breznev's personal friend) Sharaf Rashidov. A team of investigators led by T. Gdlyan and his deputy N. Ivanov was sent from Moscow to investigate cases of corruption in Uzbekistan connected with false production and sale records of cotton. More than 200 investigators worked for over four years and secured long prison sentences for thousands of former high officials in Uzbekistan, as also for Yuri Churbanov, Brezhnev's son-in-law, (former first Deputy Minister for Internal Affairs) for receiving bribes form corrupt Uzbek officials. Riots in Alma-Ata in December 1986 were sparked off by Grobachev's removal of the long-serving Kazakh Party Chief and close friend of the late Leonid Brezhnev, Dinmukhammed Kunaey, and his replacement by a Russian Party official Kollin.

The growing public resentment over these issues was expressed by Chingis Aitmatov, writer and chairman of the Kirgiz Writer's Union at the ninth sitting of the Congress of People's Deputies on 2 June, 1989. Aitmatov lashed out at the argument put forth by the influential daily *Komsomolskaya Pravda* that the Alma-Ata riots were largely a result of the continuing provision of Kazakh language school education for young people in the kazakh capital. He demanded that the languages of other nations must not be squeezed out by the Russian language which he recognised, had good historical reasons to spread out in the non-Russian republics. The Kirgiz writer asserted that each nation remains a nation only when it possesses a language of its own, and that is where its cultural sovereignty lies.

He was also critical of the mass media for not being fair towards the Uzbek nation, "when they repeatedly gloated over the "Uzbek affair to delight their readers and viewers", and demanded that organized crime should be dealt with "without smearing the honour of the entire nation". Olzhas Suleimenov, First Secretary of the Kazakhstan Writers, Union, demanded at the same meet that the Alma-Ata riots be examined by a special commission of the Supreme Soviet. Nineteen Deputies in a statement regretted references to the Alma-Ata demonstrations in the statement of the CPSU Central Committee as a manifestation of Kazakh nationalism. They demanded that the Congress approve a decree providing for offical status to the languages of the indigenous nations in the Union.

The demands for greater use of national languages, employment opportunities, environmental protection, abolition of cotton monoculture econmy etc notwithstanding, the leaders of the Central Asian Republics unitedly opposed the isolationist approach, which found strong support among the respresentatives of the Baltic Repubulics. Speaking at the First Congress of People's Deputies in June 1989, Kirgiz party Chief Absamat Masaliev pleaded for "organically" combining the independent interests of the Republics with the interests of the Union as a whole. The Tajik Communist Party First Secretary Kakhar Makhkamov took exception to the stance of general opposition as taken by a Georgian Deputy to the appointment of a person belonging to Russian nationality as the Second Secretary. "Let Georgian comrades deal with their own problems if they have them. This question must not be put on behalf of other Republics" said Makhkamov. Similarly, the Turkmen Party Chief Sapar Murad Niyazov rejected the tendency towards national isolationalism and expressed satisfaction over the policy of bilingualism. Niyazov exhorted the deputies not to forget "the dialectical priority of unity."

Contrary to the expectations in some Western circles of a "unified Muslim response to Soviet colonialism", the later *perestroika* period in 1989 saw the emergence of inter-ethnic clashes among the Central Asian Muslims when the Uzbeks attacked Meshketian Turks and clashed with Tajiks and Kirgizs. In June 1989 in the Fergane Valley armed groups of Uzbeks attacked the Meshketian Turks deported from Georgia. These riots resulted in more than 100 dead and thousands of refugees. This was followed by the Kirgiz-Tajik border clashes in July, 1989.

Economic Hardship Factor

The inter-ethnic conflicts between the Uzbeks and the Meshketian Turks, the Uzbeks and Kirgizis (in Osh) and Tajiks and Kirgizis can be largely attributed to the mounting economic hardhsips resulting from the semi-paralysed state of the economy in the later *Perestroika* period, a trend which is yet to be overcome. The clashes between the Uzbeks and Tajiks and Kirgizis owed largely to disputes over possession of rich, irrigated and fertile land, while the monopoly in small trade and distribution of consumer goods by the more enterprising Meshketian Turks contributed to the ire of the local population against them. But the nationalists also unsuccessfully tried to rouse the people against the local Russian population. Posters appeared in Fergana with slogans like "Russians must answer for everything", "Uzbekistan for Uzbeks" etc.

Several Russian women were attacked in Dishanbe during the February 1990 disturbances, and the fighting in the summer of 1992 between the Islamists and the popular National Front forces in the southern parts of Tajikistan also resulted in the killings of Russians by the Islamists. The wave of migration of Russians from Tajikistan which started in the wake of the February 1990 distrubances, reached a new heigh after the declaration by Democrat leader Shodmon Yusuf on May 10, 1992 that the entire local Russian population would be treated as hostages for the neutral conduct of the 201, Armoured Division and the Russian Republic. Out of more than 700 thousand Russians only 300 thousand were believed to have been left in Tajikistan towards the end of 1992. Russian emigration form Tajikistan would have been even higher but for the non-availability of railway containers and their prohibitive cost (of 80 to 100 thousand roubles). The situation did somewhat improve after the defeat of the Islamic fundamentalists in the Tajik civil war. The new Popular Front government made strenuous efforts to persuade the Russian emigrants to return back to the Republic as the exodus of skilled technical Russian labour adversely affected the performance of the Tajik industry.

Russians were reportedly leaving Uzbekistan, Kirgizia and Kazakhstan in large numbers sensing local hostility and apprehending the rise of Islamic fundamentalism. While the firm stand of President Islam Karimov against the Islamic Rebirth Party reduced the migration of the Russians, the situation in Kirgizia and Kazakhstan did not appear to be as harmonious despite the fact that these republics had confirmed liberal reformists as their Presidents. About 75 per cent of the native population of the Central Asian Republics is engaged in agriculture and follows a traditional pattern of life. While their population has grown during the last hundred years by 11.5 times, the area of irrigated land has increased only by 2.5 times. The problem of rural over-population exists in these republics, resulting in growing unemployment because of the disinclination of the indigenous population to take to professions other than agriculture or to migrate to the northern Russian Republic. The pressure on land has resulted in adoption of a land 'code' in Kirgizia which declares that the land in the Republic belongs to the Kirgizis alone. President Askar Akaev, however, vetoed this provision approved by the Parliament of the Republic. President Nazarbaev also withheld his assent to the Kazakh Parliament's move to change the constitution to restrict the choice of the Head of the Republic to a representative of the titular nationality. Kazakhstan has had a powerful movement for the removal of all Russian monuments and renaming of cities and settlements. Russians living in Kazakhstan began to leave for the Russian Republic as they were experiencing uncongenial atmosphere in the sphere of education and culture. On May 22, 1993 a telebridge programme between Moscow and Alma-Ata was conducted on the theme of "Russians in Kazakhstan". The correspondents of the Russian TV in Alma-Ata, Andrei Kondrashov and Alexander Sviazin, who organised this programme, were banned from entering the premises of the Alma-Ata Radio and Television station. Kazakh scholars have brought out documents to reinforce Kazakh claims on the northern territory of the Republic inhabited by a predominant Russian population. Till now, anti-Russian sentiments in the Central Asian Republics have remained confined to an insignificant section of the local population, and some bigoted religious circles. Any escalation of these sentiments, and appeals for assistance from Russian settler groups against thier oppression, is bound to lead to a resurgence of Russian imperialist mentality which, for the time being, seems to have receded in the background.

Population Distribution

But, in realpolitik terms, the new assertiveness of the national power elite in the Central Asian Republics and their urge for international recognition, notwithstanding the pervasiveness and dominant character of the Russian factor, cannot be ignored. The Russian Republic (82.6% of its population is Russian) contians 52% of the totoal population of the former USSR and 75% of its territory. Three-quarters of the minerals including oil, natural gas, coal, diamonds and gold, of the former USSR are concemtrated in the Siberi an and Far Eastern regions of the Russian Republic, which also accounts for 90% of the former USSR oil output and 70% of its natural gas production. The Slavic Republics of the erstwhile USSR—Russia, Ukraine and Belorus—together constitute about 73.5% of its population and about 80% of its territory. Central Asia and Kazakhstan, by comparison contain only 17.3% of the population (11.5% excluding Kazakhstan) and about 18% of the territory of the former USSR (5.7% excluding Kazakhstan). The three Caucasian Republics of Georgia, Armenia and Azerbaijan account for 5.5% of the total population of the former USSR and 1.51% of its population. The three Baltic Republics—Latvia, Lithuania and Estonia—contain 2.8% of the total population of the former USSR and 0.8% of its territory.

In 1989 about 26.2 million Russians were living outside the Russian Republic, comprising 10% of the total population of the then USSR. The total population of Russians settled outside the Russian Republic constituted about 18% of thier entire population. Russians comprised 52% of the total population of the former USSR, and 82.6% of the Russian Republic's population. There is hardly any CIS state which does not contain a Russian mix in its population. The following table gives an indication of the presence of the ethnic Russian factor in the population of the Central Asian Republics:

Russian Federation	82.6%
Kazakhstan	41%
Kirgizstan	26%
Turkmenistan	13%
Uzbekistan	11%
Tajikistan	10%

The cultural and linguistic dimension of the Russian factor is even more significant. A large portion of the non-Russian population of the Central Asian Republic is bilingual, with Russian as its second language.

Strange though it may appear at first sight, it is a fact that 90 to 95 per cent of the eligible voters in the Central Asian Republics favoured the preservation of the USSR, while 53.5 per cent of Russians voted for the Union. The Central Asian power elite has been notable for its attachment to the Union. Soviet modernization followed a distinctive pattern in which a large educated class rested on a largely traditional and rural society. The middle classes, which normally act historically as carriers of nationalist ideologies, were thus effectively neutralised in these Republics. As Western scholars Philip Goldmen, Gail Lapidus and Victor Zaslavasky have observed: "Dependent on a strong central state for redistributive economic policies, they pressed Moscow for increased subsidies, higher prices for local products, especially cotton, special aid from all-Union Funds to deal with severe environmental degradation and assistance in providing new jobs for the exploding populations; not for economic and political sovereignty. Under these conditions it was natural for ethnic activism to manifest itself in the form of violent clashes between titular Muslim nationality and other Muslim minorities due to competition for scarce economic gains. Whereas left-oriented leaders in Uzbekistan, Tajikistan and Turkmenistan fearing free market reforms, preferred continuation of the older ties, the Kazakh and Kirgiz Presidents were prepared to support marketization and liberalization though they also recognised the dependence of their Republics on central grants. For them the way out of this dependence was through rapid market reforms with financial and technical assistance from Western and Asian Powers.

Conflict Scenario

During the Khrushchev and Brezhnev periods the Central Asian elite had already won the battle for promoting indigenous cadres to the top managerial and administrative positions. They also had won the battle for raising the national languages to the status of state languages. What remained was to pressurise Moscow for larger allocations, investments and subsidies. With the USSR giving rise to an amorphous and loose inter-state organization, CIS, and the advance of the Russian Republic towards market economy, the Soviet redistributive state had been totally dismantled. With growing unemployment among the local educated classes. Who until recently were favourably disposed towards Russia and the possibilities of discord between the Russian Republic and Central Asia over ecological issues, particularly water management, Western observes began speculating a conflict scenario. Some built hopes on "the policies of regional leaders in countires like Iran, Turkey and Saudi Arabia and their willingness to render assistance and strengthen their respective influences in the Central Asian Republics. The scenario visualized by these scholars was for the Baltic states joining Scandinavia and Northern Europe, Ukraine with Eastern and Central Europe, the Central Asian states with Turkey and the Middle East and the Russian Far East with the countries of the Asian Pacific region. As Gail Lapidus observes. "Over time, the former republics of the Soviet Union are likely to become increasingly different from one another, politically, economically and culturally, and to draw closer to different communities outside their borders".

The situation in the Central Asian Republics was fluid, with several currents and cross-currents competing for domination of the political scene. The Pan-Islamic and Pan-Turkic trends were gaining strength day by day. Against the backdrop of supression or neglect of religion and national languages during the Soviet period, both renewed profession of Islamic faith and assertion of close Turkic linguistic affinities became vital in the Central Asian people's quest for a new national identity. Pan-Islamism provided an important basis for uniting Muslims in the erstwhile USSR against real and/or imagined Russian chauvinism, while Pan-Turkism, as an autonomous factor, united the people belonging to the broad category of a common Turkic linguistic group. The contradiction between Pan-Islamisn and Pan-Turkism has been brushed aside by none else than an ideologue of Pan-Turkism—Col. Tiurkesh—who accompanied the Turkish Prime Minister, Demirel, on his state visit to the Central Asian Republics.

Most informed observers of the Central Asian scene agree that the Soviet authorities had suceeded in only imposing a uniform, modern superstructure on what remained a relatively unaltered Islamic culture and way of life. As Edward Allworth has observed, the basic values and belief pervading the Central Asian society have not been changed by the long period of Russian rule, Michael Rywkin admits of "multiple social identities" in the case of Central Asian Muslims, where an Uzbek may view himself as an Uzbek, as Turkestani, as a Muslim, and as a Soviet, depending on the circusmstances and the person (or persons) with whom he deals or converses. After the seizure of state power by the Islamic fundamentalists in Tajikistan in May 1992, the threat of Islamic opposition cannot be dismissed lightly. The Islamists in Tajikistan lost in a civil war mainly because they tried to undo the traditional inter-regional, inter-clan power balance by ignoring the formidable northern Khojent and southern Kuliab clans and promoting the Parmir and the Garm clans to power.

The threat from Islamic opposition is particularly strong in Uzbekistan and Kazakhstan; from the underground Party of Islamic Rebirth and the *Alash* Party, respectively. The fact that the governments in these republics are fighting against this threat is a recognition of the seriousness of its challenge. Reports said of functioning of *Shariat* courts and of a parallel Islamic administration in the Namangan district of Uzbekistan. This forced President Islam Karimov to end his brief honeymoon with the new Mufti Mohd. Sadiq and come down heavily on the religious fundamentalists. The victory of the Popular Front against the Islamists in Tajikistan also owes a great deal to the hold of President Islam Karimov. Even a liberal like President Nazarbaev has been forced to hound out the '*Alash*' leader Aron Atabek from his Moscow apartment.

Towards Pan-Turic Union

The growing trend towards Pan-Turic Union of the Central Asian Republics and their participation in the Economic Cooperation Organisation of Iran, Turkey and Pakistan can be viewed differently. This vastly expanded regional grouping covers 600 million square kilometres of territory, with a population of 300 million. However, it will need much time and investment before its grandiose plans of railroad links to the Persian Gulf and the pipeline to Europe through Turkey materialise. In the meantime, the powerful old links with the north are being revived and strengthened through the CIS. Differnces exist in the approaches of the three ECO founder-members who appear increasingly as competitors rather than as cooperators.

The Tashkent initiative of January 1993 to form a Central Asian Community was the culmination of a process that began in June 1990 with the formation of a loose regional council at the initiative of President Karimov and President Nazarbaev. At a meeting in Tashkent on 15 August, 1991 the Central Asian leaders announced plans to increase its functions and expand its membership to include Azerbaijan. The January 1993 Tashkent meeting did not include Azerbaijan. The decision to form 'Turkestan' as an organisation of Central Asian states with Turkic languages was deferred to a future date at a meeting of the Heads of Central Asian Republics held in Ankara in October 1992. At the January 1993 Tashkent meet, the participants noted that not a single CIS document was being implemented. They were also critical of the "elder borther" like attitude in twice postponing the CIS summit without taking them into confidence. The Central Asian States agreed to participate in joint projects, such as refining Kazakh oil in Turkmen and Uzbek plants, construction of transit railroad links with Iran and establishment of a regional TV Centre in Tashkent and publication of regional papers from Alma-Ata. The Heads of the Central Asian Republics also took stock of the situation in Tajikistan and a Treaty of Friendship and Cooperation was signed between Uzbekistan and Tajikistan.

The promotion of the Central Asian Community of Turkestan in Tashkent early this year may be looked upon as a device to avoid the possibility of a strong neighbouring state in the south acquiring excessive influence in any of the Central Asain Republics. As President Karimov explained, the formation of the Central Asian Community was not directed at the CIS and would strive to strengthen the ties among the Central Asian Republics with the other CIS Republics. Pending activisation of the CIS, the Central Asian Community assumed the responsibility of co-ordinating the policies of the Republics in the region in different spheres. As such, these developments need not to be interpreted as formation of any Pan-Turkic state, awaiting merger with Turkey as the next logical step. In fact, President Nazarbaev of Kazakhstan continues to champion the cause of a strong CIS and has taken important initiatives to develop his Republic's tie with industries in the neighbouring Omsk region of Russia.

Reassurance of continued cooperation with the CIS notwithstanding, a note of anxiety was struck in a long write-up by the Tashkent correspondent of the Moscow newspaper *Rossiskaya Gazeta*, an organ of the Russian Parliament. Published under the provocative title "Will Turkestan move in the direction of the Bosphorous Lighthouse?" the writer, Vladimir Berezovsky made a pointed reference to Turkish President Turgut Ozal's mention of the rise of a new Muslim power with 100 million Turks during his Central Asian visit, and the failure of the Central Asian media to report the inclusion of "Fascist" Colonel Turkesh in the entourage of the visiting Turkish Prime Minister Demirel. Berezovsky also made fun of the loud talk about massive Turkish investment in

Central Asia, which did not yield any tangible results and ended up only with a leather-garment factory in Kokand and a cotton mill in Nukus, along-with a few dozens of planned joint-venture projects. The Russian journalist also referred to Demirel's appeal to the European Community to invest in a big way in the economy of the former Soviet East, as also to the plea to Saudi Arabia for creation of a special bank to finance Turkish projects in Central Asian Republics. He warned that the dumping of cheap Turkish consumer goods was likely to bury the local light industry and claimed that the economy of the Central Asian Republics was saved from imminent collapse by the multi-billion Russian credits and by their continuation in the rouble zone as also by the assumption of the repayment responsibility by Moscow of the large international debts of these young states. Calling for a more serious evaluation of the policy followed by Ankara and the re-examination of the Turkish model publicised by the West and the Russian Foreign Ministry with accent on export-oriented economy and separation of Islam from the State, the *Rossiskaya Gazeta* write-up ended by reminding the decades-long repression of the Kurd minority in Turkey, mass-killings of journalists and overgrowth of nationalism into Pan-Turkism resulting in despatch of Turkish contingents to fight in Bosnia.

An activisation of Russian policy in Central Asia can be seen, of late. The setting-up in Moscow on 8 August, 1993 of a regional security system comprising Russia and four Central Asian Republics of Kazakhstan, Uzbekistan, Kirgizstan and Tajikistan (Turkmenistan has not joined it) is a pointer in this direction. The leaders of the four Central Asian States and Russia have signed a Declaration on the inviolability of their borders in accordance with Article 51 of the UN Charter and undertaken an obligation to defend each other against outside aggression. None of the signatory states, however, will have the right to send its troops into the territory of the other States unilaterally. In another statement, the Presidents of Russia, Kazakhstan, Uzbekistan and Kirgizstan have declared their all-round support to the government of Tajikistan and stressed their commitment to reinforce the Tajik-Afghan border as the southern border of the Commonwealth of Independent States and help Tajikistan build its armed forces. While the present Russian stand on Tajikistan is a marked improvement on its attitude of non-interference and neutrality in the recent conflict between the supporters of the Popular Front and the Islamists backed by outside money and arms, the Russian President has diluted his apparently firm stand by urging the Tajik leadership to initiate a direct dialogue with all the opposition forces.

It is not known to what extent President Yeltsin's new activism in Central Asia is the result of his advisers' sober reassessment of Russia's geostrategic interests in defending the southern borders of Tajikistan, across which illegal gun-running and illicit narcotic trade threatens to subvert and destabilise not only that tiny mountainous Republic but the mighty Russia itself. It might as well be the result of recent prodding by the United States, Russia's new partner and strategic ally. It was surprising to find Russian Foreign Minister Kozyrev (who not so long ago donned the *Mujahidin* cap during his visit to Afghanistan) issuing a warning to Afghanistan against incursions across its border with Tajikistan. But President Yeltsin's plea for reconciliation with the Islamist opposition betrays his old allergy for the leadership in Tajikistan and Uzbekistan, which he considers to be neocommunist and which he blames for suppression of the democrats for whom he still seems to retain a soft corner. A weak and vacillating Russian Policy on Central Asia is not likely to produce the desired results. The Western powers and America on whom President Yeltsin appears to be relying solely, would like the Central Asian states to seek greater integration with the developing economies of the neighbouring Asia States rather than move closer to Russia which despite the demise of the USSR and communism, remains a potential rival in the near future.

POLITICS OF NATIONALISM IN CENTRAL ASIA

R.R. SHARMA

Before the disintegration of the USSR, the interest in the Central Asian region was overwhelmingly confined to a small segment of the so-called "Sovietologists". This small community was further polarised into those who analysed all developments in the region in the broader context of global politics of Cold-War. There were also other scholars whose analytical tools were sharply focussed only on religion and ethnicity. Obviously, both the approaches, characterised by 'selective research' were basically opportunistic, and thus fatuous.

However, a redirection has now taken place in a limited way. The political, economic and socio-cultural problems of the Central Asian Republics are fairly complex, therefore, these must not be examined in terms of partial categories and fitted into the pigeonholes of meagre theoretical framework, or in simplified political perceptions. A new political power-game is in the making in the region in which Pan-Islamism may be used as a major weapon to give different orientation to its geo-politics. Whether that actually takes place would depend on a host of factors.

The five republics of Soviet Central Asia which have emerged as independent countries are Uzbekistan, Kirghizstan, Turkmenistan, Tajikistan, and Kazakhstan. In fact, a large part of Kazakhstan falls outside this region. These republics, however, have many common species, which include a common Turkic ethnicity [although Tajiks project their separate identity in terms of Persian (Farsi) language], a common Muslim cultural tradition, a similarity of history, predominance of rural population, low socio-economic mobility, low level of educational/technical skills and qualifications.

Despite this apparent homogeniety, their considerable diversity is articulated in many significant ways. For example, Uzbeks, who constitute the largest national group of over 17 million people, take pride in projecting their ethnic/national identity not entirely in terms of religious (Sunni) or linguistic (Turkic) bonds, but also in terms of a superior urban civilization, which had developed an agrarian economy by the side of Amu-Darya and Syr-Darya. By contrast, Turkmens and Kirghizis are essentially nomadic, and thus devoid of a historical past. Therefore, their geo-cultural identity is regarded as constricted. Then in each republic, there is a strong tendency to identify with specific regions and districts and ethnic sub-divisions. The articulation of identitites in a variety of particularistic terms has many implications. All this makes the emerging political scenario basically friction-oriented, and hence fragile. The root of problem is not general pedigree, but self-conception and uneven development within the region.

The basic reality, therefore, is that there are a host of inner-conflicts operating on the people's minds: between their new high-pitched aspirations and objective complexities of geo-cultural nature; between the desire for change and mental reservations, and the inhibitations about accepting the consequences and paying its price. In Central Asia of the day, these have an exceptional intensity and tend to assume a unique form. The new aspirations of the political actors are separated from reality by a wide gap. The conception of reality pregnant with awsome problems is not a mere artifice, but an image that comes naturally to a perspective observer of the transition process in these Asian republics. There is a constellation of explosive potentials for change, as also formidable external difficulties and internal obstacles.

As pointed out earlier, the Central Asian republics have proximity in space. The process by which national independence was achieved by these republics was basically similar, with major and lasting consequences for both their internal conditions and their relations with the outside world. Their independence was a result of the collapse of state socialism in the former USSR The people of these republics as such, played no significant role in any struggle for independence. This was quite unlike the national struggles in the Soviet Baltic States, or even in Transcaucasia.

After achieving this unanticipated independence, their intial reaction was that modernization process could be handled much better than the Soviet Communist process. Also, it was strongly believed that the road to modernity must run directly to the outside world and not to Moscow. But the growing economic crises subsequently brought about a sea change in this perception. That explains why the concept of "closer economic union" with Russia in particular, and the Commonwealth of Independent

States (CIS), in general, has emerged as the leading idea in the political discourse. The Central Asian leaders openly pleading, not only for economic union, but also for a broad political and military alliance within the CIS.

Islamic Revival and Nationalism

Evidently, there is little clarity as to the role of religion and nationalism in the new setting. Despite the growing literature on emerging "fundamentalism", "pan-Islamism", "Pan-Turkism" in Central Asia, there is no strong evidence to show that these ideologies—the creations of the political elite—have penetrated the masses. These are seen only in a few pockets of influence in some of the Republics; of course, they do have a strong presence in Tajikistan. It is also well-known that these are aided and abetted by outside forces. President Karimov of Uzbekistan has openly accused both Iran and Afghanistan of spreading Islamic militancy in Central Asia, and more particularly in Tajikistan. A large section of the political elite is, in fact, aware that the extreme religious orientation can only destroy economic and political modernisation.

That is a strong reason why secularism has been accepted and codified in constitutional terms. However, replacement of atheism by secularism has also created an opportunity for the exploitation of religion for political purposes, being indulged in by a segment of the political elite. However, there has been no significant upsurge of Islamic fundamentalism. The tragic experience of Tajikistan has had a demonstrative effect. It has only strengthened the resolve of other Central Asian Republics to combat Islamic militancy. Islamic militancy is also being opposed by the ruling (secular) regimes for another reason. These militants have been trying to use religion to foment ethnic clashes, like the ones between Uzbeks and Kirgiz in the Ferghana Valley. This is domestically very unsettling, something the post-communist regimes cannot allow. That partly explains why President Karimov has employed harsh measures against his political opponents, who were seeking to stir up manipulated nationalistic emotions.

Saudi Arabia has also tried to be a major actor in the region. So far, it has mainly tried to put across its role as a builder of the infrastructure for the revival of Islam in Central Asia. The major advantage the Saudis have over the other powers is their considerable financial resources with which they can influence the growth of Islam. However, President Karimov of Uzbekistan is insisting that the Saudi financial assistance must be channelled through State agencies. Moreover, Saudis cannot go against U.S. interests, which are obviously opposed to fundamentalism. The Americans have taken care to popularise the so-called "Turkish" model; the only major merit of this model, in essence, is what is called Secular Islam'. Apparently, the obvious US aim is to create a pro-Western space with the help of Turkey. Therefore,by implication, the Saudis while promoting Islam in the region, would also like it to shape up as a 'liberal' and not a militant force. This logic, however, does not apply to Iran or Afghanistan.

Evidently, there is a growing interest in ethnicity and nationalism. Therefore religion has been adopted by all political elites as their base to meet these ends. Some Kind of Islamic revival was inevitable after the downfall of Soviet power in the region, but this in itself should not be a source of undue anxiety. This could be viewed as an inevitable componant of self-definition.

Notwithstanding this, a design of the future based on total negation of the past is basically flawed. A peculiar political situation now pervades in Central Asia. Practically, no political party is openly critical of religion-oriented nationalism. Of course, Karimov, Nazarbayev and many others are secular by conviction, but the reluctance of the ruling elite to openly articulate opposition to religious ideologies is perhaps rooted in pragmatism. On the surface, it appears they are seeking to project themselves as staunch nationalists, or "cultural nationalists". Since "cultural nationalism" in this case is closely associated with enthnicity and religion, future political and economic modernisation is likely to be greatly impaired. The political elites may, in the short run, find it convenient to associate too closely with readily available enthnic/religious identities, but this is bound to slow down the march towards democracy and secular state structures. As time moves forward, the present frame of reference—cultural nationalism—will increasingly make it difficult to propagate and legitimise secular goals, and ensure social change, or cultural renaissance. Cleavages and tensions within the body politic may have got entrenched by them.

The ruling political elites, therefore, have their masks on, seeking to cover the real nature of their politics. This has led them to the path of "facade-democracy", and at times it appears that the comprehension of their own nationhood is rather fragile. Whatever the reasons, the fact is that the ruling political elites have adopted the medium of cultural nationalism, which invariably gets mixed up with religion and ethnicity, weakening their internal cohesion.

Let us examine briefly the emerging political culture in each of the Central Asian republics.

Tajikistan: This is perhaps the only state in the region where the process of formation of a nation-state is grossly incomplete. The nationalist forces found it expedient to join hands with fundamentalists against the secular ruling political elites, drawn from the ranks of the former communists. The Tajik Popular Front (*Rastokhez*) and the Islamic Renaissance Party were invariably on the same side to pick up confrontation with the ruling regime. President Nabiev of Tajikistan, who had secured nearly 60 per cent votes in an internationally supervised election in November 1991, was ousted by these forced in May 1992. The nationalists-fundamentalists were actively backed by Afghan *Mujahideen*. In the final analysis, the fundamentalists were driven out and prevented from seizing power by the collective intervention of the CIS armed forced. The Tajik leaders of secular pursuasion have so far managed to stabilize the situation on the basis of a military-political alliance with Russia and three other Central Asian States. The future, however, remains uncertain, as is the future of democracy.

Turkmenistan: In Turkmenistan, there is only one political party, the 'Democratic Party', headed by President S. Niyazev, who was earlier the leader of the Communist Party. Constitutionally, there is no bar in the formation of political parties—a political party may be registered on the presentation of 1,000 signatures of supporters. There was an unsuccessful effort to form a Peasant Party, but evidently adequate support could not be mobilised. Therefore, there is no serious opposition here, either democratic or Islamic. (The *Agzbirlik* group is an insignificant force in the republic) Theoretically, however, fundamentalism could be exported from Iran as Turkmenistan shares a long border with that country. As of now, President Niyazev of Turkmenistan presides over a most stable political situation, which is the envy of other Central Asian Republics.

Kirghizstan: This independent Republic has endured one of the worst inter-ethnic relations after the demise of the USSR. Here, slavs constitute over a quarter of the population. The cultural and enthnic nationalism was primarily targetted against the Russians (and others), who were perceived as the dominant political elite. This led to a large-scale exodus of slavs from the Republic. President Akayev soon realised that this would be wholly unproductive. And since the Russians have a fairly large ethnic presence in the Republic, a viable system of sharing power is in the making. The discriminatory land law (of April 1991) was subsequently changed, the language law was similarly diluted. This happened after President Yeltsin spoke to President Akayev in March, 1993.

The ethnic situation, however, is further complicated by sub-divisions within the main group. There is sharp polarisation between the Kirghiz living in the plains, and the Kirghiz of the mountain regions. The authority structure derives its functional legitimacy from such variables as regions, clan systems, etc. The basic political struggle for power is between the Southern and Northern parts.

The Democratic structures are still fragile but there is no strong Pan-Islamic movement. Stability is there, but this has been purchased by making concessions to cultural nationalism based on religion. Victor Zapolsky, a Deputy in the Republican Parliament, has a point when he asserts that "Akaev will have to pay for stability with concessions to reactionary forces".

However, the saving grace is that the Republic is wholly oriented towards the CIS and the Asia-Pacific region rather than the Moslem world. The Islamic factor is largely superficial here.

Uzbekistan: Uzbek ethnic group is the largest and the most visible in the region. It has a common border with almost all other Central Asian Republics. After Tajikistan, this is the only Republic where armed militant Islamic movement made its presence felt, particularly in the Ferghana Valley area. The Uzbek Popular Front—*Birlik*—was constituted in November 1989. *Birlik* largely focussed its political strategy on language and religion, thus managing to gain some support. However, it got split, and a new group *Erk* made its appearance. Both of these were banned and their leaders arrested by President Karimov, Uzbekistan has a great Islamic tradition, and religious figures are influential. In case the present secular leadership grows weaker, the possibility of Islamic opposition gaining ground is the strongest in the Republic. The secular leadership may be playing into the hands of cultural nationalists by promoting the cult of Timur, Babur, etc. The new cultural renaissance has more negative than positive orientation in the Republic.

Kazakhstan: The Russians and Ukrainians constitute over 40 per cent of the population in the Republic. Additionally, another 20 per cent belong to non-titular nationalities. The ethnic divide here is therefore more complicated. Therefore, Nazerbayev has worked out a more sustainable system of power-sharing. Islamic factor is weak, and politically Nazarbayev is the most astute leader in the whole region. He is one of those who stands for a "close-knit confederation" within the CIS. Like Kirghizstan, Nazerbayev's second best option is the Asia-Pacific region. The Moslem world, with the exception of Turkey, comes lower down in his preferences.

Thus, the idea of a unified Pan-Islamic power in Central Asia appears to be wishful thinking and is sought to be propagated by vested interests. Yet, the fact is that the Central Asian society is strained by a host of centrifugal forces, which make it rather unstable. Cultural nationalism based on religion (and ethnicity) pampered by the ruling secular elite has the potential of becoming a source of regression. In broad terms, one may even draw a parallel there with the current political situation in India. Russia is anxious about the northward march of Islamic militancy. President Yeltsin has, for once, shown some clarity of thought by asserting that Russia has a major role to play as "a guarantor of peace and stability in the region". But first he has to bring peace and stability in his backyard, Russia.

PROSPECTS OF ISLAMIC FUNDAMENTALISM IN CENTRAL ASIA

AJAY KUMAR PATNAIK

During their existence as parts of the erstwhile Soviet Union, the republics of its Central Asia region were transformed from backward agrarian areas into industralized ones. This enormous transformation was done by large-scale transfer of skilled professional wrokers from its European regions to Central Asia. In spite of some progress made during the Soviet years in terms of upward mobility of the Central Asians, most of them (more than 70%) still live in the rural areas and work in agriculture. In the urban areas they are predominantly in light and food industries and in the service section. The skilled workers in industries are mostly Russians or other Europeans.

This pattern of occupational distribution has some bearing on the nationality relations. The economic position and the cultural identity of the Central Asians were barely threatened by the presence of the Europeans. Since most Central Asians live in the rural areas and cling tenaciously to their traditional ways of life, there was little perceived threat of cultural assimilation by the Russians. Knowledge of the Russian language is also poor among the Cenral Asians; even the functional utility of learning Russian by them was negligible owing to the extremely low rural ro urban mobility.

In political terms, Rober A. Lewis argues that indigens were more sucessful in gaining a privileged status in their homelands, which was an important reason for slowing down of European influx into the region.[1] During the Brezhnev years, Central Asian political elite not only came to dominate in their respective republics at the cost of the Europeans but also came to enjoy far greater autonomy in running the affairs of their republics. The stability of the leadership—Rashidov, Usubaliev, Gafurov and others and the long tenure they had—strengthened the political and administrative elite from the indigenous nationalities. In their turn the local leadership gave its unflinching support to the Central leadership on federal issues and did its utmost to discourage any discrimination against the Russians living in Central Asia.

It was no surprise, therefore, that Central Asia constituted the weakest link in the chain of nationalist movements that gained momentum in the late 1980s. Even the violent outbursts of national feelings that took the form of ethnic riots, were more or less confined to antagonism between members of the titualr group and those of the other indigenous Central Asian groups, and very rarely against the Russians.

The inter-ethnic disharmony gets further accentuated under conditions of unemployment, shortages and fall in living standards. This is also true of the series of ethnic riots that have rocked Central Asia since 1989. In countires like Tajikistan, where civil war has forced more than 100,000 people to flee to capital Dushanbe from the south, economic recession and shrinking labour market resulted in growing local hostility against non-titular groups. In all the countries of these region, difficult economic situation has put the ethnic minorities under pressure in recent years and not surprisingly there have been very violent group clashes.

Uzbeks and Kirghiz ethnic groups were involved in the violent clashes over land disputes in Uzbekistan's Andizhan oblast in 1989. Again in 1990, competing claims made by new ethnically-based associations in the Osh regions of Kirghizistan led to ethnic violence between the above two groups. Unemployment and land hunger were more acute in this region, and local politicians were willing to support nationalism openly. The ethnic Kirghiz in the region resented the fact that local Uzbeks controlled 80% of the city's trade. When the Kirghiz political leadership of the region agreeed to allot 32 hectares of predominantly Uzbek collective farm on the outskirts of Osh to settle ethnic Kirghiz families who were unable to find housing, it led to widespered violence in the Osh region between the Kirghiz and the Uzbek communities; the latter supported by compatriots from Uzbekistan who physically participated in the early statges of the fighting.[2] A dispute over claims to irrigation water and farm land led to violence between Tajik and Kirghiz villagers on the border between the two republics in 1980. Although the water dispute was eventually resolved, recriminations between the leaders of Tajikistan and Kirghizistan over the territorial dispute continued into 1991.[3] The tension between Tajiks and Uzbeks reached extreme popor-tions in August and September 1992, when tens of thousands of Uzbek refugees left Tajikistan as a result of what they describe as "pograms" in Uzbek-speaking villages.[4]

According to Laitin, minority group in any republic is threatened by (or perceives) two problems. First, the titular elites, whose positions are secured by membership in the "named" group of the republic, are administratively responsible for distributing jobs, contracts and investment funds. These elites created "family circles" to distribute jobs and favours to a wide patronage network. This problem became especially grave with the prospect of privatisation towards the end of Gorbachev years. The minority may fear that a government controlled by the titular group would distribute land and other favours to its own group, and discriminate against the former. Secondly, the minority may fear—justifiably or not—eradication or forced assimilation by the local majority as the latter gains more power. The pattern in early 1988 in the USSR shows that as soon as Gorbachev raised the question of decentralisation of power to the republics, extremely emotional uprisings began among ethnic groups within the republics. The strength of the reaction and even violence in them suggested that the local population was concerned not just about patronage, but also about its security.[5]

However, on both counts, the Russians has little to fear in Central Asia. The nature of their professional position ensured against any discrimination, and as a culturally distinct group they were not in danger of being assimilated by the titular group. It were the local minority groups who, due to inter-group marriage and linguistic similarity, were more in the danger of being assimilated.

There has been a tendency to equate social and cultural practices with religiosity in the Central Asian context. Even the Communists and other non-believers in Central Asia strongly adhered to the cultural practices which were common to believers as well. There has also been attempts to blur ethnic identity by focussing on Cenral Asian's religious identity. For many in Central Asia, tradition is confined to practices of their particular family, village, or urban quarter and not of people outside those groups. Throughout the Soviet period, the linguistic territorial identity of the different Central Asian groups had become so entrenched that any supra-national identity found it difficult to obliterate the division created by the former. Thus, the Uzbeks would not be prepared to sacrifice their Uzbek identity and merge with other Central Asians on the basis of a Pan-Islamic identity. Not to speak of merger, even co-existence has been difficult as has been shown by a series of riots among various Central Asian ethnic groups belonging to the same religious group.

Even Tajikistan, where Islamic revivalism has been the strongest, the difference with other Islamic peoples on the basis of nationality has continued to remain strong. A number of Tajik intellectuals have expressed concern that any supra-national Islamic identity would be dominated by the Turkic-speaking groups. Even one of the founders of the Tajikistan branch of the all-Union Islamic Revival Party (subsequently a separate party), Davlat Usmanov, voiced no interest in the creation of a supra-national Islamic state. Apart from the fact that he considered such a state impracticable, he also saw it as undesirable. To him, it is significant that Muslims belong to different nationalities; he thinks their national differences matter.[6]

The growth of nationalism, even on a limited scale, has not been conducive to the growth of Islamic revivalism in Central Asia. A series of ethnic riots since 1989 helped to strengthen national identity, and chances of building a Pan-Islamic identity receded. In all the Central Asian states, free elections brought to power with popular mandate, secular and former Communist leadership. Even in Tajikistan, where Islamic revivalist forces are relatively stronger compared to other Central Asian states, their hold over power was brief and secular forces were able to mobilise popular support to oust the Islamic leadership who had briefly seized power by force. The Tajik incidents (1992) have underlined factors that work against the growth of Islamic fundamentalism. It revealed that Central Asians are not one homogeneous group with one overriding identity—Islam. They are not just divided on nationality lines, but there are strong ideological and clan regional loyalties that negate and oppose the unifying appeal of Islam. North-South deivision of Tajikistan could not have been more conspicuous than it was during the days of the civil war in 1992. While the Islamic Revival Party ran its writ over Dushanbe and toppled the elected government of President Nabiyev, in Khujand the Communists were stronger and on the basis of their support in north succeeded in ousting the Islamic fundamentalists. Crowds appeared in Khujand bazaar, beside the mosque, shouting slogans, and ordering the *Katib* to break from Dushanbe's spiritual leader, the Qazi. The former agreed.[7] Another example was the Sunni Moslem Conference of the Kulyab province (Tajikistan) around the middle of 1992, where the participants resolved that the clergy of Kulyab and all the mosques in the province should secede from the jurisdiction of the *Kaziat* (principal spiritual authority of the Muslims of Tajikistan) and establish independent organs of government under the Imam Khatibolla Khodzhikhajdar

Sharifzada. It was emphasized that the orthodox Muslims of Kulyab were reluctantly forced to pass this resolution by destablising policies of the *Kaziat* and its supreme head, Khodzhiakhbar Turadzhonzoda, a supporter of the protagonists of Islamic fundamentalism at the highest levels of the Muslim leadership of the republic and who has been agitating for the foundation of an Islamic state of Tajikistan.[8]

Islamic revivalism is also likely to encounter resistance, may be passive, from many Central Asian women who have seen a progressive improvement in their economic and social position during the Soviet era and who would be required to, and might even be forced to lead a subordinate existence. Some are of the opinion that even at the religio-cultural level Central Asian women were more active in Soviet period, a role that they seem to be losing with the reassertion of patriarchal values and revival of Islam.[9]

Gillian Tett, during her fieldwork in Tajikistan, observed that with the revival of Islam across the republic, men are coming to play an ever greater role in Islamic practices. Whereas women might have *de facto* carried the greatest religious burden during the Soviet years (women performed the bulk of Islamic rituals like Ramadan fasting, Bibi-Seshambe of Grandmother's Tuesday, Mushkil-Kushoda or the Solving of difficulties, made pilgrimages to small shrines, carried out a number of domestic rituals to ward off the evil eye and orchestrated the large number of religious rituals that accompanied life cycle, rituals such as birth, marriage and death (a majority of women fasted during Ramadan in the villages in 1990 and 1991)., it is now men who dominate Islam in the public sphere and, more significantly, are setting the agenda for the discourse about what Islam should "mean" for women and it is primarily Islamic men who are calling on women to adopt a more "Islamic" role in society.[10]

Another important factor that commits the Central Asian governments and secular political and intellectual leadership to fight Islamic fundamentalism is the need to assure the skilled Russian workforce whose outmigration would seriously affect the recession-hit industries. There is also the need to have good relations with the Russian Republic on which the Central Asian states are still dependent. The treatment of Russians in Central Asia is bound to influnce Russia's relations with Central Asian states.

The phase of nationalist euphoria being over, there is a sober realisation about the possible impact of European emigration on the economy and soceity of the newly independent nations of Central Asia. Central Asian political leaders have expressed concern that the loss of professional and skilled personnel was already having a damaging effect. This included leaders in governments and members of political opposition as well. They are now urging the Europeans to stay. President Karimov of Uzbekistan has been appealing to the Russians not to leave, and so have many Uzbek intellecutals.[11]

Tajik authorities have also been making efforts to persuade the Russians to stay. Davlat Khudonazarov, a member of the special commission on normalising the situation in Kurgan-Tyube province, met with respresentatives of the local Russian minority and briefed them on the work that the commission is doing and assured them that it will do everything it can to stabilise the situation in the southern part of Tajikistan.[12]

The exodus of Russians on a large scale has aroused concern among the Kirghiz elite, who are worried about the Republic losing brains and skills. Russians make up half the population of capital Bishkek and a quarter of the country's. Although many have been leaving, President Akayev is keen to retrieve them and has been reported to have said. "I'm against emigration. I just want to keep the Russians, Jews and other minorities. We've just set up two national cultural automonous districts for the Germans". He actively solicits support and understanding of the Slavic community and has appointed two Russians to his Cabinet, the State Council, which conducts its session in Russian. His Vice-President, Kuznetsov and Interior Minister, Kulov, are both Russians. Though Akayev's allies include Kirghiz nationalists, he has refrained from pursuing a pro-Kirghiz agenda as wanted by the nationalists. In September 1991, he vetoed a land reform bill passed by the Republican Supreme Soviet that would have declared all land in the Republic the property of the Kirghiz nations, and by March 1992 had altogether vetoed the bill three times.[13]

The impact of emigration by Europeans could be so detrimental to the economies of the newly independent states of Central Aisa that it is difficult to visualise any language-based discrimination in the near future. As it is, the new language laws will take some time before coming into force and their strictest implementation under the present circumstances is doubtful. Most Republican language laws even provide for the continued use of the Russian language. Turkmen law even talks of national Russian and Russian national bi lingualism; Tajik law proclaims "the Russian language as the language of inter-ethnic communication freely in the territory of Tajikistan". The laws of Kirghizia, Uzbekistan and Tajikistan proclaim freedom of choice of language of instruction. Some argue that the transition to a native language standard will not be necessarily damaging to the position of the Russians. Rather, when the local groups have returned to their native languages and dialects, they will tend to separate from one another.

The confusion that characterises the attitude of the Central Asian leaders *vis-a-vis* Russia is an indicator of thier dependence on Russia. On the one hand there are efforts to reject the economic domination of the Russian Republic, while on the other there are statements to make the CIS stronger. Leaders of the Central Asian States and Kazakhstan agreed at a summit meeting held on January 4, 1993 on broad principles for the establishment of a common market. President Nazarbayev of Kazakhstan did not want to close all his options. He said the five should continue to co-operate with other CIS countries, preserving the rouble as a common currency, and creating a banking union to manage monetary policy and cash emission. The other leaders agreed on the need to retain the rouble for the present, but said that Russia should not remain in sole control of its emission in future.[14]

President Nazarbaev has on many occasions advocated close collaboration between CIS member-countries as the basis of future development. In an interview with *Literaturnaya Gazeta* he expressed regret that in August 1991 the opportunity to unify the economy of the CIS was missed. The result has been a drop in production of 65%. No Western generosity, no help from international giants can take the place of the collapsed space of the former USSR. The failure of the CIS states to intergrate economically is causing privation, said Nazarbaev, and politicians must justify the trust placed in them.[15] In mid-December, Nazarbayev agreed with the Russian Prime Minister Chernomyrdin that a new CIS was required to replace the now stagnant organisation. He also endorsed Chenomyrdin's proposal for a kind of mini-OPEC within the CIS. Nazarbayev's ambivalence was reflected in statements by other leaders after the Tashkent summit. Saying that the shape of the CIS needed to be changed, Kirghiz President Askar Akayev added that from the outset, Bishkek (Kirghiz capital) had suggested the CIS should be based on a core consisting of the states that were more tightly integrated, economically, politically and militarily, one which already existed in practice between Russia, Kazakhstan, Belarus, Uzbekistan and Kirghizistan. "Let the others decide on what terms they want to join the CIS", reamarked Akayev.[16]

On January 22, 1993 the head of the states of the CIS met in Minsk for the eighth summit. As this summit four Central Asian states (including Kazakhstan) along with Russia, Belorussia and Armenia signed the draft CIS charter to transform the CIS from an amorphous to a more integrated organisation. The summit's most tangible achievement was the agreement to set up a CIS inter-state bank, which is regarded as essential to the revival of inter-state trade. Most vocal advocates of the CIS integration have been the Central Asian states. All the Central Asian states, except Kirghistan, are in the ruoble zone. Central Asian states are part of the collective security arrangement signed by the six CIS states in 1992. They have been the most ardent proponents of a strong CIS military allinace and creation of a CIS peace keeping force. The Tajik government has sought Russian protection against *Mujahiddin* attacks from across the Afghan territory.

In short, Central Asian states are unlikely to encourage the growth of Islamic fundamentalism. In fact, Uzbek and Tajik governments have been very severe on fundamentalist groups. However, the growth of fundamentalism in the Central Asian states in the future cannot be ruled out. The present economic problems and growing unemployment and impoverishment could lead to a widening of the appeal of the fundamentalist groups. The protective support of the earlier system, which guaranteed employment and provided social security, is collapsing. In future, there is the possibility of increased migration to the cities (in Soviet times, rural-to-urban migration among Central Asians was negligible). These migrants would not find it easier to get employment in cities which are severely affected by recession, nor would they find it easier to link themselves to the urban cultural milieu. Religion would be one factor with which they can identify themselves in a city. According to Pran Chopra, the "marginals", the newly educated recent migrants from the rural areas to the city, lose the moorings they had in the traditional rural society which they abandon, and either fail to find any in the new urban society, or lose them if the economy shrinks. The "marginals", being totally new to the ways of market would slip even more steeply if the pace of "privatisation" remained uncontrolled by other factors, and if they lost their newly acquired middle class status, which they have aspired for years. Their bitterness makes them easy recruits to religious estremism.[17] Being aware of such problems, the goverments of Central Asia have been hesitating to plunge into rapid transition to free market economy. There is still a large degree of state intervention and regulation over the market. Hopefully, their commitment to secular principles and regulated market would succeed in preventing the growth of Islamic fundamentalism in the region.

The kind of nationality relations that existed in Central Asia towards the end of the Soviet period was not very conducive to the growth of Islamic fundamentalism. Given the economic position of the Russian and cultural resilience of the Central Asians, fear of "Russification" and targetting of Russians as antagonists from a different religion could not find substantial appeal among the population. In fact, ethnic conflicts since the late 1980's weakened the basis of religious revivalism by pitting one Muslim ethnic group against another.

The Independent countires of Central Asia find themselves gripped by recession, unemployment and the prospect of prolonged period of hardship and suffering. This prompts them to advocate the renewal of the old federation in the new way so that they can benefit from the division of labour that existed under the erstwhile U.S.S.R. Such a necessity further commits the Central Asian states to the protection of the Russian minority and maintaining the secular character of the state and government. Islamic revivalism with its Pan-Islamic appeal is also confronted with the existing division of Central Asians on diverse lines—ethnic, regional, clan and so on. The civil war in Tajikistan revealed the deep schism that exists in the society along regional and clan lines and Islam has been unable to overcome these fissures. There is also the problem related to women, many of whom would not like to go back to the veil system or accept a subordinate position in the name of Islam.

However, the growth of Islamic fundamentalism cannot be entirely ruled out. A lot depends on how these states succeed in undertaking economic reforms while minimising the suffering of the population. Unless that happens, an impoverished and disillusioned population might find the appeal of fundamentalism alluring.

References

1. Robert A. Lewis: "Are Republics becoming ethnically homogenous"? National Papers, vol. xix, No.1, 1991, p. 72.
2. Gene Huskey; "Kirghizistan: The Politics of Demographic and Economic Frustration" in Ian Bremmer and Ray Taras (eds.) Nations and Politics in the Soviet successor states, Cambridge, 1993, p. 407.
3. Mauriel *Attain*, 'Tajikistan: Ancient heritage, new politics', in Ian Bremmer and Ray Taras (eds.) op. cit., p. 372.
4. Current Digest of the Soviet Press, vol. XLIV No. 38, 1992, p. 9.
5. David D. Laitin "The four nationality games, and Soviet Politics", Journal of Soviet Nationalities vol. 2, No.1, 1991, pp. 20-21.
6. Mauriel Atkin, 'Tajikistan: Ancient heritage, new politics, in Jan Bremmer and Ray Taras (eds.) Nations and politics in the Soviet successor states, Cambridge, 1993, p. 374.
7. Jonathan Steel, "Aloof Tajiks in north few volatile south", *The Guardian*, 19-5-92.
8. *Central Asia News file*, June/July 1992.
9. Ajay Patnaik, "Women and economic changes in Central Asia, paper presented at the international seminar organized by Central Asia Research Forum and UNESO, at Soas University of London, 6-9 July, 1992.
10. Gillian Tett: "Women and Islam in Tajikistan", paper presented at International Seminar on Women and Economic Changes in Central Asia, op. cit., pp. 6-9.
11. Gregory Gleason, "Uzbekistan from statehood to nationhood", in Ian Bremmer and Ray Taras (eds.) op. cit., pp. 344-345.
12. *Rossilakiye Vesti*, Sept. 22, 1992, p. 2.
13. Bess Brown, "Central Asia emerges on World Stage", Radio Free Europe/Radio Liberty, *Weekly Research Report*, vol. 1, No. Jan. 3, 1992, Gene Huskey, op. cit., p. 410.
14. *Central Asia Newsfile*, Jan 1993, p. 3.
15. *Literturnaya Gazeta*, 19 August, 1992.
16. *Central Asia Newsfile*, No.3, Jan, 1993. p. 3.
17. Pran Chopra, 'Transition Pains of Kazakhstan', *Hindustan Times*, April 25, 1993.

MUSLIM FUNDAMENTALISM IN CENTRAL ASIA : A CRITICAL ANALYSIS

P. STOBDAN

The rise of Islamic fundamentalism was one of the obvious scenarios foreseen for Central Asia during and after the final breakdown of the Soviet Union. This renewed perception of Islamic revival, springs from the anti-Western rhetoric and impulses manifested in the past in the form of terrorism, hostages and bombings.

Unlike in the past, when fundamentalist Islam won power through revolution as in Iran, or through military coup as in Sudan, fundamentalist Islam in Algeria had almost come to power through democratic process. What happened in Algeria was sufficient enough for the West to start worrying about the shape of things to come in the post-Cold War era. In fact, questions were raised whether Islam and democracy were compatible; whether Islamic parties are part of the global democratisation; whether Islam will become a global ideology like communism and challenge the liberal democracy. While answering to these questions, the Western assessments are sharply divided along two contrasting opinions. One is that of Graham Fuller, a senior analyst at the RAND, who underlined the fact that "the Islamic (election) victory should not be a ground for panic, and the election must not be annulled. Indeed, it is time to demystify the phenomenon of Islamic fundamentalism and to see it for what it is: a movement that is both historically inevitable and politically tamable. Over the longer run it even represents ultimate political progress toward greater democracy and government". But others feel that "Islamic fundamentalism of the Sunni or Shia variety... is not merely resistant to democracy but wholly contemptuous of and hostile to the entire democratic culture... There is no spirit of reconciliation between Islamic fundamentalism and the modern world—that is the Christian secular universe". They cite example in Pakistan, "where the justice system has been obstructed by fundamentalists".

Since the early 1990's, the Western realisation of the revival of Islam has been seen in the US cutting off economic and military aid to Islamabad. The former US Senator Larry Pressler, while expressing fear over the "Islamic bomb", referred to Pakistan as a probable centre of a new geo-strategic bloc, involving Iran, Turkey, Afghanistan and the Central Asian republics.

Rise of Political Islam

On the other hand, the rhetoric of Islam is gaining popular political appeal, and it is generally articulated that this phenomenon of attraction to Islam is a response to Urbanization, poverty, economic discontent, political failure, cultural protest—all reactions to the moral bankruptcy of modernity and Western alien values. Many also view Islam as an alternative to the securalism and materialism of the West.

The emergence of Central Asia republics has evoked fresh questions, particularly about the prospects of political Islam gaining momentum to shape the future of the five republics. Answer to this question would be both yes and no. Islam is gaining tremendous popularity among the Central Asian nations, but in a manner quite different from the experiences and problems faced by the Islamic world.

The rise of political Islam can neither be a single nor a simple phenomenon. Central Asia as an Islamic civilization experienced a divergent path of historical development. Many of its national characteristics are nothing but products of dynamic interactions and tensions between religion and geography. Recent political history of Central Asian States as members of the Soviet family can be attributed to this phenomenon. Today, Islam like other forces is simply responding to the dynamics of change in the post-Soviet Central Asia, and it can be only regarded as a by-product of the *glasnost* process. Its significance lies in the evolution of a new socio-cultural framework for a post-socialist society and not necessarily to intergrate into Islamic world.

The threat of Islamic fundamentalism in Central Asia is highly exaggerated. Sure, today there is a search for Central Asian identity and the search is not for a supra-national one but for national identity. Therefore, the forces of ethnicity, the forces of history and the forces of modernity assume far more importance than the forces of religion. So far Islamic revival has expressed itself more as a cultural revival rather than religious one, and more as a religious force than a political force.

Even during the cold war period, one of the Western prophesy included that Muslims of Central Asia will pose a serious threat to Sovier authority. We have all witnessed how the Soviet empire collapsed. In fact, the Central Asian Republics reluctantly accepted their political independence. Nor the world could prove that the Central Asia Muslims suffered in any sense due to the absence of contact with the Muslim world.

However, in the changed context, several questions should be addressed:

1. To what extent Islam is important in shaping the national identities of Central Asians?
2. To what extent supra-national *(ummah*—universal Muslim unity) or (Islamic) identity is compatible (culturally and historically) with the consciousness and concept of being Uzbek, Tukmen, Kazakh, Tajik and Kirghiz nationality.
3. To what extent ethnicity (Turkism) language, tribalism, feudalism/-class etc. form essential attributes of the national identities of Central Asia.

Answers to these question can be found if we closely look and analyse the existing realities of Central Asian republics.

Irreversible Changes

In the first place, the Russians had disguised their domination by modernising Central Asia and the Tsarist colonies were turned into Soviet republics. Secondly, the Soviets created a national profile based on ideological platform of national equality. Thirdly, although the Soviets have failed in their experiment of creating an identity as Soviet man—*Homo Sovieticus*,—but they have been successful in endowing Central Asians with national identities. It is important to note that the Soviet government bestowed identities on people whose loyalties were divided between religion and ethnicity. These identities attained tremendous boost over the years and it is difficult now to denationalise these identities. Fourthly, the ideology of socialism and related welfare schemes (education, and other spheres of socio-economic development) and the set of values and behaviors deriving from them resulted in a high degree of material acculturation. Fifthly, the vast industrial infrastructural development and the communication and transport network have resulted in a high level of inter-dependency in the economy. Again, it will be incorrect to consider Central Asian societies as Sovietised by the communist rule. In the process of their intergation into the socialist system, their resistance to Soviet style modernisation became less important than the compatibility offered in other areas. For example, Central Asian traditional socio-political (clan/tribal) structure proved most suitable for communist political structure. Not only the clan-patron relationship and tribal group mentality fit easily into a Soviet system, but became stronger in the Soviet era. Then Islam was given a rational, as well as a dynamic outlook through *jadid* movement and effort was made to free Islam from the stigma attached to it as a force hindering progress. The concept of democracy was traced back to the concept of *shura* (council). The slogans of friendhsip and brotherhood raised by communists were also said by Muhammad. During the 1950's and 1960's, many *fatwas* of the religious board were lifted, including the one against the fast obligation for those who worked in agriculture and industry. They also abolished the veil. The scientific appraoch towards Islam has enabled the Central Asian religious leadership to concentrate on Central Asian *umma* rather than for the universal *umma*. It had also allowed the Central Asia to rediscover their Islamic heritage and further enhanced the awareness that if their ancestors in the past could contribute to the development of Islamic thought, culture and science, they too could make contribution to universal *umma* by sharing their technological experience with the Third World Muslims. This facet of the Central Asian identity is very important and in fact, it will shape the future status as well as relations with other Islamic countries.

Different Problems

It may not be appropriate to compare the situation of the African, Asian and Arab Muslim countries with those of the Central Asian republics. Because many of the problems faced by the Arabs are absent in Central Asia. Not only the social structure of the Muslim societies in Central Asia is different from those of Iran and the Arab world but the national psychology is also quite different from them.

Unlike in the Arab countries, the Central Asian republics are not yet victims of rapid urbanization, and their rural population is not likely to migrate to cities for economic reasons. It is another matter if the rural-urban migration takes place due to inter-ethnic problems.

Islamic resurgence was not re-sponsible for the Soviet collapse. the collapse was European in nature and related much to the rise of Baltic nationalism. The Central Asian nationalistic intensity was nowhere at par with the Baltic, who even shared Slavic affinity with the Russian. Even before the separation, the simmering discontent among the Central Asians *vis-a-vis* the Soviets was more polit ical, economic cultural (anti-Russian culture) in nature rather than religious or ideological. Compared to the Baltic republics, the democratic participation in Central Asia is unknown or confined only to the small group of intellectuals.

The Islamic world may not serve Central Asia as a model like the unifying Europe is serving for the Baltic states. Nor the life-styles and socio-economic conditions of Pakistan, Iran, Afghanistan and even Chinese Xinjiang are attraction for them. The Central Asians are confident that their present state of economy is just a passing phase.

Today's Central Asians do not suffer from the same complexes *vis-a-vis* the West as suffered by the Arab states. It will not be either easy for anyone to create a religious-psychological barrier of Islam versus West, Islam versus modernity, and so on. On the contrary, Central Asians are much ahead in adopting the Western-style democracy and market economy. It is unlikely that these republics will join other Islamic nations against the Western powers. Western technical experts etc., will find it easier to work with Central Asians than in the countries of the Arab world. In fact, exposure to the West will further accelerate Central Asian demand for change. Whereas, the track record of Tehran and Islamabad would act as a deterrent rather than inspiration for the socially and intellectually liberated Central Asians.

Sectarian Politics

Like anywhere else, Islam in Central Asia has its own religious politics. Apparently, there are over 30 differnt Islamic sects with varying degrees of differences among them. In the case of Central Asia, historical, cultural, tribal and national contexts furthet complicate the web of relationships among and within different kinds of Islamic sects. Besides, the rivalries among external Islamic forces may further prevent the development of a cohesive strong Islamic movement for Central Asia. Proselytisation of Wahbi sect by the Saudi Arabians, Pakistanis and Afghans have exacerbated inter-ethnic tensions in Uzbekistan, particularly between Uzbeks and Shia Meshketian Turks. So far, Iranian effort has been hampered by linguistic and cultural problems. The Tajiks although belonging to Persian stock, adhere to Sunni Islam. However, Tajik mosques, particularly Tajikistan's spiritual as well as *Qaziat* Party leader Akbar Toradzhon Zoda and other anti-government parties like IRP and DP are reported to have received Iranian support during the recent crisis.

Notwithstanding Muslim predominance in the republics as a whole, they are in a minority in most cities of Central Asia. Besides, only five to 10 million Muslims in Central Asia are said to be practising their faith.

At the moment the fundamentalists are strong only in Uzbekistan and Tajikistan. So far it has been witnessed that the movements in these republics have no links with each other. Even otherwise Islamic movements in these republics appear to be progressing separately in response to their local political conditions.

Tajikistan

The larger confrontation between the ideologies, Islamic fundamentalism versus communism, seems to have ended with the withdrawal of Sovier troops from Afghanistan. The spatial as well as tribal-based conflicts not only appear to be gaining serious dimensions but also becoming a divisive factor for religions unity. Afghan *mujahidin* or Islamic fundamentalist, ultimately got divided along ethnic lines. The ongoing fighting in Tajikistan is not so much a tussle between Islam versus communist, as much as a traditional power struggle between various regional entities *(Mahalgaroi* or regionalism), *(Khojent* and *Kulyab* against *Garm* and *Pamir)*. Conflicts within a clan and sub-clan become more important than politics or even religion.

In Tajikistan, 23 per cent of total population is constituted by Uzbeks. Most of them are settled in the city of Leninabad. They are crossing the border in Uzbekistan in fear of the ethnic war. The Ismaeli Muslim sect has also been victimised by both Islamic fundamentalism and communists in the civil war. Growing nationalism has prompted millions of ethnic Russians to leave Central Asia.

Uzbekistan

There are about a million Tajiks in Uzbekistan who have become victims of growing Uzbek or Pan-Turkic nationalism. Many of these Tajiks are migrating from the cities of Samarkand and Bukhara to Tashkent. Other ethnic groups including Meshketian Turks have been fleeing from Uzbekistan and Kazakhstan.

In Uzbekistan, Saudi Arabia has been pushing hard to proselytise its principle creed of Wahabism, an austere and extremist sect within the mainstream branch of Sunni Islam. Wahabis are the most extremist form of Islam in Central Asia, particularly in Uzbekistan where they have displayed tremendous strength across the country. They have seized prime sites in the cities for *mosque* and *madrasa* construction. Many Central Asian youths are joining the Wahabi military training. Their prime aim is to create an Islamic state through revolution. The Wahabis strongly differ with '*sufism*' and rejects it as nothing but Zionist and Turkish conspiracy to undermine Islam. Similar differing attitudes are also shown towards other sects such as Shias and other branches of Sunni Islam. Wahabis also differ with the other fundamentalist party like the Islamic Renaissance Party (IPR) which is spread across Central Asia. The IPR's aim is to bring about an Islamic state through democratic process.

So far the Wahabi movement has only sharpened the sectarian differences in Uzbekistan. Many liberal sects like *Sufis*, the pro-government Imams and mosques are accusing the Wahabis for introducing sectarianism of the Arab world. The vast majority of the Central Asian countryside Muslims who belong to the *Hannafi* sect of Sunni Muslims strongly reject the sectarian militancy propagated by externeous Islamic zealots. There are other ultra-nationalist (Uzbek or Pan-Turkic) forces like *Birlik* (unity) and *Erk* (independence) which are bitterly opposed to the Islamic fundamentalism.

Kazakhstan

Islamisation of Kazakhastan is a late phenomenon. Largely a nomadic population, Kazakhs got converted to Islam in the early 19th century. The Kazakh nomads continue to uphold the traditional beliefs of pre-Islamic period. Moreover, ethnic composition of Kazakhstan, some 47 per cent of them being non-Kazakhs, is the most important factor and goes against fundamentalism. There is no major known Islamic fundamentalist group in Kazakhstan. Only the *Alash ordo* Party advocates the idea of integrating Pan-Turkism with Islam and democracy.

Kirghistan

Like in Kazakhstan, the Kirghis's attachment to Islam is far from strong. Here too, Islam arrived much late. The easy-going nomadic life style of the Kirghis has prevented Islam from penetrating deep into the society. The liberal attitudes of the Kirghis show high inclination for economic progress. Their leaders have shown more interest for the Asian dragon as model for development, rather than for the Iranian or Pakistani kinds. Because of the geographical proximity Kirghistan and Kazakhstan are likely to be pre-occupied more with Russian, Siberian, Chinese and other East Asian affairs rather than in development in West Asia or Islamic world.

There is no doubt that Islamic fervour is strong in southern Kirghistan in the region of Osh, partly as a result of the spillover from northern Tajikistan and Uzbekistan. But here too, tribalism prevails stronger than fundamentalism. Various tribal groups—Uzbeks, Kazakhs, Tajiks and Kirghis—frequently fight for land, housing and water. Inter-ethnic clash between Kirghis and Uzbeks has forced the Uzbeks to migrate from the Osh region to Uzbekistan.

Interestingly, there have been conversion of Kirghis to Christianity. No answers have been found so far for this unique phenomenon. But explanations would range from their lack of religious fanaticism, strong desire for modernity and change, disorientation after the socialist system, short-term monetary gains from the missionaries, attraction for English language to genuine religious belief.

Turkmenistan

The Turkmen tribes are traditionally noted by the Russians as the least religious fanatics. Here too, major impediment to Islam is the division among them along tirbal loyalties. Akshabad had no mosque for its Muslims for the past 40 years after the only Mosque existed earlier was destroyed by an earthquake in 1948. In the recent years Islamic movement has progressed rapidly, but more in the cultural life than in politics.

Iranian missionaries are active in Turkmenistan but they are faced with two major obstacles. First, Turkmens are Sunnis, and secondly, Turkmens have objection to learn Islam in the Persian language.

It does not appear as yet that the present Turkmen leaders are willing to compromise with the secular practice. President Saparmurad Niyazov's prime thrust is to improve the economic standard of the people. The ruling government uses the opposition Nationalist Party *Agzbirlik* (unity) as a force to counter the Islamists. The problems in Turkmenistan are more economic in nature. Nationalist movements are stimulated by more awareness of low standards of living.

The threat of Muslim fundametalism in Central Asia is greatly exaggerated. The consciousness of Uzbek, Turkmen, Kazakh, Kirghis and Tajik identities is deeply rooted in the respective republics. The possibility of establishing a collective identity remains a matter of speculation. But Islam assuming a common denominator to unify Central Asia into a cohesive organic whole has little scope as compared to the assertion for a Pan-Turkic state.

The five republics of Central Asia are soon going to complete two years of their independence, but so far there are no signs of their moving in the direction of forming either an Islamic bloc or a Turkic empire. In fact, it has been established that each of them has a distinct personality of its own. Two years of their independence have been marked by both continuity and stability, except in the case of Tajikistan which can be considered as an odd man out. Each of them has adopted the local language as the sole official language and the national agenda also varies from one republic to another. They are ruled by regimes of different hues, from liberal President Askar Akayev of Kirghistan to the authoritarian leader Saparmurad Niyazov of Turkmenistan. If Turkmenistan believes in a secular and democratic state, Kirghistan wants to have a Switzerland type status of permanent neutrality.

Central Asian transition from centralised economy to market economy is also proceeding at a varied pace. All of them are fast reorienting themselves to retain closer economic as well as stragetic alliance with Russia. Their efforts to strengthen the CIS and related collected security and economic treaties are important steps to defend themselves against internal as well as external exploitative elements particularly from fundamentalist forces, which would destablise their respective countries. Civil war in Tajikistan has opened the eyes of a lot of people in other republics, and it is increasingly being felt now that Russia is the only power which would act as guarnators of stability in Central Asia.

Moscow has been unable to dissociate itself from any of the current happenings in any of the former Soviet republics. Anti-Russian attitudes proved quite costly for Georgia and Azerbaijan. Today, they are back in the CIS security system. Islamic fundamentalism in Central Asia also concerns Russia, not only because of the large Russian diaspora in the region, but also because of the possible spillover effect into Russia.

The future peace and stability in Central Asia depends not only on the rise of Muslim fundamentalism but also on many other complex issues. The possibility of the Pan-Islam and Pan-Turkism concept not taking proper shape does not mean that Central Asia will transform into secular, democratic and stable political unit. All the aforementioned factors will continue to be sources of instability in the region for a long time to come. There will be as many Islamic fundamentalists as ethnic resurgents whose numbers will be sufficient to foment trouble in the region. But all the same, there will be a series of checks and counter-checks to prevent any of these forces from assuming total control. Islamic fundamentalism will be countered by non-religious measures, and regionalism will be countered by tribalism, etc.

Islamic Fundamentalism in Central Asia and Tajik Factor

V.D. CHOPRA

With the world attention focussed on the recent internal developments in Russia, another active spot in the troubled Central Asia seemed to get ignored. There exists a close relationship between Islam and nationalism in this region of the erstwhile Soviet Union. Evidence is there that at one stage Islam was used as a central force of opposition by certain neighbouring states to the Soviet regime in some of the traditionally Islamic regions. Islam did, and continues to play an important role in the national consciousness of the people of this region. As such no water-tight division can be made between Islamic revivalism and nationalism in these regions.

After the withdrawal of the Soviet troops form Afghanistan and dislodgment of the Najibullah regime, religious fundamentalist forces captured power with the active support of Pakistan, Saudi Arabia and Iran. These forces, internal as well as external, instead of creating political stability set in motion armed conflicts among themselves.

These very religious fundamentalists and ethnic factors are now attempting to destabilise the Central Asian Republics. The strategic position of Afghanistan has always been recognised by the countries around it. During the British reign over India, Afghanistan was treated as a buffer state. However, in modern times with winds of change ushering in international relations on democratic footing, and without interference in the internal affairs of other countries, it was expected that the situation in South-West Asia, including Afghanistan, too would change. These expectations rose higher after the developments in the erstwhile Soviet Union, East Europe and in Afghanistan because the so-called threat of communism "Vanished. But, unfortunately, the US-Russian detente did not radically change the political climate. One reason for this anomaly is that certain countries are still to shed old concepts of their geopolitical interests. One tends to believe that after the disintegration of the Soviet Union, an unipolar world has begun to emerge and this trend is manifest in this region, as well as evident from the policy of the Clinton administration *vis-a-vis* India and Pakistan.[1]

It is pertinent to mention that Kashmir played a significant role in India's relations with Central Asia because of its gegraphical proximity and cultural affinity with the religion. Kashmir assumed new importance in the context of the Anglo-Russian rivalry over Central Asia. This rivalry lost some of its intensity with the conclusion of the 1907 convention, and with the emergence of a common threat from Germany; but it got revived in the wake of the October revolution in Russia. The British felt tempted to interfere in Central Asia owing to the chaotic conditions of the civil war there. The Soviets tried to embarass the British by encouraging anti-British activities of the Indian revolutionaries, which in turn resulted in the further tightening of British stranglehold over Kashmir and its frontier dependencies.[2]

The 'Third Strategic Theatre'

A major factor in the Afghan conflict has been the policies and actions of Pakistan. Starting January 1980, India took a number of initiatives to seek a regional solution, but the latter was more interested in fuelling the conflict. In fact, in recent years it has tried to wrongly project the Afghan problem, more in terms of an Indo-Pakistan dispute while pursuing military option to impose a solution of its choice. The failure to obtain a military solution has not deterred its leadership from the visions of a "strategic consensus", and a confederation of Pakistan, Afghanistan, Iran and Turkey, ostensibly with U.S. support, in what was termed by Brzezinsky as the "third strategic theatre". However, it is difficult to understand Pakistan leadership talking of such a strategic consensus even in 1990, for at the minimum it ignores the drastic change in international environment. But it does clearly indicate an intention to seek a friendly government in Kabul willing for such an arrangement (with undoubted Pakistani hegemony). Despite past failures, Pakistan has not given up the military option to impose a regime of its choice. The United States, apparently, is quite willing to sit back and give Pakistan another summer-fighting season to achieve its objective, and provide a face-saving formula for the US, through its success or faliure. The only hurdle, ironically, may be the *Mujahideen*. The other option would be to seek impose a division of Afghanistan through the creation of a Pushtoonistan. Pakistan's interest in such a solution is for the possible access to uranium deposits in southern and south-eastern Afghanistan which would make

Pakistan more independent in terms of basic resources for its nuclear weapon programme.[3]

Pakistan's strategic perception about Kashmir, Afghanistan and Central Asia, therefore, needs to be seen in its totality. In a 'secret' document as published by the *Kabul Times* on January 24, 1990, Lt. Gen. Hamid Gul, the Director General of the Inter Services Intelligence, had underlined that after the withdrawal of the Soviet troops from Afghanistan "in which Pakistan had a decisive role", "unprecedented historical opportunities" have been provided to Pakistan, and Pakistan should not "let go this historical opportunity". He also underlined that "to counter Indian expansionism, which has created a powerful military mechanism, it is imperative that Pakistan should set up a confederation with Afghanistan. This may be done under the banner of rallying Islamic countries for the sake of peace, security and stability in the region, thus preventing communist infiltration.

He was candid about Pakistan's objective when he said that the "majority of Muslim countries will welcome the unification of Pakistan and Afghanistan, with the exception of Saudi Arabia which may voice objections, but not go as far as aggravating relations with Pakistan". He felt that Pakistan "has every right to seek a confederation with Afghanistan. All these years Pakistan has exposed itself to serious risks and cannot permit Afghanistan to remain as it was prior to 1978...." This strategic perspective of Pakistan speaks for itself.

That being the position, the developments in Afghanistan, Kashmir and the Central Asian Republics have their own links and cannot be viewed in isolation from each other. It is, therefore, natural that New Delhi cannot afford to ignore these linkages. The harsh reality is that fundamentalist forces have made Afghanistan as its springboard to destabilise the Central Asian Republics on the one side and India on the other, Events, both in Kashmir and the Central Asian Republics, need to be objectively assessed from this perspective.

Essential Differences

The ground situation in the Central Asian Republics is different from most other Muslim-dominated countries in the region in two respects.

First, in these backward regions of the erstwhile Soviet Union there have been regeneration of their economies, and in this sense these states have laid out their own course for modern nation-states. It is a paradox that these states are now more politically stable than most of the erstwhile Republics of the Soviet Union. This has naturally baffled those who had expected that after the collapse of the Soviet Union, this region would witness unprecedented upsurge of religious fundamentalism.

Secondly, the Soviet policy on the question of religion in this region was more flexible, and had kept in mind the religious aspirations of the people.

Like institutions representing other religions in the former USSR, official Islam had sought its own ideological and existentialist compromise with the official secular state to which it owed its sustenance. It had insisted that Islam was not opposed to, rather it was capable of coexisting with Marxism-Leninism, and had devoted considerable attention to expounding the possibilities of reconciling what would seem to be two inherently contradictory doctrines. In this sense religious freedom existed.

As part of the inevitable tightrope walking of the Muslim clergy, like the clergy of other religions. Islam has tended to show considerable moderation in its requirements for the faithful conforming to the five pillars of Islam, the forceful imposition of three of which (the 'Zakat', the obligatory alms tax; the 'Haj', the pilgrimage to Mecca, and the fast of Ramadan) have been officially legal since the 1920's—and the practice of religious rites. This flexibility had ensured compromise formulae that led to the continued adherence to Islamic traditions. Thus, virtually all Central Asians buried their dead, married in accordance with Muslim custom and circumcised their sons. Instead of being a part of the gradual process of abandoning religion and embracing total secularisation and modernisation, or updating of Islam, such flexibility enabled even those Muslims who were integrated into the socialist ssystem to observe Islamic practices as they understood them without sensing any fundamental contradiction between socialism and their religion. Thus, certain reformism of Islam did take place.

Islam, generally, also played a positive role in implementing some of the social goals such as combatting crime, corruption, alcoholism, and drug abuse. In a deteriorating moral situation manifested by the serious growth of social ills and malaise, such usefulness of religious beliefs has been displayed by the adherants of other faiths as well, the Russian Orthodox Church in particular.

However, it would be naive at the same time to ignore or minimise the fact that the growing religious fundamentalism is not being used against the existing establishment in this religion.

Sufism, Wahabis And Marxism

A significant portion of this Islam is the by-product, or the offspring, of Sufism. The traditional conservative, the Sufi brotherhood, which focuses not on the mosque but on private prayers at home or in any house of worship, and on pilgrimages and other devotions at holy places, are basically *murid* or *darvesh*. Sufism propounds its own system of rites and rules for spiritual training, empowering the master (the *shyakh, murshid* or *ustad*) to help the individual mystic reach higher levels of spiritual knowledge, as a result of which the 'master' comes to command total obedience. It is this section of the population which provides social base to the religious fundamentalists outside the religion.

The numbers of active Sufi practitioners, or holy men and women, involved in this movement are not known. But evidence points to the fact that such adepts are much more numerous than appear on the surface. Moreover, although their natural sphere of action is the countryside, there are numerous unofficial *mullahs* even in some urban centres. Some of the Sufi groups have specifically been described by the authorities as manifesting a blend of religiosity and nationalism.

In some areas of Central Asia, particularly in central and southern Tajikistan, there has also been a resurgence of Wahabism, a Sunni fundamentalist movement that seeks pristine Islamic purity. Wahabi *mullahs* are said to have accused the regimes of following a negative policy towards Islam, of having denounced the official Muslim establishment, criticised the war in Afghanistan, and charged Moscow with having invaded that country in order to turn the Afghans into infidels.

Two other factors have also contributed to the religious revivalism in this region.

First, mechanical interpretation of the Marxist theory, failure to create a new humanism in the society and the centuries-old urge to have a spiritual value system and build a "God-fearing" society, and above all, the one-sided anti-religious propaganda had driven women and the younger generation towards religious revivalism. However, this trend cannot be equated with religious fundamentalism.

Secondly, the new political elite which emerged in the communist movement and commanded a dominant position and the lack of democracy and pluralism, were some of the factors that has alienated a section of the population in the region; albeit not to the extent it had in other parts of the former USSR.

The collective consciousness of the Central Asian people, however, seems to be nationalistic. Whatever may have been acts of omission and commission by the communists during the last seven decades a new sense of nationalism had developed within the womb of the essentially tribal and feudal socio-economic scociety.

Nevertheless, the tribal or clan consciousness seems to be particularly important in the economic, cultural and political spheres. Colletive farms are often based on clan kinship, while the cadres are frequently selected for government positions as well as to posts in scientific and higher educational institutions by virtue of their tribal affiliation. This tendency seems to be especially salient in two of the Central Asian republics, Kirgizia and Turkmenistan.

Effects of Pan-Turkism

Quite a few members of the intellectual elites among the Turkic peoples are beginning to refer to themselves as Turks, and see their Turkic identity as a potential rallying point. That Pan-Turkism has perhaps some appeal for the local population may be inferred from the anti-Armenian slogans and the general feeling of solidarity with the Azeris in their quarrel with the Armenians.

But this is only one aspect of the region's reality. Equally important is the fact that among the people of Central Asia a strong consciousness of national identity pervades. This section of the population is largely urban, yet it developed a secular modernistic outlook. However, the recent disintegration of the Soviet Union has been a serious setback to the trend. Some American scholars now admit that "secularism has become an essential part of their credo." They developed a peculiar "fundamental loyalty" to the Soviet Union, while at the same time taking pride in their national consciousness of being Uzbeks or other national and ethnic groups.

Till the disintegration of the Soviet Union and the political instability in Russia, a section of the elite in this region has been in search for a new "spiritual value" system—a combination of nationalism, pride in their ethnic identity and in the positive role of Islam in generating a new ethical value system (fight against alcoholism, drugs, crime, corruption and prostitution). That is why there has been a marked tendency among them to veer to their religious traditions.

The Central Asian elite has been jealous of any infringement of what they see as their right with regard to appointments to local official positions, and have resented their lack of authority in decision-making on internal issues, including education, art, literature and religion.

A closely related issue is the study of the Arabic script. One of the Soviet leadership's reasons for switching from the Arabic to the Latin and then to the Cyrillic script for Central Asia was to create a *common culture* That is why, students graduating from the language and literature departments in Uzbekistan's universities and scientific institutions could not read the Arabic script, and were ignorant of their literary heritage which had been written in Arabic, Persian and Chagatay.

To remedy this situation, it was first suggested that the Tashkent State University should train specialists for the study of Central Asia's classical literature. By the summer of 1978 it was further advocated that the study of the Arbic script be introduced as a subject in the high school curriculum. Some of the activities connected with making the language of the respective republic as the state language had raised the issue of the Arabic script as well.

Thus, at a nationalist demonstration held in Dishanbe early in 1989, demands included not only the recognition of Tajik as the Republic's official language, but also return to the Arabic script. By the school year

1989-90, the Arabic script was being taught in some schools in the Tajik Republic. Another issue of interest and passion was translation of the *Quran* into the local tongue, in all the Central Asian Republics.

The general tendency in Central Asia is to focus on secular matters, and play down the issues of religious significance. The national movements had become increasingly politicised, and broadened their base.

Two parallel developments seem to be taking place in this region. While secularisation of polity has created a new national consciousness, religious revivalism too is growing. The intensity of these two trends varies from republic to republic. Extremist expression of Islamic nationalism seems to be more common in Tajikistan than in other parts of Central Asia. Some people, however, believe that Islam never incited believers to fight against their own government, or to disregard the laws of their country.

Another important factor here has been the religious propaganda from abroad, particularly from Iran, Saudi Arabia and Pakistan. Calling "religious believers to holy war", they have been preaching the need for believers to 'save Islam" in all its aspects.

One-third of Türkmenistan's young people are said to listen to Turkmen-language broadcasts from Iran and Afghanistan. The Turkmen authorities regularly complain of the negative influence of Iranian radio and television on its people. No less than 38 radio stations that discuss "Islam and the exporting of the Islamic revolution" are said to be active along the border. Since the withdrawal of Soviet troops from Afghanistan, Afghan *Mujahedin* are reported to have doubled their efforts to smuggle subversive materials and weapons into the area.

Islam the Cementing Force?

Does this mean that Islam will cement the various Central Asian national movements? So far, the answer is no. The effect on the contrary has rather been to split them from inside on the basis of nationalities.

Although not much can be said now on what the future holds for Central Asia, there seems no doubt that at least some among the younger generation are looking simultaneously to Islam and to nationalism. Thus, although Central Asians do identify themselves as Muslims, the political implications of this identification are not clear beyond the fact that separates the collective Muslim of the Central Asian periphery from the Russian or Slavic "they" at the Centre.

The Serious mistakes made in the past are being used to give a new direction to the polity of this regions. But these attempts have their own limitations as religious revivalism has its own specific characteristics.

Seen in this background, the solution of the Tajik problem assumes a key factor in Central Asia because it is directly related to the attempts to spread Islamic extremism in this region, and, thereof to other neighbouring areas, including India. It must be kept in mind that Tajikistan is encircled by states in which Islamic fundamentalists are politically strong, such as Pakistan, Iran and Afghanistan.

The Afghan and Tajik extremist groups are supported by influential political circles of the so-called Islamic states. These political elements consider the conflict in Tajikistan as a new theatre: of the "holy war" in the region. In their estimate, Tajikistan can be transformed into a springboard in the struggle for setting up Islamic regimes in the Central Asian states, in a political situation in which Russia has entered into a prolonged period of political instability.

According to the Western mass media, some of these extremists have been recruited from among the young and misguided Arabs. Some of them are reportedly connected with an organisation called "Jamaat-al-Islamia", which is under the control of Imani-a-Zalvaliri, who was active in the Muslim Brotherhood of Egypt and a veteran of the Afghan war against Russian occupation. These terrorist groups are being financed by affluent fundamentalist elements based in the Western countries, including the United States. Recently, the *Time Magazine* (October 4, 1993) disclosed how an immigrant cab driver from Egypt was the alleged ringleader of the gang that planted the powerful bomb at the World Trade Centre in New Jersey. The report portrayed him as a "commando leader who relied on his guerilla training in Afghanistan. But there is something more to this. As after obtaining permanent resident status in the United States in 1988, Abouhalima, the mastermind, made "several trips" to Pakistan and joined the "Afghan *Jehad*", the report said adding that large number of Muslim fundamentalists from various countries joined this" *Jehad*" This makes it clear that religious fundamentalists becoming terrorists have emerged as a new factor in the post-cold war period. Some of them are operating in Kashmir, but this is not the point under discussion here. The crux is that in Central Asia, at the moment, religious fundamentalists have made Tajikistan as their centre of operation. This omnious development cannot be ignored by those engaged in building a modern nation-state based on secularism, nor can one afford to ignore its impact on the regional stability.

References

1. V.D. Chopra, *Super-Power Detente and Afghanistan* p. 64.
2. K. Warikoo: *Centre Asia and Kashmir;* p. 221-222.
3. Air Cdr. Jasjit Singh: *Super-Power Detente and Future of Afghanisthan:* p. 7 and 8.

WHY NEHRUVIAN CONCEPT WAS DEMOLISHED BY WEST

DARBARA SINGH

Jawaharlal Nehru will go down in the world history as an outstanding statesman, one of the top leaders of national liberation movements, a fighter for peace, the architect of modern India and, above all, one who immensely contributed to the realisation of the noble concept of a modern Indian nation-state. For decades his name was synonymous with the struggle of the Indian people for independence. It was at midnight, as 1930 was being ushered in, that the flag of Indian independence (saffron, white and green) was unfurled and Jawaharlal Nehru made the declaration on the banks of the Ravi in Lahore (now in Pakistan) that it would be a "crime against man and God to submit any longer" to the British rule. After this declaration India's struggle for independence entered a new phase. Rising strikes, powerful mass demonstrations, the Chittagong Armoury raid in Bengal, the incidents in Peshawar when the Royal Gurkha Rifles refused to fire, spontaneous "no-rent" movements by the peasants in a number of provinces, United Provinces in particular, were some of the highlights of this heightened struggle. And then the final blow on British imperialism was inflicted in the forties, and India won its freedom. It was again Jawaharlal Nehru who unfurled the National Flag on August 15, 1947 at the historic Red Fort in Delhi and remained at the helm of affairs of the country till his death on May 27, 1964. During this period he built the edifice of a new India and gave a new direction to its socio-economic development. During his life-time, India faced two aggressions one from Pakistan in 1947 and the other from China in 1962. After both these aggressions were successfully met, Indian freedom emerged stronger. After his death, Lal Bahadur Shastri, Indira Gandhi and then Rajiv Gandhi shaped the destiny of the country, excepting for a short period between 1977 and 1980. The country had to face two more aggressions from Pakistan, one in 1965 and the other in 1971. And on both occasions, the country foiled the game of the aggressors.

These facts of history need to be recalled especially as the country is passing currently through a most critical period. Threat to the secular edifice built by Gandhiji and Jawaharlal Nehru has increased, calling for certain amount of introspection by all patriotic Indians, Congressmen and those who believe that Nehruism is still relevant to the solution of contemporary Indian problems. One is immediately reminded of the lines of Robert Frost's poem, which lay on Nehru's bedside table, underlined in his own hand:

> *The woods are lovely, dark and deep,*
> *But I have promises to keep*
> *And miles to go before I sleep.*

One cannot but conclude that Jawaharlal Nehru had some premonition about his last hour, and met it worthily; as befits one who was completely immersed in his life's task. Mighty industrial complexes had transformed the face of ancient India in such a short period, which has no parallel in history. While inaugurating the mighty Bhakra Dam project, which changed the entire socio-economic face of Punjab, Haryana and parts of Rajasthan, Nehru had rightly said that such projects were the "new temples" of India. How prophetic he was.

Again, as early as March 1947, at the Asian Relations Conference held at the initiative of India, he said:

> "Far too long, we, of Asia, have been petitioners in Western courts and chancellaries. That story must now belong to the past. We propose to stand on our own feet and to cooperate with all others who are prepared to cooperate with us. We do not intend to be playthings of others."

Jawaharlal Nehru not only laid the foundation of an independent and self-reliant economy, but also laid the basis for building a modern Indian nation-state based on secularism and democracy.

Imperialists' Ire

Nehru's internal and external policies came under heavy fire, both from the imperialist countries, America in particular, and their internal allies, the domestic reactionary forces. It is for scholars and academics to analyse the relationship between his internal and external policies, but on the basis of experience of mass movements, certain observations can be made here.

In the early fifties, Indian public opinion was outraged at the ruthless ways of American warfare in Korea. It was clearly evident that American policy in Asia was not a series of isolated and erratic moves but based on a firm pattern of action without any concern for Asian interests. It was in this situation that Jawaharlal Nehru repeatedly pressed the proposal at all international forums for a peaceful solution of the conflict in Asia. This Nehruvian stand was described in the American press as "the voice of abnegation" and a policy of "appeasement". Abuse was supplemented by political pressure when India requested US a loan for wheat purchases.

On August 28, 1951, the New York Daily Mirror accused Jawaharhal Nehru of "Asiatic intrigue" and charged that "one of the enemies of this country is the India of Nehru." The New York Times declared in an editorial that "Jawaharlal Nehru is fast becoming one of the great disappointments of the post-war era."

These facts are evidence that hostility of the American administration towards India has been a continuous policy.

But the emergence of India as a secular democratic state had begun to change the course of history, in the newly-liberated countries in the first instance. India, under Jawaharlal Nehru's leadership, threw up a new model of nation-state building, different from the Western model on the one hand and the Russian model on the other.

Since a clear line of demarcation has now begun to emerge between secular and communal forces, primarily under the compulsions of parliamentary politics, it is essential to grasp two basic parameters of Jawaharlal Nehru's concept of secularism.

First, Jawaharlal Nehru had again and again brought into focus that the communal problem in India was "one of adjusting the claims of the minorities and giving them sufficient protection from majority action". He knew more than anybody else that minorities in India were not "racial or national minorities "as in Europe; they were religious minorities. He, therefore, concluded that religious differences do not come in the way of nation-state building. However, he was aware of the attempts being made to communalise politics by distorting religious teachings for the sake of power politics.

Secondly, Jawaharlal had a most rational approach towards religion. While he believed that Indians should get rid of any narrow outlook of religions, he took a series of measures to ensure that all religions co-existed in India. That is why right from the beginning, Jawaharlal Nehru, his ideas and policies became the main target of attack by all communal, casteist and obscurantist forces.

It was in this scenario that the blackmailing pressure of the imperialist countries increased against India and the Indian right wing started regrouping. In the late fifties the right-wing opposition with the support of the RSS played a prominent role in sparking off a new wave of religious fanaticism. This intensified the activities of both the Jana Sangh and Hindu communalism. This led also to increased counter-activities by Muslim communalists. In addition, the Christian Church also began to intervene in political affairs. In Punjab, the Akalis became more aggressive with their demand for the creation of a Punjabi-speaking state. These developments need to be seen in their totality.

Along with the rise of communalism in India, the situation was further compounded by caste conflict. The 'dominant' caste', i.e., which had control over the bulk of the land and which included the upper layer of the land-owning classes, made use of their caste solidarity to strengthen their hold on the organs of the state machinery—from the Panchyats to the Zilla Parishads.

The Chinese attack on India in 1962, was the biggest blow to Nehru's vision. After the Chinese aggression, the right-wing offensive against Jawaharlal increased further. They started demanding that a "national Government" be formed. The Jana Sangh went a step further, and demanded that India should invite the "American nuclear umbrella". It must also be admitted that within the Congress, the right-wing forces too became very active. In the last phase of his life, Jawaharlal was actively thinking of taking some more radical steps, and in one of his speeches underlined that something drastic would have to be done to check the concentration of economic wealth. But the cold hands of death snatched him away from the Indian nation at a most crucial period of its history.

Post-Nehru Period

In the post-Nehru era, particularly after the death of Lal Bahadur

Shastri, rightist forces both within the Congress and outside made a common cause to reverse the policies laid down by Jawaharlal Nehru. Since Indira Gandhi not only symbolised these policies but was also determined to carry them forward, she bacame the main target of their attack. This offensive became very intense after the 1967 elections. The leadership of the Congress, headed by Indira Gandhi, had then to expel from the party certain conservative elements in order to keep the doors open for a progressive democratic policy. Measures were taken to nationalise banks and general insurance. Many closed concerns, particularly textile and engineering, were taken over. The crucial measure of coal nationalisation was put into effect; overall, the public sector was elevated to a still higher position.

And when the princes were pensioned off, followed by other radical steps, the right reaction was put on the defensive. But during the eighties, a major change had taken place in the tactics and the policies of both internal and external reaction. Asia had become the main target of Washington to change the correlation of global forces, and the changes taking place in our sub-continent need to be seen in that light—terrorism in Punjab and Jammu and Kashmir.

Some naive or ill-informed politicians have led themselves to believe that there is no threat to India's security and that the Congress is blowing the situation out of proportion with an eye on the next election to the Lok Sabha. There are others who believe that though the threat exists, these challenges cannot be met without changing the internal policies and also dislodging the Congress form power. It has been alleged both by American and Pakistani journalists that Zulfikar Ali Bhutto had to go to gallows because he was trying to assert the independence of his country. Even if one doubts the authenticity of this fact, in country after country political leaders have been dislodged from power because they were resisting American pressure. One has to read the American press to find out how the CIA has been meddling in the affairs of some of the Latin American countries.

It is not difficult to understand that a country of India's size, following a policy of independent economic development and leading the non-aligned movement has in her the capacity to tilt the balance of international power. Hence it has been made a special target of American attack.

India's internal situation in general and attempts at subversion need to be seen in this context. Is it a mere coincidence that our north, north-eastern and western borders are in turmoil today? Rajiv Gandhi had put the spotlight on the "foreign hand" in the recent spurt of secessionist and terrorist activities in Punjab, and Jammu and Kashmir.

Certain foreign powers have been very active among the Sikhs and Kashmiris abroad. If one takes a close look at the press reports in the US, Canada, and UK, it is not difficult to see that there is a direct encouragement to the separatist movements based in these countries, with the active support of their intelligence services.

Attack of Pincer Arms

What all these boil down to? The two sinister arms of the pincer, one, the threat from external forces, and the other, internal subversion, cannot be fought by state measures alone. Though the Congress is the biggest party in the country, it alone cannot mobilise the broadest sections of the people belonging to different political parties. It has differences with some of the other parties on the path of India's economic development. But these differences can be resolved through a frank and friendly debate. Other differences can be resolved on the basis of mass experiences. But there can be no differences as far as the defence of the country's security and unity is concerned. What is at stake is not the future of one party or the other; the country's security and unity are being threatened by external forces and its internal allies. Threats of nuclear war too are being voiced.

India's history is replete with some of the most shining examples of struggles against imperialism. The many foreign invasions over the centuries, including four invasions after independence, and the inherent disposition of the patriotic people of our great country have all combined to throw up at various periods of its chequered history some of the finest and noblest specimens of human endurance and glory. India's vast plains are covered with the blood of freedom fighters, who laid down their lives so that we can remain free and independent. Its precious soil has been hallowed by the memories of youthful parties rushing headlong to the gallows and the old stalwarts braving cheerfully the blows of naked British imperialism for the liberation of their motherland and its unity. After four decades of freedom we are facing the same challenges once again. As Jawaharlal Nehru said: "Freedom is in Peril", let us sink our differences and build a broad anti-imperialist and anti-communal front. The challenge is formidable but equally strong is the determination of our people. If we do not rise to the occasion, posterity will never forgive us.

The rise of religious fundamentalism in our country and in other developing countries has wider ramifications than what appear on the surface. It destabilises all the countries and paves the way for foreign intervention. However, what is new in the situation is that religious and ethnic conflicts in a large number of developing countries have become the biggest disintegrating force. This in turn, is unleashing new regional conflicts, and new perilous situations.

Index